THE
PERSONAL
TOUCH

THE ART OF SEWING

THE PERSONAL TOUCH

BY THE EDITORS OF TIME-LIFE BOOKS

TIME-LIFE BOOKS, NEW YORK

TIME-LIFE BOOKS

FOUNDER: Henry R. Luce 1898-1967

Editor-in-Chief: Hedley Donovan
Chairman of the Board: Andrew Heiskell
President: James R. Shepley
Chairman, Executive Committee:
James A. Linen
Group Vice President: Rhett Austell

Vice Chairman: Roy E. Larsen

MANAGING EDITOR: Jerry Korn
Assistant Managing Editors: David Maness,
Martin Mann, A. B. C. Whipple
Planning Director: Oliver E. Allen
Art Director: Sheldon Cotler
Chief of Research: Beatrice T. Dobie
Director of Photography: Melvin L. Scott
Senior Text Editor: Diana Hirsh
Assistant Art Director: Arnold C. Holeywell

PUBLISHER: Joan D. Manley
General Manager: John D. McSweeney
Business Manager: John Steven Maxwell
Sales Director: Carl G. Jaeger
Promotion Director: Paul R. Stewart
Public Relations Director: Nicholas Benton

THE ART OF SEWING
SERIES EDITOR: Carlotta Kerwin
EDITORIAL STAFF FOR
THE PERSONAL TOUCH:
Assistant Editor: David L. Harrison
Designer: Virginia Gianakos
Text Editors: Gerry Schremp,
Bryce S. Walker
Chief Researchers: Wendy A. Rieder,
Gabrielle Smith (planning)
Staff Writers: Sondra R. Albert,
Carol I. Clingan, Michael T. Drons,
Marian Gordon Goldman, Angela D. Goodman,
Frank Kappler, Marilyn Kendig,
Joan S. Reiter, Suzanne Seixas
Research Staff: Rhea Finkelstein,
Nancy J. Jacobsen, Ginger Seippel,
Vivian I. Stephens, Reiko Uyeshima
Art Staff: Sanae Yamazaki (design assistant),
Patricia Byrne, Catherine Caufield,
Robert McKee
Editorial Assistant: Kathleen Beakley

EDITORIAL PRODUCTION
Production Editor: Douglas B. Graham
Assistant: Gennaro C. Esposito
Quality Director: Robert L. Young
Assistant: James J. Cox
Copy Staff: Rosalind Stubenberg (chief),
Mary Orlando, Ricki Tarlow, Florence Keith
Picture Department: Dolores A. Littles,
Jessy S. Faubert
Traffic: Feliciano Madrid

Portions of this book were written by Hazel
Arnett, Helen Barer, Don Earnest, Margaret
Elliott and Wendy Murphy. Valuable assistance
was provided by these departments and
individuals of Time Inc.: Editorial Production,
Norman Airey; Library, Benjamin Lightman;
Picture Collection, Doris O'Neil; Photographic
Laboratory, George Karas; TIME-LIFE News
Service, Murray J. Gart. Correspondents Margot
Hapgood and Dorothy Bacon (London), Ann
Natanson (Rome), Maria Vincenza Aloisi (Paris),
Sue Wymelenberg (Boston).

THE CONSULTANTS
Gretel Courtney taught for many years at the
French Fashion Academy in New York City. She
has studied patternmaking and design at the
Fashion Institute of Technology in New York and
haute couture at the French Fashion Academy.

Annette Feldman is a knitting and crocheting de-
signer, both for clothing and interior decorating.
She is the author of *Knit, Purl and Design!* and
Crochet and Creative Design.

Tracy Kendall has worked in many capacities for
various fashion firms in New York. She is pres-
ently a freelance costumer and set designer for
television commercials and print advertising.

Julian Tomchin is a textile designer who has been
awarded the Vogue Fabric Award and a Coty
Award of the American Fashion Critics. A grad-
uate of Syracuse University's Fine Arts College,
he has been chairman of the Textile Design Department at the Shenkar College of Fashion and
Textile Technology in Tel Aviv and now teaches
at the Parsons School of Design in New York.

CONTENTS

1

PROCLAIMING YOURSELF

ame Edith Sitwell, the late English poet, held a strong and outspoken opinion of the way most people, especially her own countrymen, wore their clothes. "We are a nation of mice," she once declared. "We dress and behave with timid circumspection. Why not be one's self? If one is a greyhound, why try to look like a Pekingese?"

Nobody could ever accuse Dame Edith of looking like a mouse or a Pekingese. Yet

THE BOLD CHALLENGE OF PERSONAL STYLE

Dame Edith thought there was someone else she did favor. "I resemble Henry VII," she once remarked. "He was an ugly old man." Six feet tall, with a strong aquiline nose and hooded eyes, Dame Edith indeed bore herself like the reincarnation of some Renaissance monarch.

The way she dressed exaggerated her unique looks still further. She arrayed herself in long flowing gowns of brocade and velvet, elaborate turban-like headdresses and dramatically outsized jewelry. And the figure she cut, despite that severe self-appraisal, was an unmistakably fascinating one. It was handsome and appealing because it was so assuredly her own.

"Why not be one's self?"

A stirring, seductive thought but not always easy to bring into reality. Individuality for most of us has been for a long time a pretty but rather frightening toy. We are, after all, herd animals, whose earliest instincts warn us not to stray. But another powerful instinct tugs us in the opposite direction, urging us to be our own persons, behaving and dressing to suit ourselves. In today's superfluid society, we have not only the opportunity but the persuasion of our peers to do just that. And by the clothes we choose —pantsuits or mini skirts, grannies or dashikis, funky fatigues or bared satin halters —we can testify to the world the kind of persons we really are.

Usually, the most successful individual statements in dress are the least self-conscious ones—styles not adopted from a fad but invented by a single person to impress nobody but himself. One example is the "Lilly," the short, bright-printed chemise dress that young Palm Beach socialite Lilly Pulitzer devised for herself in the early '60s. "I hate anything tight," said Lilly, a barefoot type, explaining why she was tired of blouse and skirt or blouse and shorts. Forthwith she designed an above-the-knee chemise, lined it so that she could wear the barest nothing underneath, and prettied it up with a well-placed dart or two, a mandarin slit up each side and bold-spirited fabrics. The result was so handsome on Lilly that other Palm Beach ladies clamored for duplicates. And Lilly herself became a thriving fashion tycoon whose "Lillies" (and their numerous progeny) blossomed nationwide.

Many of history's great stylistic innovators set out like Lilly to please only themselves. Consider, for example, Dwight Eisenhower and the field jacket he wore as Commander of the Allied forces in Europe during World War II. Ike found the hip-length U.S. officer's jacket bulky and constricting, so he asked his tailor to run up one that ended at the waist—like the standard British infantry jacket. The resulting garment, besides being comfortable, was remarkably becoming to Ike. Subsequently the jacket was not only adopted throughout the U.S. Army but quickly became an item among civilian haberdashers back home.

As with most items of contemporary dress, the Ike jacket and its British brother had a distinguished ancestry. Both garments owed some paternity to another short, tailless jacket, born of individuality and called the spencer. One day in the 1790s, the story goes, Lord George John Spencer, England's First Lord of the Admiralty, was warming himself by the fire and burned his coattails. Lord Spencer did the sensible thing: he cut the damaged tails off.

Furthermore, Lord Spencer avowed, so absurd were the vagaries of fashion, he could start a new style simply by strolling around London in his chopped-off attire. He was entirely correct. "In two weeks," according to one chronicler, "all London was wearing the 'spencer.'"

The sartorial whims of other powerful men—and powerful causes—have been broadly noted and often copied all through history. During the early days of the American Revolution, the canny Benjamin Franklin arrived as emissary at the foppish French court in Paris, wearing a suit of somber Quaker brown. Dr. Franklin was the instant rage of Paris, not only drawing attention to himself and his mission as intended, but strongly proclaiming the advent of a new independence and homespun democratic virtue. Shortly thereafter, upon the cresting wave of its own revolution, all France abandoned the breeches-and-hose style long established by the aristocracy and switched to humble Republican trousers. And during that same revolution the fanatical Robespierre made his own views chillingly and sartorially explicit by wearing buttons engraved with an image of the guillotine.

A less celebrated and far gentler revolutionary, who nonetheless set a new fashion, was the early feminist leader Amelia Jenks Bloomer. Around 1851, Amelia and a few sister pioneers started wearing what quickly came to be called the Bloomer Costume, featuring ankle-length pantaloons, worn under a dress cut a few inches below the knee. Mrs. Bloomer's bloomers amply suited their innovator's unconventional inclinations; she found them far more comfortable and con-

The history of clothing is full of famous people who gave their names to a particular garment. Thus Lord Chesterfield *(above, left)* made fashionable a new style of topcoat with a straight silhouette. So too, Lord Raglan, while fighting the Crimean War, devised a sleeve that extended in one piece to the neckline. And reformer Amelia Bloomer tried to put women into baggy Turkish-style pantaloons—known as bloomers ever since.

venient than the conventional layers of long petticoats and hoop skirts that proper ladies of her era were supposed to wear.

In those Victorian days, however, Amelia and company were hooted back into their long skirts. But gradually, various derivatives of the bloomers took hold—as part of women's bicycling wear in the 1890s, then as the lower half of the first ladies' bathing suit, and finally as knee-length gym costumes for young girls, lasting right up through the 1950s.

Perhaps the most potent of history's style setters, one whose name—and with it the garment he popularized—has become a basic item in today's world of women's fash-

ions, was none other than the Daring Young Man on the Flying Trapeze. From 1859 to 1869, the matinee idol of France was a handsome, steel-nerved circus performer named Jules Léotard. Dressed in an eye-boggling costume that consisted of a skin-tight neck-to-toe body suit of knit jersey (with a demure little skirt discreetly draping the mid-latitudes), he sent pulses of awe and delight through packed audiences of admiring Victorian ladies. His aerial feats inspired the song in his honor, now a classic. And they made his costume, the leotard, a classic as well. Where it once enhanced the athletic masculinity of Jules, it now proclaims the feminine allure of modern woman.

More recently, the Duke of Windsor set a fashion for a thick, double knot in men's neckties—called a Windsor, though the Duke acknowledged he did not invent it himself. A fad for Nehru jackets in the 1960s took as its source the native coat favored by the Indian Prime Minister. And the abbreviated tunic known as the Eisenhower jacket is named for the World War II general who had the prototype cut to his personal order.

This kind of self-proclamation has become part of the essence of now-generation living. In fact, today almost anything goes, so long as it fits the mood and inclination of the wearer. Among the celebrities attending a Paris fashion show in 1973 was rock singer Mick Jagger's wife, Bianca, who upstaged both the other guests and the professional models when she stalked in clad in a dandyish pantsuit complete with dangling watch fob and walking stick. Smashing, was the consensus; not for everyone, perhaps, but exactly right for Bianca.

Also not for everyone but decidedly right for the lady herself is the careless individualism exhibited by Katharine Hepburn, who once said she had worn the same clothes for 40 years ("literally, even the shoes"). In 1971 she granted an interview, wearing what was for her a standard off-stage costume: her favorite black turtleneck sweater, beige slacks, bright red socks, brown buckled shoes and a Civil War-style uniform cap under a white head scarf. "She is a stunning sight," wrote the enchanted reporter, "and you wonder why more people don't dress that way."

The answer is that more and more people are learning to dress—not in imitation of famous movie stars—but like themselves. The sewing and dressmaking techniques described in this volume can help you take

Leaders in the evolution of personal style include these six personalities, whose modes of dress have made them instantly recognizable and much imitated. Benjamin Franklin is unmistakable in his sober Quaker garb. Poet

Edith Sitwell achieved her own uniquely dramatic look with such items as outsized antique jewelry and Tudor headdress. And who could miss the power and pomp of Queen Elizabeth's habitually ruffle-clad presence?

a giant step toward exploiting and perfecting this innate preference for what is distinctively your own. One easy and natural way to begin is by remodeling clothes that are already in your wardrobe. From there, you can move naturally into combining patterns, experimenting with fresh fabrics, introducing novel trimmings, adding artful monograms and emblems. All these devices can provide routes to a heightened feeling of self-expression and creativity.

Yet these essential techniques, liberating and satisfying though they may be, are only part of the formula for achieving the goal of a personal style. Like Dame Edith Sitwell in her Renaissance brocades, or Katharine Hepburn in her Civil War cap, or even Lilly Pulitzer in her novel chemise, you must practice a certain courage and assurance to be truly yourself. Such self-assurance has nothing to do with the style of the moment, the rise and fall of hemline or the decrees of couturiers in Paris and New York; it has only to do with what seems right for you. Indeed, one of the most revered and distinctive designers of the 20th Century admitted as much herself. Madeleine Vionnet, who brought a new and elegant simplicity to women's clothes in the 1920s and '30s, once said, "Remember, I never made fashion, I never saw fashion, I don't know what fashion is. I made the clothes I believed in."

The subdued personal elegance of Jacqueline Kennedy, expressed in softly tailored suits, white gloves and demure pillbox hats, set a new style for the Western world. So too did the tough-guy flamboyance of Elvis Presley, as he strutted his stuff in boots, tight breeches, lank hair and jackets or shirts worn unbuttoned to the waist. And Greta Garbo, three decades after her last movie, still boasted legions of admirers and imitators.

The subtle art of borrowing

Clothing design, like cooking, is sometimes improved by improvisation. On these and the following pages some classic dishes have been seasoned to taste with distinctive personal touches.

In this first trio the key is in the combinations: a fashion note is lifted from one design to enliven another. Thus, the body-skimming pink satin sheath at right acquires a softer silhouette when the sleeves are knitted in fine, silver-slivered wool. Another combination of knitted elements produced the pert ensemble at center. The tube top is a cut-down turtleneck of cotton knit, which sets off a color-matched, wool jersey pantsuit. And at far right, the jaunty layered look of a two-piece, two-tone dress has been underscored by adding long sleeves from another pattern. The relationship is further emphasized by making the new sleeves with the same material as the skirt.

15

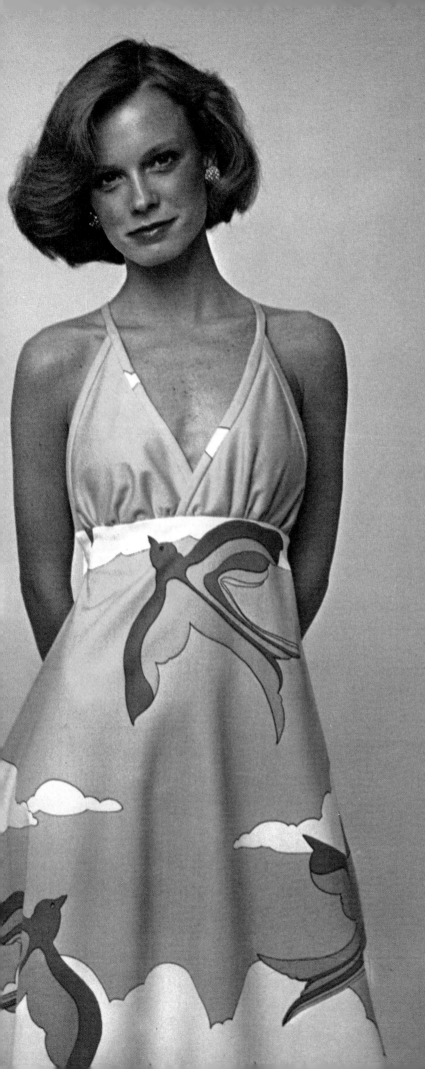

The medium is the material

One of the traditional emblems of haute couture is the venturesome use of fabric. Here that spirit is applied to three basic designs with eye-catching results. A striped polished cotton is played to bold advantage *(far left)* when wrapped across the figure on the diagonal. Contrasting panels of vertical stripes complete the neckline and remaining sleeve.

The beige and brown ribbed pullover at center becomes something special when oversized epaulets in matching cotton poplin are superimposed. A running stitch in a thread of the darker brown crisscrosses the poplin to simulate quilting. And a pretty little slip of a dress *(left)* takes on unexpected drama when rendered in a vivid pink and orange cotton print. By deft cutting of the pattern, the birds are made to circle skirt and waist. but the bodice remains a clear and pristine pink.

17

Accents that make the difference

Even the slightest additions of trim or ornament can bring strong personal accents to clothes. Here, a red silk jersey cocktail dress *(right)* gains distinction when punctuated with a brilliant waistband of silk ribbon.

A peach gabardine sheath *(center)* finds a subtle grace note in a monogrammed cravat. The large-scale initial, finely worked, becomes the focal point of the understated design. And gray velvet pants *(far right)* are promoted to parade dress when a two-inch strip of crocheting is run down the leg; a matching strip cinches the sweater top.

2
BRIGHT IDEAS
IN FABRIC

During the great days of British grouse shooting in the mid-19th Century, Prince Albert, the dandified consort of Queen Victoria, had a habit of turning out for a day on the moors in a jacket of resplendent black velvet. The Prince's choice of fabric appalled the gentry, who all knew enough to go shooting only in proper British tweed. Nor was Albert's aura of chic in any way helped by his fondness for high scarlet

CUTTING LOOSE WITH SOME NEW NOTIONS

boots. He looked, according to a wit of the time, "like some foreign tenor."

Albert's problem arose not so much from his resemblance to a Tannhäuser-on-the-Heath, but from the fact that in his free-wheeling taste in fabrics he was simply 100 years ahead of his time, even for royalty. However, in today's wide-open fashion world, no one questions another person's right to pick whatever materials he wants —any texture, any color, any weave—or to set any style that pleases him. We choose from a range of fabrics that would flabbergast our grandparents—not just the perennials like velvet and linen and cotton, but a profusion of acetates, nylons, polyesters and acrylics. And we mix these fabrics in colors that would confound a Victorian's eye, matching vibrant oranges with reds, greens with electric blues, pinks with lemon yellows. The only limit is a person's own sense of what is right for himself. However, as Albert, and the members of a hundred other generations, might have attested, such unbounded freedom in matters of clothing is something very new. Throughout most of history, not only fabrics but the way they were cut, the trim they were given, and even the accessories worn with them were governed by stern rules. Until quite recently, seersucker for suits, straw hats, and even patent leather were deemed acceptable among upper-class Americans only between Memorial Day and Labor Day. And no proper gentleman appeared in a striped shirt after sundown. In many older societies much stricter rules prevailed. Indeed, some governments even passed laws that dictated just who could wear what.

Most of these regulations, known as sumptuary laws and covering in some cases not only clothing but a whole range of personal habits, were designed ostensibly to prevent extravagance on the part of the common people. In fact, they served to protect the rich and highborn from imitation by their social inferiors. Thus, in ancient Rome, only free citizens were allowed to drape themselves in the long, undyed wool robe

called a toga. Slaves, foreigners, exiles and other lesser orders had to make do with simple tunics, either wool or linen.

In addition, the color and decoration of a citizen's toga became a sure sign of his rank. No one but the emperor or a victorious general marching in a triumphal procession could flaunt an all-purple toga with gold embroidery. A decorous purple border, to be sure, was permitted to magistrates, priests or chief officers of towns or colonies. And boys under 16, as a special privilege of youth, could also wear a broad purple hem.

For the ordinary citizen, the plain toga was considered distinction enough—except when he ran for public office. Then, to signal his availability, he would dust his toga with chalk. The result was a brilliant white that the Romans called *candida*—and the wearer became a candidate.

After Rome fell and a new civilization sprang up in northern Europe, even more elaborate sets of sumptuary laws came into force. One regulation in 13th Century France determined the size and trim of cloaks. Only a nobleman could adorn the hood of his cape with the long, conical extension known as a liripipe. The higher his rank, the longer his liripipe. By the later Middle Ages the laws spelled out the length of people's trains, and the cost not only of the fabrics they wore, but of their buttons, belts, jewels and furs.

During the 14th Century, long pointed shoes came into style. They grew to such dimensions that in some cases it became necessary to hold up the pointed toes with gold chains attached to the ankles or knees.

While commoners were allowed to sport a six-inch toe, a gentleman's toe could be twice that long, and a nobleman could indulge himself in a toe of two feet. Finally, Charles V ended the frivolous competition by banning pointed shoes altogether.

Though Charles was clearly a bit of a bluenose for his day, at other times and places the nobility indulged itself with unabated frivolity and egotism. No monarch guarded the sartorial privileges of high rank more jealously than England's Elizabeth I. None of her courtiers was permitted to wear a starched linen neck ruff wider than her own, and she gave strict orders to her palace guards to snip off the ruffs of any offenders. Elizabeth's clothing decrees extended downward through all ranks of society. No subject with an income of less than £200 a year could adorn either himself or his horse with velvet or embroidery in gold, silver or silk. Only members of the royal family could sport garments of crimson cloth—though some people, resentful at being pushed around, donned underwear of red flannel.

In the face of such restrictions, people in every age and civilization devised ingenious ways to express their own individuality. In Japan around the year 1000 the requisite costume for a lady at court consisted of a heavy outer garment and a set of 12 unlined silk robes, worn one on top of the other. Even some of the basic colors were determined by statute. Nonetheless, Japanese ladies invented ways of making their costumes their own by means of subtle differences in the hue of each robe.

A Japanese woman chose her color variations to reflect the seasons. In spring, kimono silks might echo the delicate hues of cherry and plum blossoms, and in winter, accent the contrast between green pine trees and white snow. To show off her selection, she wore each sleeve slightly shorter than the one beneath it, so that the entire spectrum was delicately displayed.

Despite such artful evasions, ordinary folk the world over despised clothing laws. During the egalitarian fervor that swept France during the French Revolution, any association with the styles of the French nobility could bring personal disaster. One fabric that was singled out for particular revolutionary vengeance was lace, which had been manufactured at Chantilly under royal patronage—and only for the members of the court. When Chantilly fell to the republicans in 1793, angry mobs demolished the lace factories, patterns and all, and led many of the lacemakers to the guillotine.

Eventually, as monarchies everywhere collapsed and the rigid class structures of the past began to fall apart at the seams, the whole rigmarole of clothing regulations eroded away. Today a person can strut down the street in a harlequin costume, a burlap overcoat or a bathing suit made of rabbit fur, and hardly anyone will raise an eyebrow. And with fabrics now available in an astonishing richness of textures and colors, the possibilities for blending clothing into a unique personal style are limitless.

One designer who has used a novel approach to fabrics is the fashion pioneer Anne Fogarty. She began her career in 1950 by turning out street clothes and evening dresses in denim, mattress ticking and calico—all fabrics that designers had previously scorned. The resounding applause—and business—she earned from this experiment prompted her to try other offbeat fabrics. Many of her departures have since found their way into the standard fashion repertoire: a tailored shirt made of organdy; an evening ensemble combining a gingham blouse trimmed in rickrack with a faded blue denim skirt and a red patent belt; evening dresses with wool jersey bodices and satin or taffeta skirts; and satin jeans.

By using fabrics of your own choice, you can find equally ingenious methods of varying your wardrobe. The following pages show a number of novel concepts for using fabrics and trims to achieve a personal touch. You can even make up your own fabric, by piecing together strips and patches of different materials, or sewing together ribbons and scarves.

Another noted designer, Julian Tomchin, summed up the possibilities with this bit of general advice: "Take a simple paper pattern with its pedestrian suggestions, then close your eyes and imagine the garment in other fabrics, other colors, another time of day, another state of mind. Who says you have to use the same color or colors for both skirt and jacket? If the pattern says you can use flannel or velvet, why not both? It's the anachronistic, unexpected use of fabric that makes a garment personal."

This 1807 engraving from Napoleonic France pokes a bit of gentle fun at some customers of a Paris millinery shop who embellish their bonnets in various frivolous ways with feather and ribbons and extra odds and ends of fabric. Only a few years earlier, during the French Revolution, these same ladies would have demonstrated their republican loyalties—and their stylistic conformity —by wearing tricolored caps of red, white and blue.

A splash of bold prints

One sure-fire—and often amusing—way to draw attention is to wear a bold print. Clever showmen have done this ever since the first brightly clad harlequin pranced across a Renaissance stage. Clever women still use it today by sewing their own unique costumes from a spectrum of prints that might upstage the most knowing harlequin.

Thousands of dazzling prints are available in factory-made designs such as the one unfurling from the model at right. The surest way, though, to obtain a bold print that is distinctly your own is to make it yourself. Those shown here, surrounding the model's green and white pattern, have been created simply by sewing together silk scarves. The bull's-eye pattern, all brilliance and boldness, produces color contrasts within color contrasts. A less boisterous but equally vibrant effect comes from stripping together scarves of solid contrasting colors, as at upper right. The choice is entirely yours, but once you have chosen, check the chart on pages 32 and 33 to be certain you handle the fabric correctly as you sew.

Fabrics made from frills

Traditionally, ribbon has taken the role of a frilly afterthought, a decorative—though frequently useful—touch such as a hair bow, a corsage fastening, a bit of dress trim or a bright wrapping for a gift box. Yet under a pair of skillful hands, the most fragile and tinselly strips of ribbon can suddenly reappear as a dress fabric with far more dazzle per square inch than any standard piece of yard goods.

For example, the 26 strips festooning the model at right make a whirligig of colors and patterns, ranging from simple geometric forms to designs as complex as those on a miniaturized electronic circuit. All those shown here are of rayon, cotton or wool (silk is too expensive in ribbon form to be practical as a fabric base), and some are enhanced with metallic thread. The widest one measures an inch and a half. But there are some ribbons that span four inches or more—which could save the fabric maker a lot of sewing.

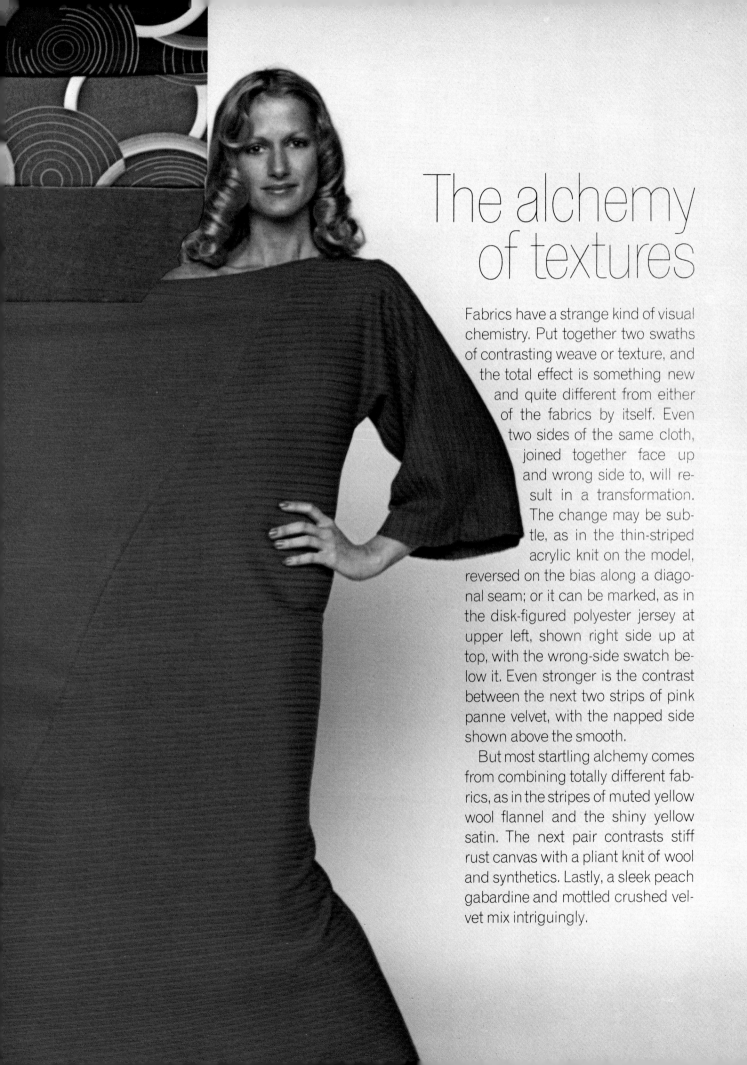

The alchemy of textures

Fabrics have a strange kind of visual chemistry. Put together two swaths of contrasting weave or texture, and the total effect is something new and quite different from either of the fabrics by itself. Even two sides of the same cloth, joined together face up and wrong side to, will result in a transformation. The change may be subtle, as in the thin-striped acrylic knit on the model, reversed on the bias along a diagonal seam; or it can be marked, as in the disk-figured polyester jersey at upper left, shown right side up at top, with the wrong-side swatch below it. Even stronger is the contrast between the next two strips of pink panne velvet, with the napped side shown above the smooth.

But most startling alchemy comes from combining totally different fabrics, as in the stripes of muted yellow wool flannel and the shiny yellow satin. The next pair contrasts stiff rust canvas with a pliant knit of wool and synthetics. Lastly, a sleek peach gabardine and mottled crushed velvet mix intriguingly.

Secrets of individualizing fabrics

A fabric that you make yourself —from scarves, ribbons or lengths of standard yard goods—represents the ultimate in personalized dressmaking. Assembling it takes not only creativity, but also a certain amount of technical expertise, of the kind explained in the chart at right.

When you have picked out the patterns and textures that please you, examine the materials to be certain they will be compatible. Look for a description of fiber content on the end of the bolt or on a tag hanging from the fabric itself. Check labels on scarves and ribbon packages. And select threads, pins and other sewing accessories that are appropriate for the fabrics you choose.

Fabrics that consist of bands of ribbon should be sewn together before the individual garment pieces are cut out; ribbon trims, on the other hand, may often be added after the parts are assembled. In creating a garment from scarves or mixed textures or prints, the materials may also be combined before the pattern is laid out for cutting; or—more simply—different garment parts can be cut from separate fabrics.

TYPE OF FABRIC	COMBINING FABRICS
TEXTURED AND REVERSED FABRICS	With distinctively textured fabrics, you can play off slick finishes against nubby ones, shiny textures against dull ones, soft textures against stiff ones. Or you can cut napped fabrics so that the nap runs in different directions on different parts of a garment. With fabrics that have an interesting texture on the reverse side, you can turn the fabric wrong side up for some parts of a garment. In this way both the face and back surfaces will be visible in the finished design.
PRINTED FABRICS AND SOLID-COLORED OR PATTERNED SCARVES	Contrast solid-colored scarves with one another or with printed fabrics or patterned scarves. For subtle pattern variations, mix prints and patterns that are similar in scale and color. For more dramatic emphasis, contrast small patterns with large ones or vice versa, or juxtapose bright colors with pale or somber ones.
RIBBONS AS FABRIC OR TRIM	To create a ribbon-covered fabric from which to fashion all or some parts of a garment, sew bands of identical or contrasting ribbon together on a backing of firm, light- to mediumweight fabric. To trim fabrics or finished garments, apply ribbons singly or in sets as bands on collars or cuffs, around necklines and along hems and button closures, or as inserts into seams.

SHOPPING SUGGESTIONS	SEWING ACCESSORIES	SEWING SUGGESTIONS	CARE AND HANDLING
As you buy your fabrics, bear in mind that it is easier to work with materials whose fiber content is similar. At the least, choose fabrics that require similar care and handling. Choose lightweight facing fabric for velvet and brocade to minimize the bulk of the finished garment. Buy all the necessary sewing accessories at the same time you buy the fabric. This will ensure that the color and fibers are compatible.	*Thread:* polyester or silk *Pins:* silk pins for silks, ballpoint for knits *Needles:* ballpoints for knits *Equipment:* even-feed sewing-machine foot for satin, velvet and other slippery fabrics; sharp shears to avoid snags on knits	Preshrink all washable fabrics before laying them out for cutting. Mark silk, velvet and brocade with tailor tacks. For satin, make the tailor tacks with silk thread and position them inside the seam or dart allowances to avoid scarring the fabric with permanent pin or needle holes. Test a doubled swatch of fabric to determine the proper stitch and tension setting for machine stitching. When stitching two fabrics together, place the one more difficult to handle on the top. Let knits, or knit combinations, hang for 24 hours before hemming them.	Dry-clean all fabrics unless the labels or tags specifically suggest washing. Follow the cleaning instructions carefully. If only one fabric in a combination is washable, dry-clean the garment. Always test fabrics for the proper setting before ironing or pressing them. Press knits along the lengthwise grain. Press velvet with a needle board to avoid crushing the nap. Press satin on the lowest possible setting, using a pressing cloth and inserting thick paper between the seam allowance and the wrong side of the garment to prevent marking the fabric.
In planning a combination of prints or scarves, choose fabrics that will require similar care and handling. Allow extra yardage to match directional or oversized designs. Buy all the necessary sewing accessories at the same time you buy the fabric. This will ensure that the color and fibers are compatible.	*Thread:* polyester or silk *Pins:* silk pins for silks, ballpoint for knits *Equipment:* even-feed sewing machine foot for silk and other slippery fabrics	Preshrink all washable fabrics before laying them out for cutting. When laying out prints or scarves, position the brightest and boldest areas where they will be most flattering in the finished garment. Use rolled or hemmed scarf edges as the edges for the finished garment wherever possible. Create decorative seams with embroidery stitches or machine zigzag stitching in a matching or contrasting thread. Accentuate prints by embroidering parts of the design.	Dry-clean the fabric unless the print or scarf labels specifically suggest washing. Follow the cleaning instructions carefully. When only one fabric or scarf in a combination is washable, always dry-clean the garment. Always test fabrics for the proper setting before ironing or pressing them.
As with prints and scarves, select ribbons that will require similar care and handling. Match the weight and flexibility of ribbons to the fabric they trim or cover so that the ribbons will not pull the finished garment out of shape. For use as curved trimming, select grosgrain ribbons—especially the scalloped types—which can be shaped readily. Buy all the necessary sewing accessories at the same time that you buy the ribbons to ensure that the colors and fibers are compatible.	*Thread:* polyester or silk *Pins:* silk pins for silks *Equipment:* basting tape to use for aligning ribbons on fabric backing	Use seam tape to determine the exact length required before cutting ribbon trim. Pin the tape to the garment—mitering and shaping it as necessary. Then unpin and measure the tape. Add 4 inches to the measurement to allow for finishing the ends of the ribbon. Preshrink all washable ribbons and backing fabrics before laying them out for cutting. Preshape grosgrain ribbons by pressing them into curves with a steam iron while they are still damp. Use tailor tacks to mark pattern symbols on ribbon-covered fabric. Baste and machine stitch silk and velvet ribbons with silk thread.	Dry-clean ribbon-trimmed garments unless both the ribbon and fabric labels specifically suggest washing. Follow the cleaning instructions carefully. Always test ribbons for the proper setting before ironing or pressing them. Velvet ribbons should be pressed wrong side up on a terry towel with a dry iron. Most other ribbons should be pressed wrong side down with a steam iron set for synthetics.

Preparing fabric for cutting

Whether you are working with a new pattern or remodeling a garment by adding contrasting bands or inserts, the fabric must be checked to make sure that the grain has not been pulled out of shape by handling. For woven fabrics, find the true crosswise grain *(top right)*. Fold the fabric in half lengthwise and align the fold with a table edge. If the raw edges do not match or the corners do not form right angles, the grain is off and must be corrected.

Begin to straighten a washable fabric by immersing it in cold water, squeezing it gently and pulling on diagonally opposite ends. Then refold the fabric in half lengthwise, wrong sides out; lay it on a flat surface until almost dry. To finish the straightening, pin the edges and steam press.

For nonwashable fabrics, simply fold and press. For knits, lay the fabric on a flat surface for 24 hours before cutting to allow the yarns to assume their natural shape.

When the fabric is straight, cut out your pattern pieces as shown on the opposite page. When working with knits, make sure to align the grainline arrow of your pattern with a lengthwise rib of the fabric.

FINDING THE TRUE CROSSWISE GRAIN

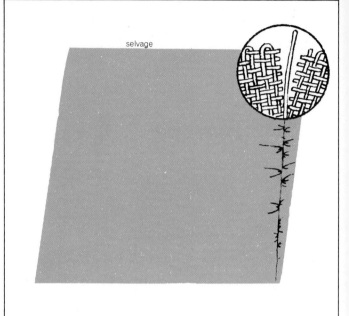

selvage

1. Make a small cut into one finished, or selvage, edge of the fabric and snag a crosswise thread with a pin. Gently pull on the thread so that it shows up as a puckered line along the width of the fabric.

2. Cut along the puckered line from one selvage to the other; this is the true crosswise grain.

3. Repeat at the opposite end of the fabric so that the ends can be matched for straightening the grain as explained at left.

FINDING THE TRUE BIAS

1. After straightening the fabric *(left)*, place it on a flat surface and fold it diagonally so that one selvage is parallel to the crosswise edge and perpendicular to the other selvage. The diagonally folded edge is the true bias.

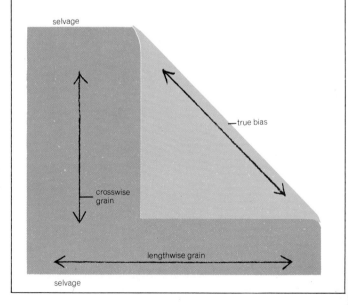

selvage

true bias

crosswise grain

lengthwise grain

selvage

LAYING OUT ON-GRAIN PATTERNS

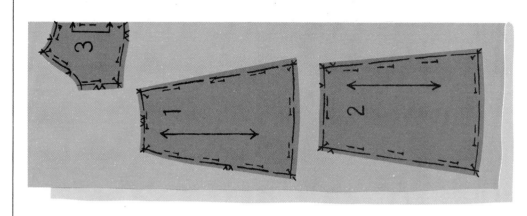

1. Pin all pattern pieces having a line that is marked "place on fold" to the fabric so that the line marking aligns with the fold.

2. Arrange the other pieces according to the pattern cutting guide, placing the printed grain-line arrows parallel to the fold and to the selvage edges.

3. Pin each pattern piece diagonally at the corners; then pin parallel to, and just inside, the cutting line.

LAYING OUT BIAS-CUT PATTERNS

1. Trace a duplicate pattern for each pattern piece that will be used more than once. For example, a left skirt back must be flopped to cut a right skirt back. Trace the grain-line arrow in each duplicate piece.

2. Spread open the straightened fabric and loosely arrange the pattern pieces according to the accompanying pattern cutting guide, making certain the grain-line arrows are parallel to the selvage edges.

3. Pin each pattern piece diagonally at the corners; then pin parallel to, and just inside, the cutting line. Arrange and pin all pattern pieces before cutting any.

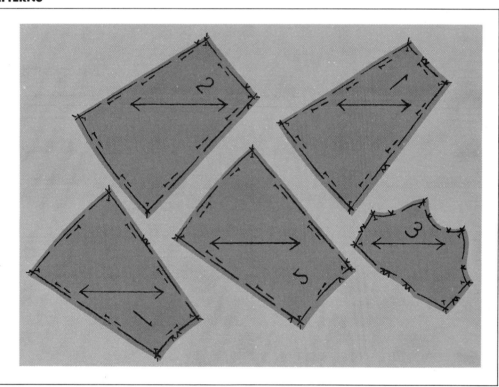

MARKING GRAIN LINES ON HOMEMADE PATTERNS

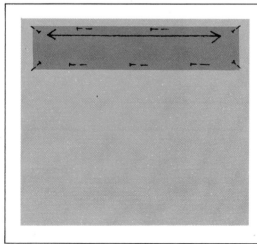

1. If the fabric section is to be cut on the grain, mark an arrow parallel to the lengthwise edges of the homemade pattern.

2. If the fabric section is to be cut on the bias, make a mark about midway along one lengthwise edge of the homemade pattern. Using a protractor, rule the grain line at a 45-degree angle from this point.

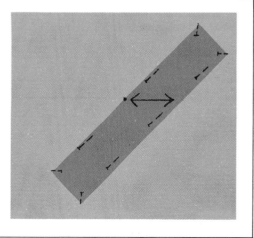

SKIRT FRONT

SKIRT FRONT

SKIRT FRONT

Center front: place line on fold of fabric

Center front: place line on fold of fabric

SKIRT FRONT

3
MIXING PATTERNS TO MATCH YOUR STYLE

Never does a designer in one of New York City's garment factories face a more unnerving moment than the day she shows her new line to her toughest critics—the salesmen, with their enormous power to influence what women will wear. Yet the very fact that she can mount the show indicates that this hard-working woman has survived another season in one of the world's most pressurized industries. For this survival, she

DESIGNING WITH BITS AND PIECES

needs a flair for fashion, business acumen and the constitution of an ox. She must be able to produce in quantity, churning out hundreds of styles each year, without repeating herself.

She works in a setting that is a far cry from popular conceptions of designers' studios. She has no plush workrooms, no legions of assistants. Generally she uses one harassed helper and an office the size of a walk-in closet where she sketches her ideas for new dresses on a drawing pad. To this office, with its mélange of drawings, swatches and samples on pipe racks, comes an unending stream of people—fabric and trimming salesmen, seamstresses, the production chief. In the midst of this confusion, amounting at times almost to pandemonium, she must create her collection.

Amazingly enough, she does. By cannibalizing some of her old styles, she can create something new from the proven elements of previous bestsellers: uniting the bodice of one number with the skirt of another and the belt of a third. Or she may give a fresh shape to the season's hot silhouette —lengthening an A-line skimmer, perhaps.

Outside the designer's office, in the factory proper, other skilled workers translate her sketches into actual garments. First there is the sample maker, who runs up hundreds of sample styles for each collection. Those accepted for production are sent to a cluttered corner where dozens of paper patterns hang from pegs—sleeves from one peg, skirts from another, bodices, collars and cuffs from others. Each pattern is identified and numbered and, all together, they form the parts of a fascinating puzzle. This room is the patternmaker's niche, where that master puzzle-solver works at a long table, elbow-deep in pattern parts.

He begins by taking apart the sample garment—say, a blouse. Then, acting quickly, he chooses a pattern for a bodice, one for a collar, another for a sleeve. This amalgam becomes the new blouse pattern.

Once satisfied, the patternmaker sends his product out to the factory floor, to the cutting tables, each one fed by long tributaries of flowing fabric. Here, the cutters chop out parts that ultimately land on sewing-machine benches to be stitched together.

Any energetic home seamstress can learn these designer and patternmaker techniques of mixing random parts to make an exciting whole. When she does, she will be able to make a pattern—and ultimately a dress—that is exactly what she wants.

A good way to start is by dividing a few patterns into categories (dresses, blouses, etc.) and laying the corresponding pattern pieces (bodices, sleeves, collars) side by side to analyze them. The various pieces will probably share similarities of style. The chances are that the home seamstress has developed her own fashion image, based on knowledge of her figure's good features. Thus she will combine pieces that play up the good points and tone down the bad, and so sharpen the image.

Certain common-sense rules should be kept in mind: when two patterns are combined, the new design may call for more fabric or less. Since Junior and Misses sizes are proportioned differently, they do not mix successfully. If a bodice and a skirt are to be combined, both patterns should be examined to be sure that the openings correspond and the lines are similar. And though it is not always necessary, pattern-mixing usually calls for tests in muslin.

The neophyte pattern-mixer may want to start small, adding a collar here, scrapping a cuff there. But she will soon find herself switching parts with confidence—at which point she starts being her own designer.

A sleeve for all fashions

Charles Worth, the creative Englishman who dominated the world of haute couture from the 1860s until the turn of the century, was perhaps the most imaginative and surely the most energetic man in the history of his profession. His ingenuity helped him build his clientele from a single, home-grown model—his Paris *vendeuse* wife—to the most extravagant and demanding women on the Continent and in America. His most striking contribution to 19th Century style was the bustle. But a more lasting one was in developing the technique of mixing patterns—which designers the world over still use today.

As a result of such shrewd pragmatism, his design house did a volume of business that would strain the capacity of any modern mass producer. To fill orders like the one for 1,000 ball gowns he sewed for guests at a single imperial fete in 1866, he developed patterns consisting of standardized parts to be used interchangeably. One example was the bell sleeve (so called because it is narrow at the top and widens at the bottom) that he fitted to any number of garments, like those at right, by skillfully varying details of trim and tailoring.

Worth's protean bell sleeve appears in five guises: at near right a frothy evening coat, then a casual full-length travel coat, a short coat with ruffles, a boldly braided suit jacket and a boxy daytime tunic with bow-tied neck.

Preliminary pattern adjustments

Before you begin stitching together pieces from different patterns—perhaps a skirt from one and a bodice from another—take the time to double-check the fit of the patterns you plan to use. Few women have measurements that match the patterns precisely. Thus, even with styles that are easy to make, adjustments may become necessary.

Begin by trimming all the pattern pieces you plan to use on the printed cutting lines; then press each piece. Next, compare your body measurements with those on the pattern envelopes and add or subtract the difference on the pattern pieces, as shown at right. Adjustments for horizontal measurements (such as bustline and waistline) are made on the side seam lines of the pattern pieces; for vertical measurements they should be made on the printed adjustment lines.

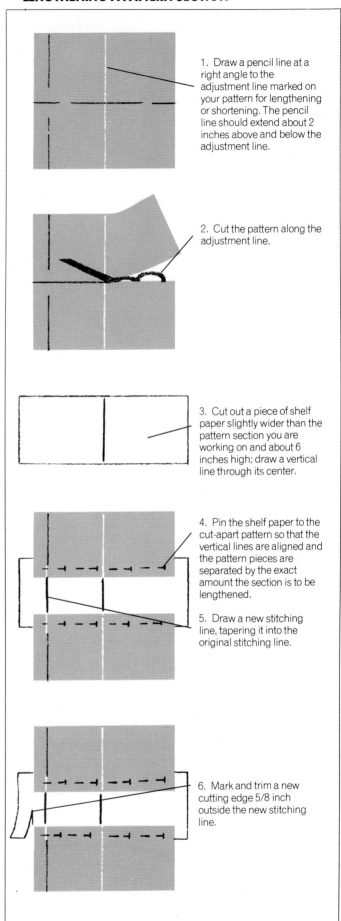

1. Draw a pencil line at a right angle to the adjustment line marked on your pattern for lengthening or shortening. The pencil line should extend about 2 inches above and below the adjustment line.

2. Cut the pattern along the adjustment line.

3. Cut out a piece of shelf paper slightly wider than the pattern section you are working on and about 6 inches high; draw a vertical line through its center.

4. Pin the shelf paper to the cut-apart pattern so that the vertical lines are aligned and the pattern pieces are separated by the exact amount the section is to be lengthened.

5. Draw a new stitching line, tapering it into the original stitching line.

6. Mark and trim a new cutting edge 5/8 inch outside the new stitching line.

SHORTENING A PATTERN SECTION

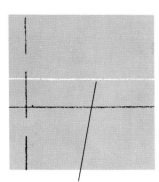

1. Draw a line above the adjustment line marked on your pattern for lengthening or shortening. The distance should be exactly equal to the amount the pattern section is to be shortened.

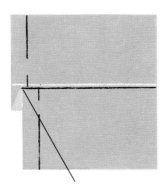

2. Fold the pattern so that the adjustment line meets the new line.

3. Press the fold flat with a warm iron.

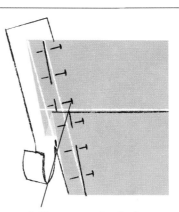

4. Pin a paper extension to your pattern.

5. Draw a new stitching line, tapering it into the original stitching line.

6. Mark and trim a new cutting edge 5/8 inch outside the new stitching line.

REDUCING A PATTERN SECTION

1. Divide the total amount to be reduced by the number of side seams on your garment. At the point where your pattern piece needs to be reduced, measure in from each stitching line and mark a distance equal to the resulting figure.

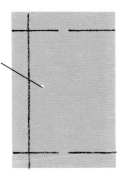

2. Draw a new stitching line, making a graduated curve from the point of reduction to the original stitching line.

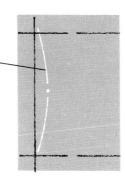

3. Mark and trim a new cutting edge 5/8 inch outside the new stitching line.

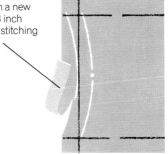

ENLARGING A PATTERN SECTION

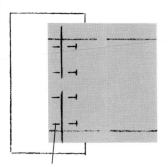

1. Lay your pattern piece on a strip of shelf paper cut to extend about 2 inches underneath the pattern and about 2 inches beyond the edge. Pin the pattern to the shelf paper.

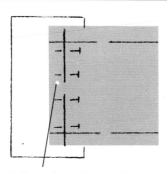

2. Divide the total amount to be enlarged by the number of side seams on your garment. At the point where your pattern piece needs to be enlarged, measure out from each stitching line and mark a distance equal to the resulting figure.

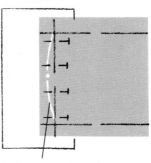

3. Draw a new tapered stitching line from the point of enlargement into the original stitching line.

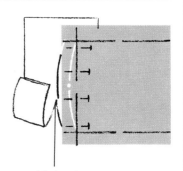

4. Mark and trim a new cutting edge 5/8 inch outside the new stitching line.

Combining the patterns

Adding a collar to a collarless bodice *(right)* is just one of the ways you can use pieces from one pattern to improve—and to individualize—another pattern. The procedure described here is a basic one in patternmaking. It may be used to redesign a neckline, to exchange collar styles or even to remove a collar from a bodice pattern that includes one. All these transformations are worked by tracing the neckline from one pattern onto the neckline of a second pattern, as shown.

Similarly, the techniques for substituting sleeves *(overleaf)* may be applied to any pair of set-in sleeve styles—provided that both sleeve patterns meet the bodice shoulder at the same point, and that the circumferences of both armholes are within 1/2 inch of being identical.

Whether for style or fit, or both, mixing the bodice from one pattern with the skirt of another can result in a striking new design. The success of the mix hinges on matching the waistlines of the two units flawlessly. Detailed instructions on the pages that follow show how to combine bodices and skirts when they meet at a natural waistline or in an A-line or classic princess dress.

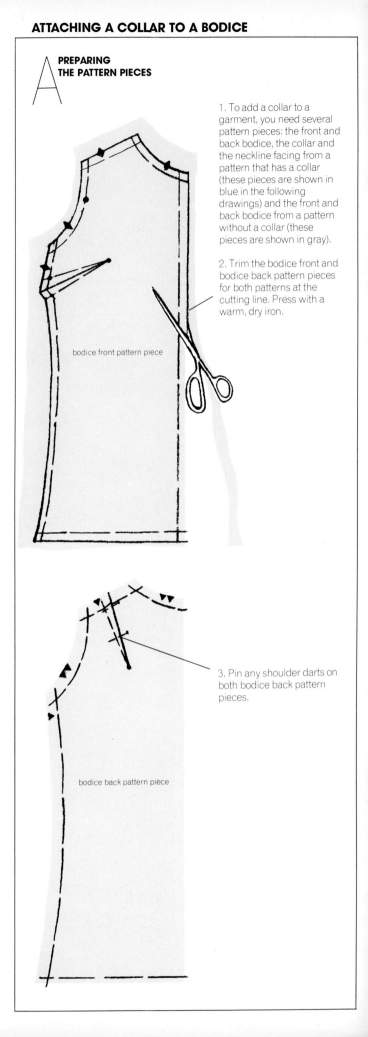

A PREPARING THE PATTERN PIECES

1. To add a collar to a garment, you need several pattern pieces: the front and back bodice, the collar and the neckline facing from a pattern that has a collar (these pieces are shown in blue in the following drawings) and the front and back bodice from a pattern without a collar (these pieces are shown in gray).

2. Trim the bodice front and bodice back pattern pieces for both patterns at the cutting line. Press with a warm, dry iron.

bodice front pattern piece

3. Pin any shoulder darts on both bodice back pattern pieces.

bodice back pattern piece

B ALIGNING THE PATTERN PIECES

4. Place the bodice front pattern piece for the garment with a collar on a flat surface and position the bodice front pattern piece to be altered on top of it, matching the center front markings.

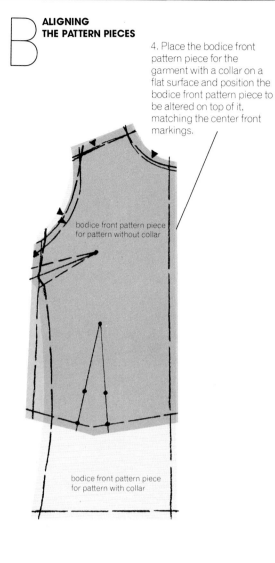

bodice front pattern piece for pattern without collar

bodice front pattern piece for pattern with collar

5. Move the top pattern until the shoulder seam line intersects the bottom pattern at the point where the neck and shoulder seam lines cross.

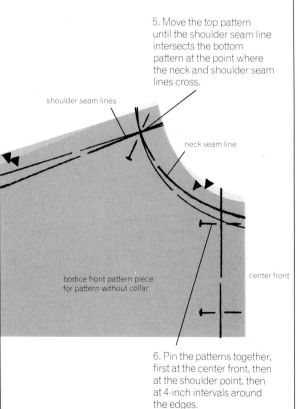

shoulder seam lines

neck seam line

bodice front pattern piece for pattern without collar

center front

6. Pin the patterns together, first at the center front, then at the shoulder point, then at 4-inch intervals around the edges.

C ALTERING THE PATTERN AT THE NECKLINE

7A. If the neckline of the top pattern piece is too high, trace the neckline of the bottom pattern onto it, noting the cutting line, seam line, notches and any other pertinent markings.

7B. If the neckline on the top pattern piece is too low, pin a piece of transparent paper to the piece as shown and transfer the neckline and other markings of the bottom pattern onto it.

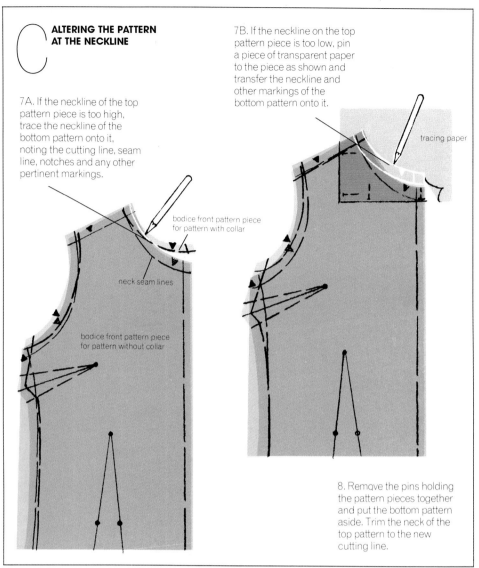

tracing paper

bodice front pattern piece for pattern with collar

neck seam lines

bodice front pattern piece for pattern without collar

8. Remove the pins holding the pattern pieces together and put the bottom pattern aside. Trim the neck of the top pattern to the new cutting line.

D ADJUSTING THE FACING

9. Place the front neck facing pattern piece for the pattern with a collar on top of the bodice front pattern piece to be altered, matching the center fronts and neck seam lines. Pin the two pieces in place.

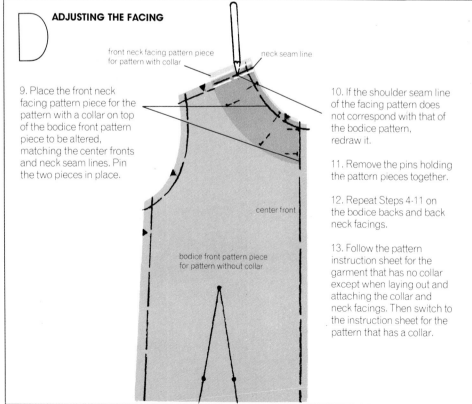

front neck facing pattern piece for pattern with collar

neck seam line

center front

bodice front pattern piece for pattern without collar

10. If the shoulder seam line of the facing pattern does not correspond with that of the bodice pattern, redraw it.

11. Remove the pins holding the pattern pieces together.

12. Repeat Steps 4-11 on the bodice backs and back neck facings.

13. Follow the pattern instruction sheet for the garment that has no collar except when laying out and attaching the collar and neck facings. Then switch to the instruction sheet for the pattern that has a collar.

SUBSTITUTING SLEEVES

A MEASURING THE ARMHOLE CIRCUMFERENCE

1. To substitute a sleeve for the one in your chosen pattern, you will need the pattern pieces for the front and back bodice that accompany the substitute sleeve, as well as the sleeve piece itself (these pieces are shown in blue in the following drawings) and the front and back bodice pieces from the basic pattern you are altering (these are shown in gray).

2. Determine the circumference of the armhole by measuring the armhole seam lines on the front and back bodice pattern pieces, omitting seam allowances and darts.

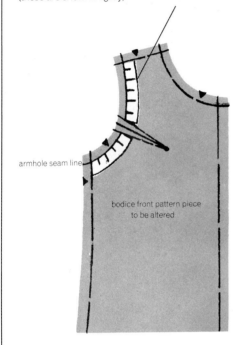

armhole seam line

bodice front pattern piece
to be altered

3. Repeat Step 2 on the bodice front and back pieces with the desired sleeve.

4. Compare the two armhole circumferences.

B ALTERING THE ARMHOLE CIRCUMFERENCE

5A. If the armhole on the bodice you are altering is larger than the one the sleeve was designed to fill, pin a piece of shelf paper to the bodice front pattern piece at the underarm.

6A. Raise the underarm seam line one half the total amount the circumference needs to be reduced, tapering the new seam line into the original at the vertical turn of the curve.

7A. Draw a new cutting line on the shelf paper 5/8 inch beyond the new seam line and parallel to it.

8A. Trim away the excess shelf paper. Repeat on the bodice back pattern piece.

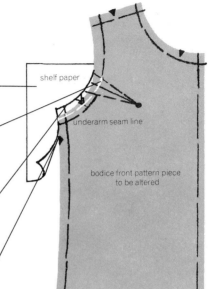

shelf paper

underarm seam line

bodice front pattern piece
to be altered

5B. If the armhole on the bodice you are altering is smaller than the one the sleeve was designed to fill, lower the underarm seam line on the bodice front pattern piece one half the total amount the circumference needs to be increased. Taper the new seam line into the original at the vertical turn of the curve.

6B. Draw a new cutting line 5/8 inch beyond the new seam line and parallel to it.

7B. Trim away the excess pattern tissue to the new cutting line.

8B. Repeat on the bodice back pattern piece.

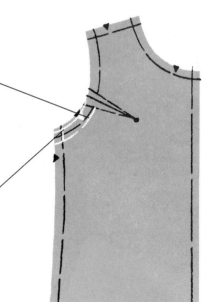

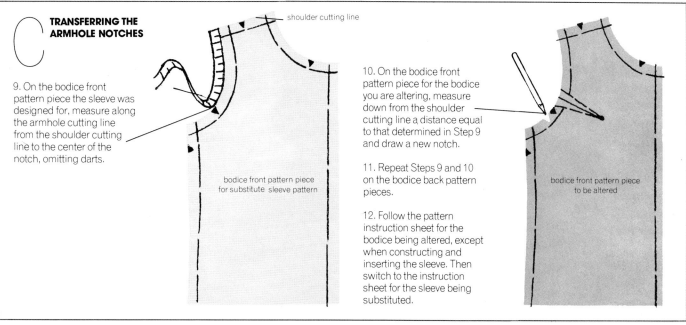

C TRANSFERRING THE ARMHOLE NOTCHES

9. On the bodice front pattern piece the sleeve was designed for, measure along the armhole cutting line from the shoulder cutting line to the center of the notch, omitting darts.

shoulder cutting line

bodice front pattern piece for substitute sleeve pattern

10. On the bodice front pattern piece for the bodice you are altering, measure down from the shoulder cutting line a distance equal to that determined in Step 9 and draw a new notch.

11. Repeat Steps 9 and 10 on the bodice back pattern pieces.

12. Follow the pattern instruction sheet for the bodice being altered, except when constructing and inserting the sleeve. Then switch to the instruction sheet for the sleeve being substituted.

bodice front pattern piece to be altered

COMBINING PATTERNS THAT HAVE NATURAL WAISTLINES

A PREPARING THE PATTERN PIECES

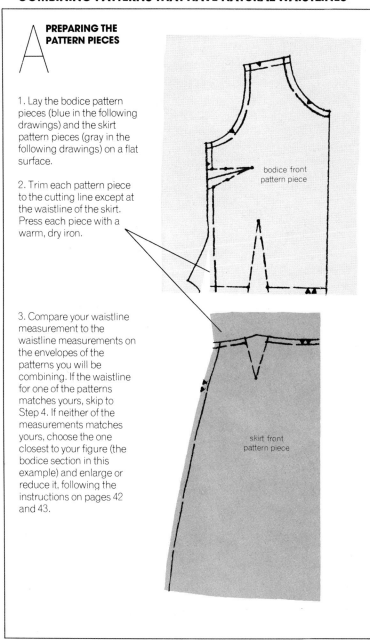

1. Lay the bodice pattern pieces (blue in the following drawings) and the skirt pattern pieces (gray in the following drawings) on a flat surface.

2. Trim each pattern piece to the cutting line except at the waistline of the skirt. Press each piece with a warm, dry iron.

bodice front pattern piece

3. Compare your waistline measurement to the waistline measurements on the envelopes of the patterns you will be combining. If the waistline for one of the patterns matches yours, skip to Step 4. If neither of the measurements matches yours, choose the one closest to your figure (the bodice section in this example) and enlarge or reduce it, following the instructions on pages 42 and 43.

skirt front pattern piece

B MEASURING THE WAISTLINES OF THE BODICE AND SKIRT

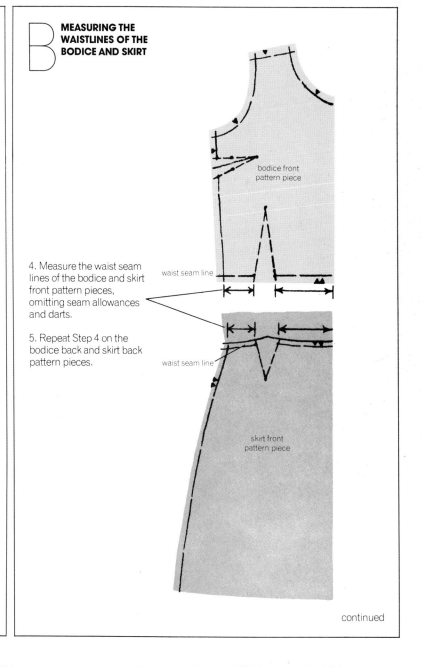

bodice front pattern piece

4. Measure the waist seam lines of the bodice and skirt front pattern pieces, omitting seam allowances and darts.

waist seam line

5. Repeat Step 4 on the bodice back and skirt back pattern pieces.

waist seam line

skirt front pattern piece

continued

C ADJUSTING THE SECTION THAT DOES NOT FIT

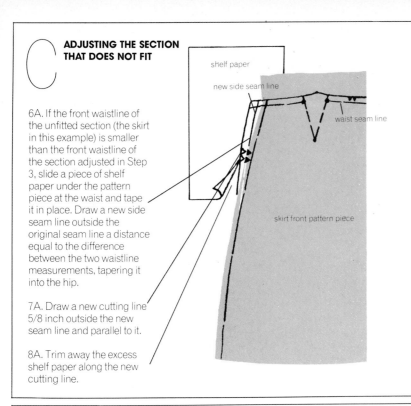

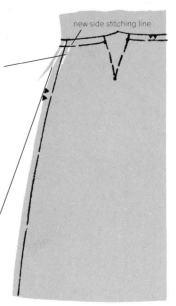

6A. If the front waistline of the unfitted section (the skirt in this example) is smaller than the front waistline of the section adjusted in Step 3, slide a piece of shelf paper under the pattern piece at the waist and tape it in place. Draw a new side seam line outside the original seam line a distance equal to the difference between the two waistline measurements, tapering it into the hip.

7A. Draw a new cutting line 5/8 inch outside the new seam line and parallel to it.

8A. Trim away the excess shelf paper along the new cutting line.

6B. If the front waistline of the unfitted section (the skirt in this example) is larger than the front waistline of the section adjusted in Step 3, draw a new seam line inside the original seam line a distance equal to the difference between the two waistline measurements, tapering it into the hip.

7B. Draw a new cutting line 5/8 inch outside the new seam line and parallel to it.

8B. Trim away the excess pattern tissue along the new cutting line.

9. Repeat Steps 6-8 on the back pattern pieces of the section that does not fit.

D DETERMINING WHETHER THE WAISTLINE DARTS ALIGN

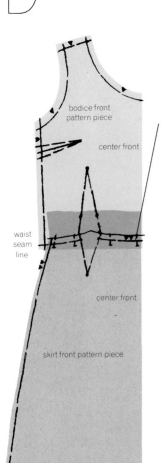

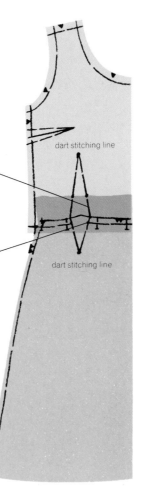

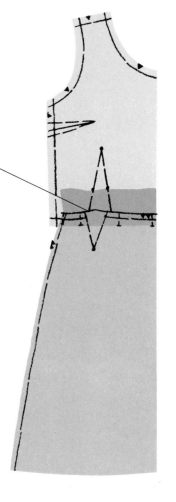

10. Place the bodice front pattern piece on a flat surface.

11. Place the skirt front pattern piece over the bodice front pattern piece, matching the center fronts and the waist seam lines. Pin in place.

12. Check the dart stitching lines closest to the center front of the garment to determine whether the darts on the bodice and skirt pattern pieces align.

13A. If the dart stitching lines intersect at the waist seam lines, the darts align. You can now transfer all notches, easing symbols and other pertinent markings from the bodice to the skirt. Trim away the excess pattern tissue at the waist to the cutting line. Repeat the procedure on the back bodice and back skirt pattern pieces; if they also align, proceed to make the garment.

13B. If the dart stitching lines do not intersect at the waist seam lines, the darts are not aligned and the dart on the skirt must be moved. If there are two darts close together on the skirt and only a single corresponding one on the bodice, both skirt darts must be moved to keep the distance between them the same as it was originally.

14. Repeat Steps 10-13 on the bodice and skirt back pattern pieces.

E MOVING THE SKIRT DART

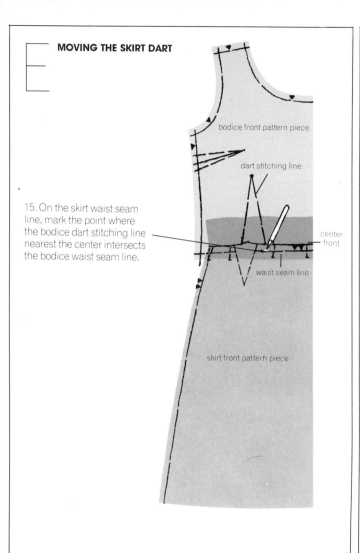

15. On the skirt waist seam line, mark the point where the bodice dart stitching line nearest the center intersects the bodice waist seam line.

bodice front pattern piece

dart stitching line

center front

waist seam line

skirt front pattern piece

16. Separate the pattern pieces.

17. Draw new darts on the skirt front pattern piece exactly parallel to the original darts, starting at the mark made in Step 15.

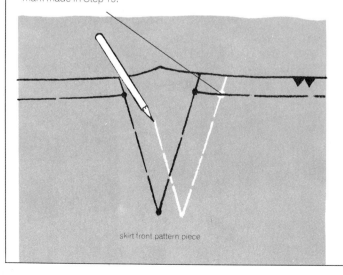

skirt front pattern piece

F REDRAWING THE WAISTLINE DART POINTS

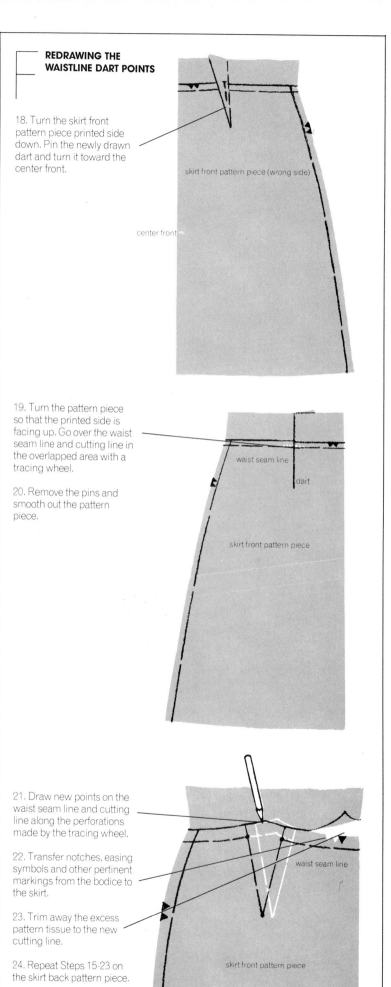

18. Turn the skirt front pattern piece printed side down. Pin the newly drawn dart and turn it toward the center front.

skirt front pattern piece (wrong side)

center front

19. Turn the pattern piece so that the printed side is facing up. Go over the waist seam line and cutting line in the overlapped area with a tracing wheel.

20. Remove the pins and smooth out the pattern piece.

waist seam line

dart

skirt front pattern piece

21. Draw new points on the waist seam line and cutting line along the perforations made by the tracing wheel.

22. Transfer notches, easing symbols and other pertinent markings from the bodice to the skirt.

23. Trim away the excess pattern tissue to the new cutting line.

24. Repeat Steps 15-23 on the skirt back pattern piece.

waist seam line

skirt front pattern piece

COMBINING TWO PRINCESS-LINE DRESS PATTERNS

A PREPARING THE PATTERN PIECES

1. Cut all of the pattern pieces at the waistline, and select the bodice pattern pieces (blue in these drawings) and the skirt pattern pieces (gray in these drawings) that you want to use.

2. Trim each pattern piece along the cutting line and press with a warm, dry iron.

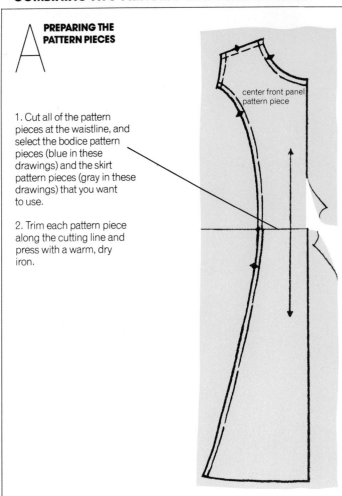

center front panel pattern piece

3. Compare your waistline measurement with those on the envelopes of the patterns you will be combining. If the waistline for one of the patterns matches yours, go on to Step 4. If neither of the measurements matches yours, choose the one that is closer to your figure and enlarge or reduce it, following the instructions on pages 42 and 43.

B ADJUSTING THE CENTER PANELS

4. Tape the bodice and skirt pattern pieces for the center front panels together at the waistline, matching center front markings and keeping the grain lines straight.

5. Slide a piece of shelf paper under the combined pattern piece at the waistline and tape it in place.

6. Draw a new seam line by starting at the seam line adjusted in Step 3 and gradually tapering it into the other seam line.

7. Draw a new cutting line 5/8 inch outside the new seam line.

8. Trim away the excess shelf paper along the new cutting line.

9. Repeat Steps 4-8 on the center back panels.

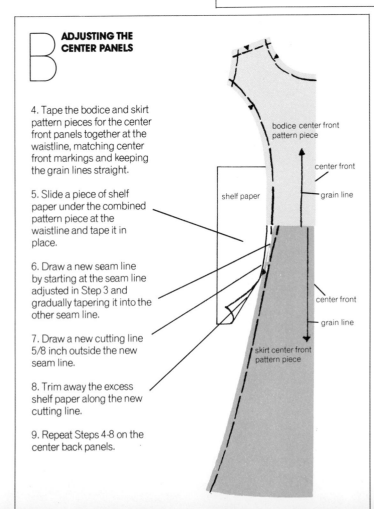

bodice center front pattern piece

center front

grain line

shelf paper

center front

grain line

skirt center front pattern piece

C ADJUSTING THE SIDE PANELS

10. Center the bodice side front pattern piece over the skirt side front pattern piece. Tape the two pieces together, keeping the grain lines straight.

11. Slide a piece of shelf paper under the combined pattern piece at the waistline and tape it in place.

12. Draw new seam lines on each side of the panel by starting at the seam lines adjusted in Step 3 and gradually tapering them into the other seam lines.

13. Draw new cutting lines 5/8 inch outside the new stitching lines.

14. Trim away the excess shelf paper along the new cutting line.

15. Repeat Steps 10-14 on the side back panels.

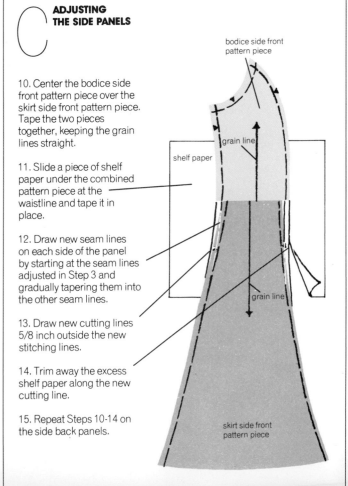

bodice side front pattern piece

grain line

shelf paper

grain line

skirt side front pattern piece

COMBINING TWO A-LINE DRESS PATTERNS

A PREPARING THE PATTERN PIECES

1. Cut all the pattern pieces apart at the waistline, and select the bodice pattern pieces (blue in these drawings) and skirt pattern pieces (gray in these drawings) that you want to use.

2. Trim each pattern piece along the cutting line and press with a warm, dry iron.

3. Compare your waistline measurement to those on the envelopes of the patterns you will be combining. If the waistline for one of the patterns matches yours, go on to Step 4. If neither of the measurements matches yours, choose the one that is closer to your figure and enlarge or reduce it, following the instructions on pages 42 and 43.

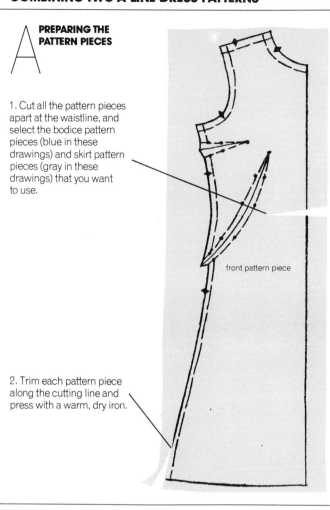

front pattern piece

B ADJUSTING THE DRESS FRONT PATTERN PIECE

4. Tape the bodice front and skirt front pattern pieces together at the waistline, matching the center front markings.

5. Slide a piece of shelf paper under the combined pattern piece at the waistline and tape it in place.

6. Draw a new seam line by starting at the line adjusted in Step 3 and gradually tapering it into the other line.

7. Draw a new cutting line 5/8 inch outside the new seam line.

8. Trim away the excess shelf paper along the new cutting line.

9. If your pattern has a dart that runs from the bust to the hip—known as a French dart—adjust it as follows: Draw a new fold line, maintaining the original curve. Draw new stitching lines parallel to the fold line.

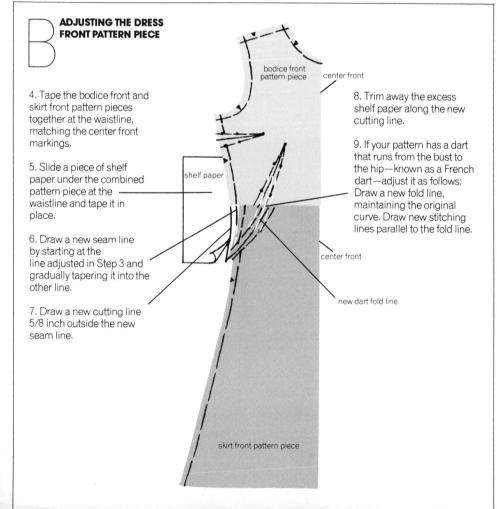

bodice front pattern piece

center front

shelf paper

center front

new dart fold line

skirt front pattern piece

C ADJUSTING THE DRESS BACK PATTERN

10. Repeat Steps 4-8 on the bodice back and skirt back pattern pieces.

11. Adjust the position of the dart on the back of the combined pattern piece by moving the markings on the skirt piece directly below the markings on the bodice.

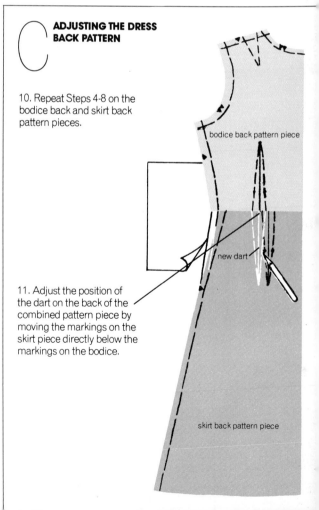

bodice back pattern piece

new dart

skirt back pattern piece

4
FRESHNESS FROM RESTYLING

Once there was a time when young ladies remodeled their clothes because they had to: the piggy bank was empty, or the stores too far away. And if Cinderella wanted to get to the ball in anything worth wearing, it was up to her to perform her own magic with a clever needle and an old dress hauled from the back of the closet.

Today, on the whole, we restyle our wardrobes because we choose to. We have

A SPRIGHTLY REPRISE FOR OLD FAVORITES

emerged from the compulsion to be always mint-new at all costs. And it has become downright chic to hang onto last year's—or last decade's—favorites, and to find ways of converting them into something fresh and fanciful. In fact some of the country's smartest boutiques have thrived by turning wardrobe discards into with-it wear for the young and adventurous.

Consider, for example, Madame Cherie Dervin, who in the early 1970s became proprietor and presiding creative genius of a New York City shop devoted to just this kind of sartorial revivification. Mme. Dervin began buying up closets full of old dresses —some dating back to the 1890s—together with scarves, jewelry, hats and other oddments. Much of her trove came from used-clothes salesmen, though she often has picked up a choice item from either a client or friend who knew her work. If the old dresses were attractive and in good condition, she might modify them only slightly or simply refurbish them with a little mending or replacing of buttons. Dresses too bulky or otherwise troublesome to restore have been cut up to create entirely new garments, using a technique called piecing that was an important part of virtually every woman's homemaking repertoire a century ago.

Mme. Dervin might, for instance, take the skirt of an old dress and cut from it a new one-piece bodice. Then she might cut up the old bodice and combine it with pieces of another dress, or dresses, to create a long, wide patchwork skirt. Lastly she could add ruffles made from still another dress to the neckline and wrists of the new garment.

Some Dervin gowns grew from patchwork medleys of 1920s and '30s prints. In others, she has used old silk neckerchiefs as her raw material, combining as many as 12 or 14 to produce anything from a bikini to an entire dress. Her clients have included young men from rock bands who like the color mixtures and ruffled sleeves.

Other boutique operators have worked equally ingenious reincarnations from even humbler discards. They originated the art of recycling worn-out workaday blue denim into high-priced toggery. Under their touch, a pair of frazzled jeans might turn into a long skirt with triangles of bright, contrasting fabric inserted fore and aft. Beat-up denim jackets or coveralls sprouted embroidery, glittering paillettes and appliqué flowers. All this fanciful sprucing up makes little effort to disguise the ancient origins of the garment beneath it. Quite the contrary. The softer, more faded and frayed the original fabric, the more it is coveted.

Giving new life to retired garments emerged as a contemporary impulse among the younger generation of the '60s. It is they who first made beat-up old clothes really fashionable—to the consternation of their tradition-bound elders, many of whom, besides an inbred preference for the conventional mold, remembered having nothing to wear *but* castoffs and hand-me-downs during their own youth in the Depression and post-GI days. Indeed, during the '30s and into the '40s the only pajamas, underwear and even dresses that some back-country youngsters owned were fashioned from old flour and feed sacks.

But in the boom times of the '60s, youngsters who had never known hard times began to prize the scrubby look of old discards and rough work clothes. They started haunting secondhand dealers and army-surplus stores for garments that had more character and individuality—or better yet, soul—and hence were more satisfying to wear than unripened, easy-come clothing just off the assembly line. Indeed, the desire to appear in soul clothes has since become so strong that many people try to give brand-new clothing an instant antiquity, for example, by dunking such items as jeans in bleach to impart a soft patina.

But no ersatz oldies have the appeal of real ones that have aged naturally—especially ones that we ourselves have worn over the years. As with certain old friends, we tend to be most comfortable with them —and feel they bring out the best in us. A certain vintage blouse may have a warm, flattering color that has rarely failed to evoke compliments. Or the fabric of a skirt may have been particularly handsome or supple, or perhaps cut in a way that was somehow uniquely, personally right. Garments like these make prime candidates for restyling; and to bring them back into circulation can be in many ways more satisfying than buying a brand-new couturier creation.

The secret of success in restyling is to think big. All too often, the timid half measure—the little band of fabric added at the bottom to lengthen a dress—will look exactly like what it is: an afterthought. By contrast, the restyling ideas that appear in the following section all strive to give the remodeled garment a totally new look. And in most cases the trick is turned by some simple —yet bold—device; a touch of fabric may be added in unexpected places, or entire panels of material may be slashed away.

Narrow pants, for example, are flared and lengthened by cutting into the side seams and adding a brightly printed godet and border. A mini skirt is cleverly cut even shorter, this time on the bias, and wide, contrasting bias strips are added to achieve whatever length you please. A classic shirt acquires an elegant high-standing stock. Or a conventional gored skirt takes on new style with a burst of low, narrow pleats inserted in the front seams.

Whether you follow these design suggestions or develop your own, before you begin make sure that the clothes you have earmarked for restyling are worth the time and effort. Inspect the major seams, and check the condition of the fabric at the elbows of long sleeves, the seats of dresses and skirts, and the stomach panels on skirts and pants. If any important seams are pulling out or the fabric has worn noticeably thin at crucial points, the garment as a whole may be too far gone for successful revival. Look critically also, at the overall luster and color of the fabric; if it is too tired or stained, these flaws will show up dramatically the minute you add sections of new material.

Another vital consideration as you plan remodeling changes is to establish the correct proportions of the new look. Exactly how wide, for instance, should you make the godet to give the proper flare to a pair of narrow pants? And how far up the leg do you start it? Precisely how much fabric should you add to extend the skirt? The answers lie in your own personal proportions. What looks right on a long, lean figure may be disastrous for a short, plump one.

Once you have calculated the rough parameters of the intended change in front of a full-length mirror, it may help to make a paper or muslin pattern. You can then pin or baste the pattern pieces to the old garment for test fittings. Such fussiness at the preliminary stages can pay handsome dividends. When you get the dimensions of the proposed restyling exactly right, the results will leap out at you from the mirror.

When you are selecting new fabric to be added, take your old garment along to the store. There, under natural light, you will be able to judge how well the two materials will look when sewed together. And be sure to judge carefully, for color in a fabric can change dramatically with different textures and weaves. If your plan is to pick up in a solid fabric one of several colors in a print or plaid, you should select a slightly darker hue than the original; the darker color will seem like a closer match than one that misses by being too light. If you can't get a good match, switch to a color that is distinctly dif-ferent but that mixes harmoniously with the original. Remember, however, that the two materials to be combined should be similar in weight and weave if the seams where they join will be under constant functional stress; otherwise, the seam will pucker.

All of the lively restyling ideas in these pages begin with classic garments that are probably hanging in your closet right now —a simple long-sleeved blouse, a plain man-tailored shirt, a jewel-neckline sheath, an A-line or six-gore skirt, and tapered pants. With the expenditure of very little time—and a good deal of pleasure—you can give them a second chance to play an active role in your fashion life.

Hollywood designer Edith Head created concepts such as these when the 1947 New Look devastated wardrobes. She remodeled the wartime dress at left, giving it a boat neck, pushed-up sleeves and a lace overskirt.

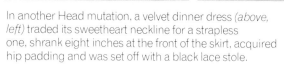
In another Head mutation, a velvet dinner dress (above, left) traded its sweetheart neckline for a strapless one, shrank eight inches at the front of the skirt, acquired hip padding and was set off with a black lace stole.

Variations on a basic theme

Restyling a dress can be as creative as making a new one—and as easy, because most of the seams are already sewn. As these three variations on the basic A line at the far left show, you can go to any length you want, figuratively and literally.

By simply inserting godets into the side seams, you can achieve a bright new flair *(second from left)*. Or you can try a more challenging variation by reshaping and banding the neckline, then adding cuffs *(third from left)*. Another band around the hem extends its length. Finally *(near left)*, if the old dress is of a lightweight fabric, you can turn it into a blouson shirtwaist by sewing a new A-line skirt to the top, replacing the zipper with front tabs and adding a sash. (Instructions for these alternatives appear on the following pages.)

Before you begin, be sure the original dress and the new fabric are compatible in weight and washability. Be sure, too, that the original stitch and crease lines can be removed so that no trace of the old style mars your new invention.

CONVERTING A DRESS INTO A FLARED TUNIC

A PREPARING THE HEM

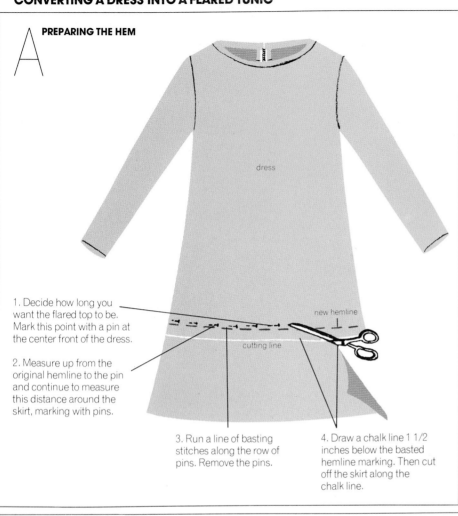

dress

new hemline

cutting line

1. Decide how long you want the flared top to be. Mark this point with a pin at the center front of the dress.

2. Measure up from the original hemline to the pin and continue to measure this distance around the skirt, marking with pins.

3. Run a line of basting stitches along the row of pins. Remove the pins.

4. Draw a chalk line 1 1/2 inches below the basted hemline marking. Then cut off the skirt along the chalk line.

B PREPARING THE SIDE SEAMS

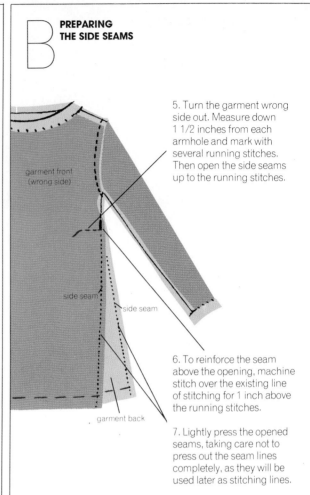

garment front (wrong side)

side seam
side seam

garment back

5. Turn the garment wrong side out. Measure down 1 1/2 inches from each armhole and mark with several running stitches. Then open the side seams up to the running stitches.

6. To reinforce the seam above the opening, machine stitch over the existing line of stitching for 1 inch above the running stitches.

7. Lightly press the opened seams, taking care not to press out the seam lines completely, as they will be used later as stitching lines.

C CUTTING OUT THE SIDE GODETS

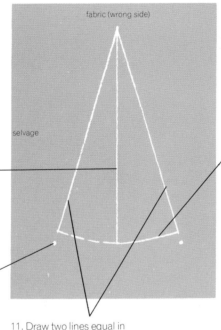

fabric (wrong side)

selvage

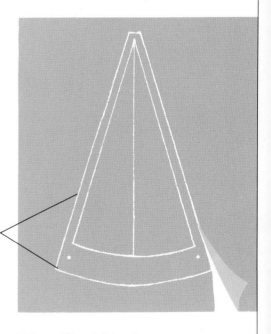

8. For the side godets you will need 3/4 yard of fabric in any of the standard widths—36, 45 or 54 inches.

9. Straighten the grain of the fabric (page 34) and place it wrong side up on a flat surface. Draw a vertical line parallel to the selvage and equal to the length of the opened side seam from the running stitches to the basted hemline.

10. Make a dot on each side of the bottom of the vertical line at a distance equal to 1/4 of the width of the cutoff front of the garment at the hemline.

11. Draw two lines equal in length to the vertical line, running diagonally from the top of the vertical line toward the dots. These new lines will become the stitching lines.

12. Connect the bottom of the triangle with a curved line.

13. Draw two cutting lines 1/2 inch outside the lines drawn in Step 11. Where the lines intersect, square off the tip to 1/2 inch above the point where the stitching lines meet. Then draw a line 1 1/2 inches below—and parallel to—the bottom curved line. Cut out the godet along these lines.

14. Repeat Steps 9-13 to cut out the second godet. Then mark the hemlines with lines of basting stitches.

D ATTACHING THE GODETS TO THE GARMENT

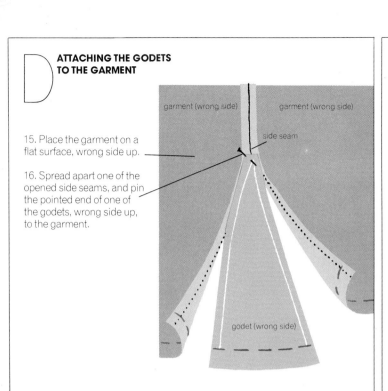

15. Place the garment on a flat surface, wrong side up.

16. Spread apart one of the opened side seams, and pin the pointed end of one of the godets, wrong side up, to the garment.

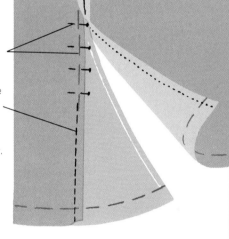

17. Pin the garment to one side of the godet. Baste and remove the pins.

18. Machine stitch along the seam lines and remove the basting.

19. Attach the godet to the other seam in the same way.

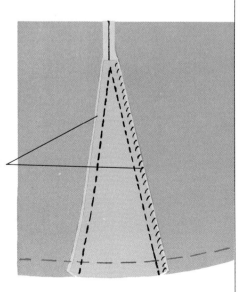

20. Press the seam allowances toward the garment. Then sew them together using an overcast stitch (Appendix).

21. Repeat Steps 16-20 to attach the second godet.

E HEMMING THE FLARED GARMENT

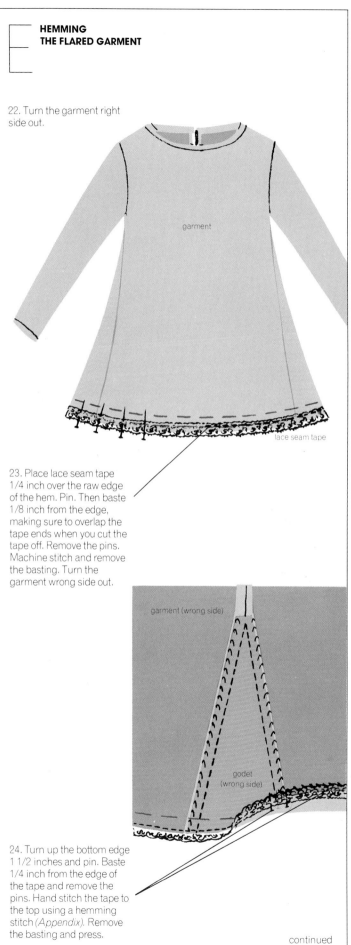

22. Turn the garment right side out.

23. Place lace seam tape 1/4 inch over the raw edge of the hem. Pin. Then baste 1/8 inch from the edge, making sure to overlap the tape ends when you cut the tape off. Remove the pins. Machine stitch and remove the basting. Turn the garment wrong side out.

24. Turn up the bottom edge 1 1/2 inches and pin. Baste 1/4 inch from the edge of the tape and remove the pins. Hand stitch the tape to the top using a hemming stitch (Appendix). Remove the basting and press.

continued

PREPARING THE SLEEVES

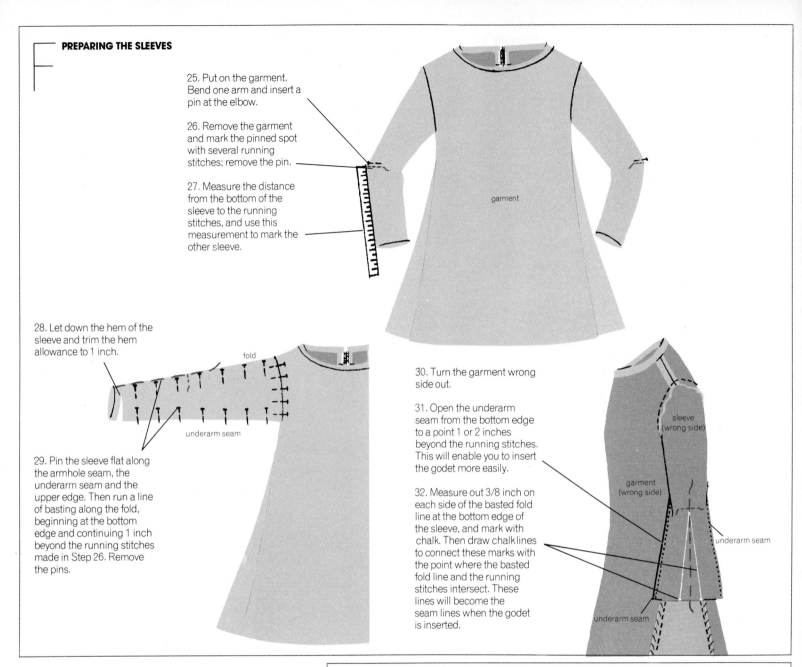

25. Put on the garment. Bend one arm and insert a pin at the elbow.

26. Remove the garment and mark the pinned spot with several running stitches; remove the pin.

27. Measure the distance from the bottom of the sleeve to the running stitches, and use this measurement to mark the other sleeve.

garment

28. Let down the hem of the sleeve and trim the hem allowance to 1 inch.

fold

underarm seam

29. Pin the sleeve flat along the armhole seam, the underarm seam and the upper edge. Then run a line of basting along the fold, beginning at the bottom edge and continuing 1 inch beyond the running stitches made in Step 26. Remove the pins.

30. Turn the garment wrong side out.

31. Open the underarm seam from the bottom edge to a point 1 or 2 inches beyond the running stitches. This will enable you to insert the godet more easily.

32. Measure out 3/8 inch on each side of the basted fold line at the bottom edge of the sleeve, and mark with chalk. Then draw chalk lines to connect these marks with the point where the basted fold line and the running stitches intersect. These lines will become the seam lines when the godet is inserted.

sleeve (wrong side)

garment (wrong side)

underarm seam

underarm seam

G CUTTING OUT THE SLEEVE GODETS

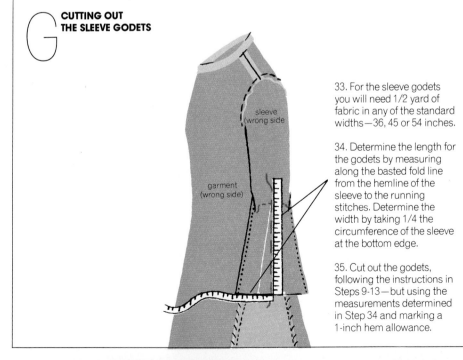

sleeve (wrong side

garment (wrong side)

33. For the sleeve godets you will need 1/2 yard of fabric in any of the standard widths—36, 45 or 54 inches.

34. Determine the length for the godets by measuring along the basted fold line from the hemline of the sleeve to the running stitches. Determine the width by taking 1/4 the circumference of the sleeve at the bottom edge.

35. Cut out the godets, following the instructions in Steps 9-13—but using the measurements determined in Step 34 and marking a 1-inch hem allowance.

ATTACHING THE SLEEVE GODETS

36. Set your sewing machine to 15 stitches to the inch. Starting 2 inches below the running stitches on the sleeve, stitch one side of the chalk-marked stitching line to the point where the stitching lines intersect. Pivot (Appendix). Take one stitch across the point, then stitch down the other side for 2 inches.

37. Slash the sleeve along the basted fold line. Cut up to—but not through—the horizontal machine stitch at the point.

38. Place the godet, wrong side up, in the slashed opening. Push a pin through the point of the opening and through the godet where its seam-line markings intersect. Then align the seam-line markings of the sleeve and the godet along one side, and push the pin through both, keeping the pin parallel to the seam line.

39. Align the sleeve and godet seam-line markings along the other side, insert a second pin in the same way. The two pins should cross at the point of the godet.

40. Pin the godet to the sleeve along the seam lines. Baste and remove all pins except the two crossed pins at the point of the godet.

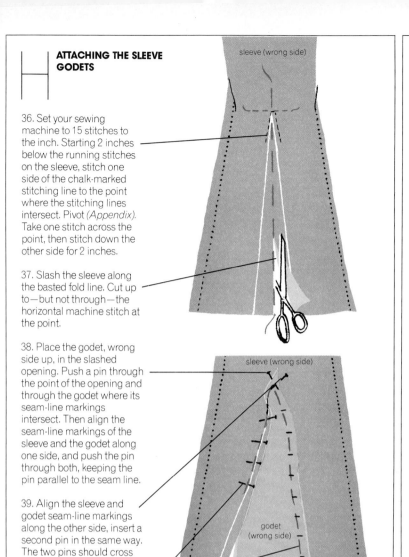

STITCHING THE SLEEVE GODETS

41. Reset your machine to the normal 12 stitches to the inch, and stitch the godet to the sleeve as follows: start at the bottom edge and sew along one side of the godet. When you reach the pin at the point, stop the machine. Remove the pin and stitch up to the point.

42. Pivot (Appendix). Remove the remaining pin and continue stitching down the seam line to the bottom of the sleeve. Remove the basting.

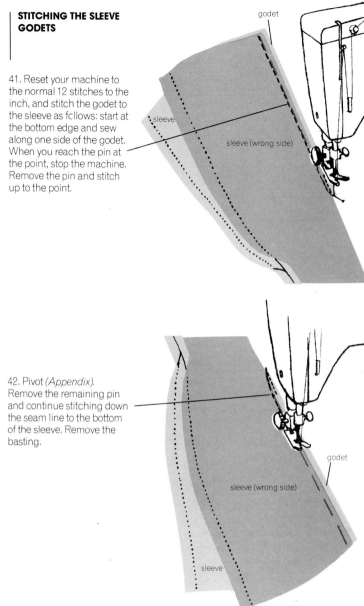

COMPLETING THE SLEEVE GODETS

43. Press the seam allowances toward the sleeve and sew them together, using an overcast stitch (Appendix).

44. Stitch the underarm seam closed. Then hem the sleeve, following the instructions in Steps 22-24.

45. To insert the godet in the other sleeve, repeat Steps 28-44.

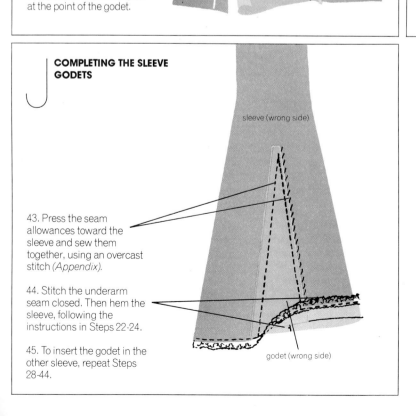

ADDING A V NECKLINE AND HEMLINE BANDS TO A DRESS

A PREPARING THE NECKLINE

1. Decide how deep you want the V-shaped neckline opening to be. Mark this point with a pin on the center front of the dress; re-mark the spot with a line of horizontal running stitches. Remove the pin.

2. Measure down the center front of the dress from the neck edge to the running stitches.

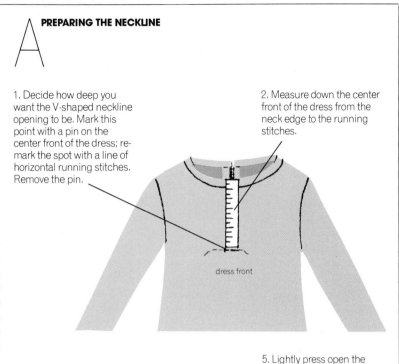

dress front

3. Remove the existing neckline band or neckline facing.

5. Lightly press open the neckline seam allowance; then trim away the seam allowance along the stitching line.

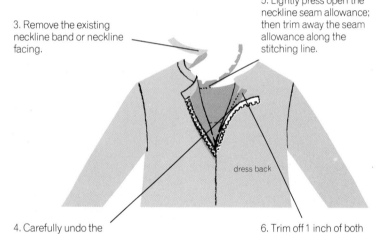

dress back

4. Carefully undo the stitching securing the zipper to the dress for about 3 inches below the neck seam line.

6. Trim off 1 inch of both sides of the center back seam, cutting along the stitching line.

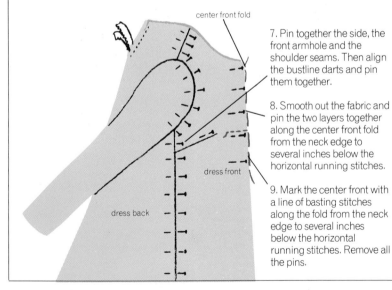

center front fold

dress front

dress back

7. Pin together the side, the front armhole and the shoulder seams. Then align the bustline darts and pin them together.

8. Smooth out the fabric and pin the two layers together along the center front fold from the neck edge to several inches below the horizontal running stitches.

9. Mark the center front with a line of basting stitches along the fold from the neck edge to several inches below the horizontal running stitches. Remove all the pins.

B MAKING A PATTERN FOR THE NECKLINE BAND AND FACING

10. Place a piece of muslin on a flat surface.

11. Draw a vertical line down the center of the muslin, following the lengthwise grain.

12. Open the zipper and spread out the neckline of the dress over the muslin, making sure that the basted center front on the dress is in alignment with the vertical line on the muslin.

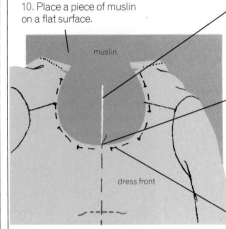

muslin

dress front

13. Pin around the neckline.

14. Using a tracing wheel and dressmaker's carbon paper, mark the outline of the neckline. Next trace along the trimmed center-back stitching lines; then mark along the shoulder lines for about 2 inches.

15. Remove the pins and set the dress aside.

16. Measure down the vertical center line on the muslin from the curved edge, and mark a distance equal to the measurement taken in Step 2.

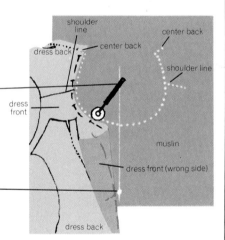

shoulder line

center back

dress back

center back

shoulder line

dress front

muslin

dress front (wrong side)

dress back

17. Extend the center-back lines to 1 1/2 inches. Then, beginning at the shoulder lines, mark the outer back neck curves 1 1/2 inches from the inner back curves.

18. Mark the inner edges of the V neckline by ruling chalk lines connecting the inner end of each shoulder line with the mark on the vertical center line.

19. Starting at the shoulder lines, mark the outer edges of the V by ruling chalk lines 1 1/2 inches outside and parallel to the lines drawn in Step 18.

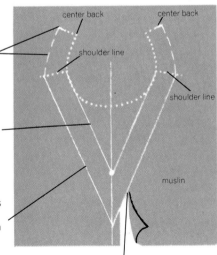

center back

center back

shoulder line

shoulder line

muslin

20. Cut out the muslin pattern for the V along the chalk lines and the tracing wheel markings.

C MARKING THE NECKLINE ON THE DRESS

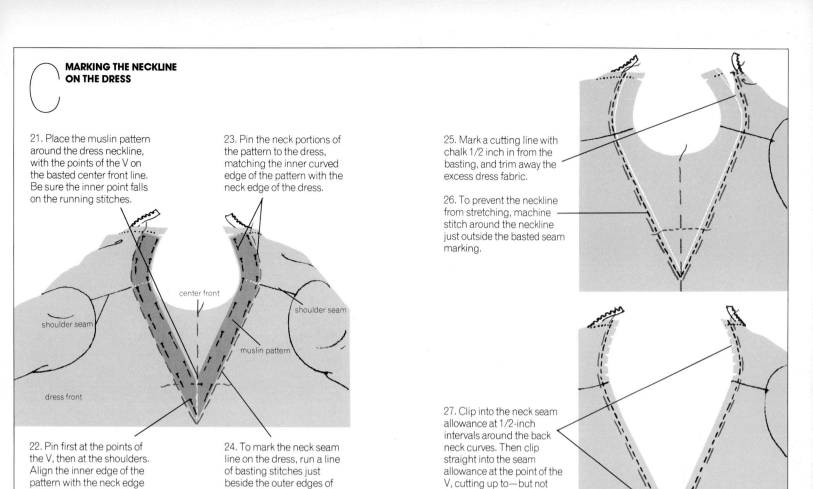

21. Place the muslin pattern around the dress neckline, with the points of the V on the basted center front line. Be sure the inner point falls on the running stitches.

23. Pin the neck portions of the pattern to the dress, matching the inner curved edge of the pattern with the neck edge of the dress.

25. Mark a cutting line with chalk 1/2 inch in from the basting, and trim away the excess dress fabric.

26. To prevent the neckline from stretching, machine stitch around the neckline just outside the basted seam marking.

shoulder seam

center front

shoulder seam

muslin pattern

dress front

22. Pin first at the points of the V, then at the shoulders. Align the inner edge of the pattern with the neck edge of the dress and match at the shoulders. Now pin along the inner and outer edges of the V.

24. To mark the neck seam line on the dress, run a line of basting stitches just beside the outer edges of the pattern. Remove the pins and set the pattern aside.

27. Clip into the neck seam allowance at 1/2-inch intervals around the back neck curves. Then clip straight into the seam allowance at the point of the V, cutting up to—but not through—the stitching.

D PREPARING THE NECKLINE BAND AND FACING

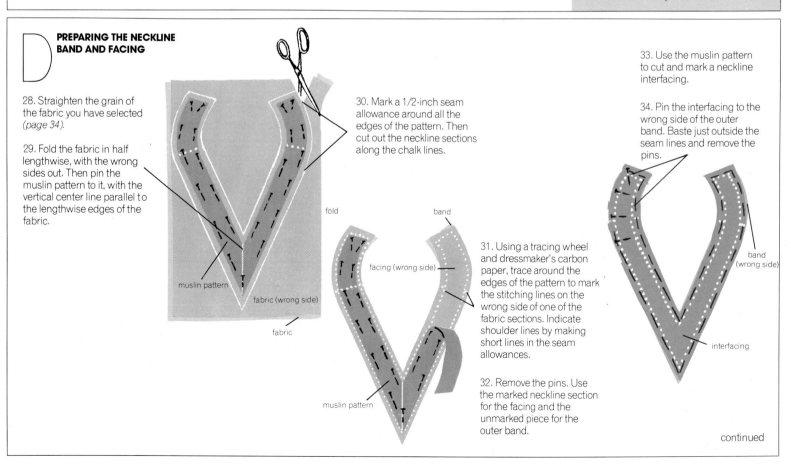

28. Straighten the grain of the fabric you have selected *(page 34)*.

29. Fold the fabric in half lengthwise, with the wrong sides out. Then pin the muslin pattern to it, with the vertical center line parallel to the lengthwise edges of the fabric.

30. Mark a 1/2-inch seam allowance around all the edges of the pattern. Then cut out the neckline sections along the chalk lines.

33. Use the muslin pattern to cut and mark a neckline interfacing.

34. Pin the interfacing to the wrong side of the outer band. Baste just outside the seam lines and remove the pins.

fold

band

muslin pattern

fabric (wrong side)

fabric

facing (wrong side)

muslin pattern

band

band (wrong side)

interfacing

31. Using a tracing wheel and dressmaker's carbon paper, trace around the edges of the pattern to mark the stitching lines on the wrong side of one of the fabric sections. Indicate shoulder lines by making short lines in the seam allowances.

32. Remove the pins. Use the marked neckline section for the facing and the unmarked piece for the outer band.

continued

E | ATTACHING THE NECKLINE BAND

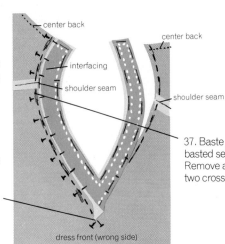

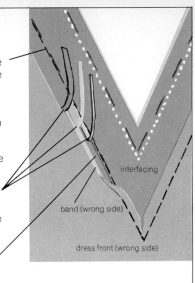

35. Turn the dress wrong side out. Place the neckline band, wrong side out, in the neckline opening, matching the outer point of the V with the clipped V of the dress.

36. At the point of the V, insert two crossed pins parallel to the seam lines. Then match the band at the shoulder seam lines and center back, and pin the band to the neck along the basted seam markings.

37. Baste just inside the basted seam markings. Remove all pins except the two crossed pins.

38. Machine stitch along the seam markings, pivoting the material (Appendix) and removing the crossed pins at the point of the V as shown in the instructions on page 63, Box I, Steps 41-42.

39. Trim the seam allowance of the interfacing to the stitching line around the band seam. Trim the seam allowance of the band to 1/8 inch; then trim the seam allowance of the dress to 1/4 inch.

40. Press all seam allowances toward the band.

F | ATTACHING THE FACING TO THE NECKLINE BAND

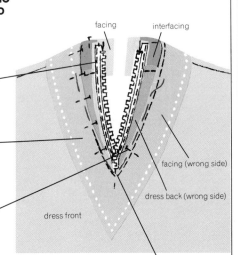

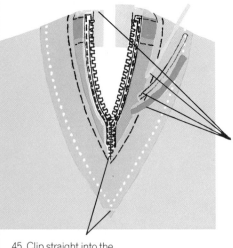

41. Turn the dress right side out and restitch the zipper to the dress and to the neckline band.

42. Place the facing, wrong side up, over the neckline band, matching the inner points of the V.

43. Pin the facing to the neckline band along the inner neck seam line. Baste and remove the pins.

44. Machine stitch along the inner neck seam line, pivoting at the point of the V. Remove the bastings.

45. Clip straight into the inner neck seam allowances at the point of the V, cutting up to but not through the stitching. Then trim the outer seam allowance of the facing up to the stitching lines at the tip of the V.

46. Trim the inner seam allowance of the facing to 1/4 inch and the seam allowance of the neckline band to 1/8 inch. Trim the interfacing down to the stitching line. Then clip into the seam allowances around the back neckline curves at 1/2-inch intervals.

G | FINISHING THE NECKLINE

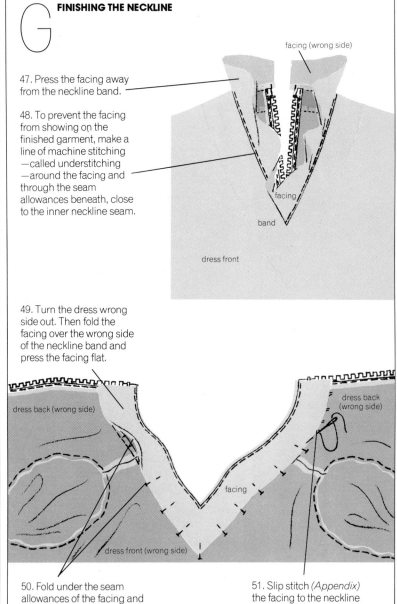

47. Press the facing away from the neckline band.

48. To prevent the facing from showing on the finished garment, make a line of machine stitching —called understitching —around the facing and through the seam allowances beneath, close to the inner neckline seam.

49. Turn the dress wrong side out. Then fold the facing over the wrong side of the neckline band and press the facing flat.

50. Fold under the seam allowances of the facing and pin the facing to the neckline band. At the back neck opening, pin the facing to the zipper tape.

51. Slip stitch (Appendix) the facing to the neckline band and to the zipper tape. Remove the pins and any remaining bastings. Press.

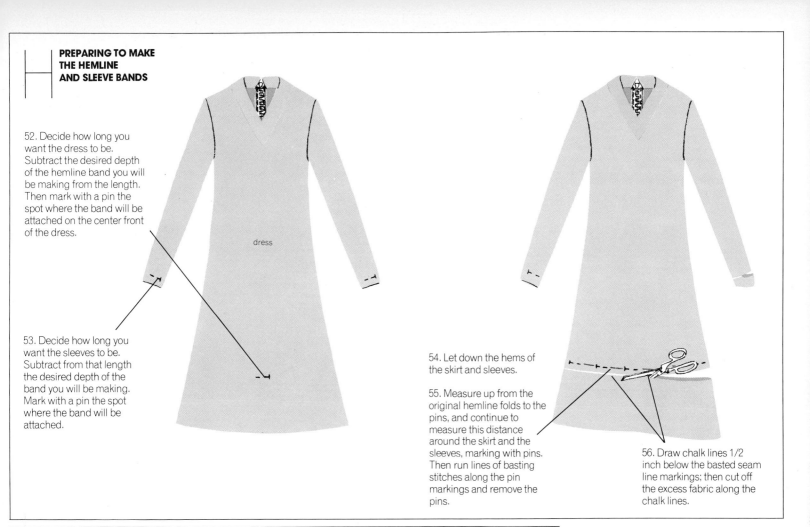

PREPARING TO MAKE THE HEMLINE AND SLEEVE BANDS

52. Decide how long you want the dress to be. Subtract the desired depth of the hemline band you will be making from the length. Then mark with a pin the spot where the band will be attached on the center front of the dress.

53. Decide how long you want the sleeves to be. Subtract from that length the desired depth of the band you will be making. Mark with a pin the spot where the band will be attached.

dress

54. Let down the hems of the skirt and sleeves.

55. Measure up from the original hemline folds to the pins, and continue to measure this distance around the skirt and the sleeves, marking with pins. Then run lines of basting stitches along the pin markings and remove the pins.

56. Draw chalk lines 1/2 inch below the basted seam line markings; then cut off the excess fabric along the chalk lines.

CUTTING THE HEMLINE AND SLEEVE BANDS

57. Lay the fabric wrong side up on a flat surface.

58. Measure the hemline of the dress front along the basted seam marking.

59. Mark on the fabric, with chalk, a rectangle for the front hemline band. Use the measurement made in Step 58 for the long sides of the rectangle, and draw them parallel to the crosswise edge. To determine the measurements on the short sides, double the desired depth of the band.

60. Add 1/2-inch seam allowances with chalk to the four sides of the rectangle.

61. Repeat this procedure to mark a rectangle for the back hemline band.

62. Measure the hemline of one sleeve along the basted seam marking.

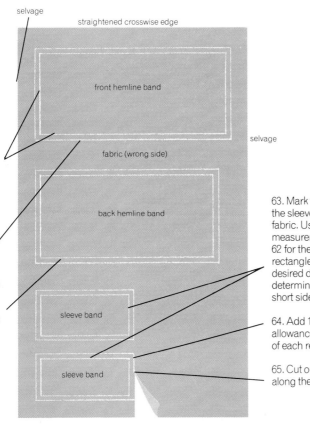

selvage

straightened crosswise edge

front hemline band

fabric (wrong side)

selvage

back hemline band

sleeve band

sleeve band

63. Mark two rectangles for the sleeve bands on the fabric. Use the measurement made in Step 62 for the long sides of the rectangle, and double the desired depth of the band to determine the length of the short sides.

64. Add 1/2-inch seam allowances to the four sides of each rectangle.

65. Cut out the rectangles along the outer chalk lines.

continued

J ATTACHING THE HEMLINE BAND

66. With the wrong sides of the fabric facing out, pin the front and back hemline band sections together along the side seam lines. Baste and remove the pins.

67. Machine stitch on the seam lines and remove the bastings.

68. Press open the seam allowances.

69. Slip the hemline band, wrong side out, over the dress, matching the side seams. Pin along the seam markings. Baste and remove the pins.

70. Machine stitch and remove the bastings.

71. Trim the seam allowance of the band to 1/4 inch; trim the seam allowance of the dress to 3/8 inch.

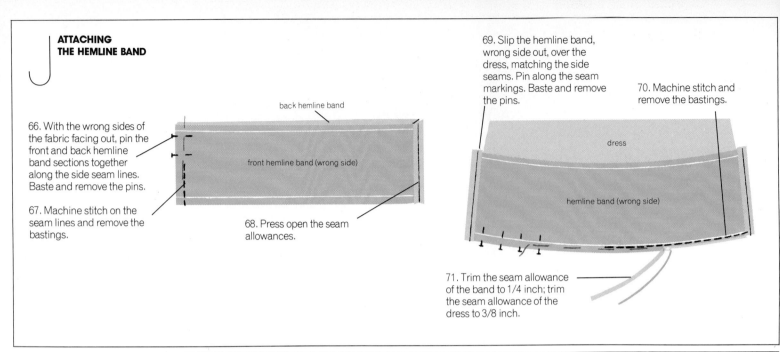

K FINISHING THE HEMLINE BAND

72. Turn the dress wrong side out. Then turn the band away from the dress and press the trimmed seam allowances toward the band.

73. Turn the unattached edge of the band to the inside of the dress. Fold the band along the seam line. Pin the folded edge to the dress just over the stitching made in Step 70.

74. Baste and remove the pins. Using a slip stitch, attach the band to the dress. Remove the basting and press.

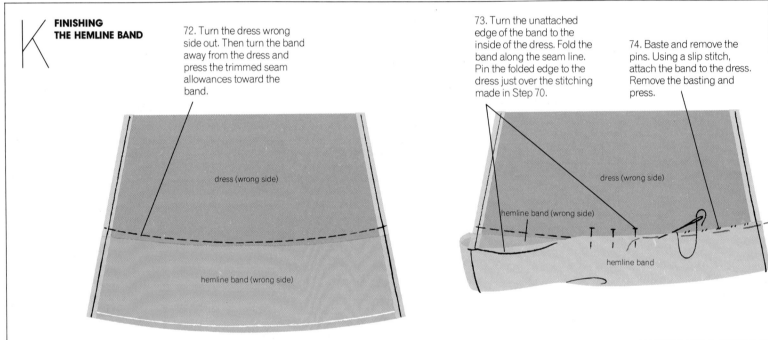

ATTACHING THE SLEEVE BANDS

75. With the fabric wrong side out, pin the two short ends of each sleeve band together along the side seam lines. Baste and remove the pins.

76. Machine stitch and remove the bastings.

77. Trim the seam allowances of both bands to 1/4 inch.

78. Press open the seams.

79. Match the seams of the bands with the seams of the sleeves; attach and finish the bands, following the instructions for the hemline band, Steps 69-74.

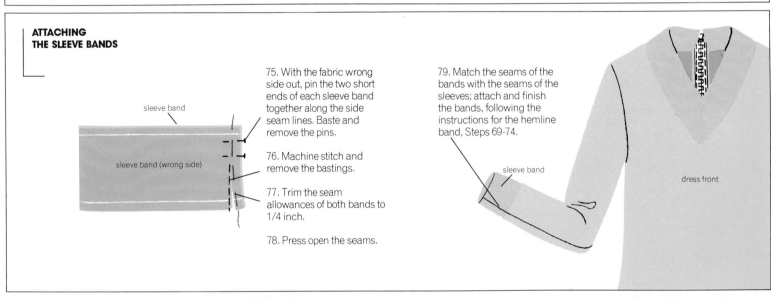

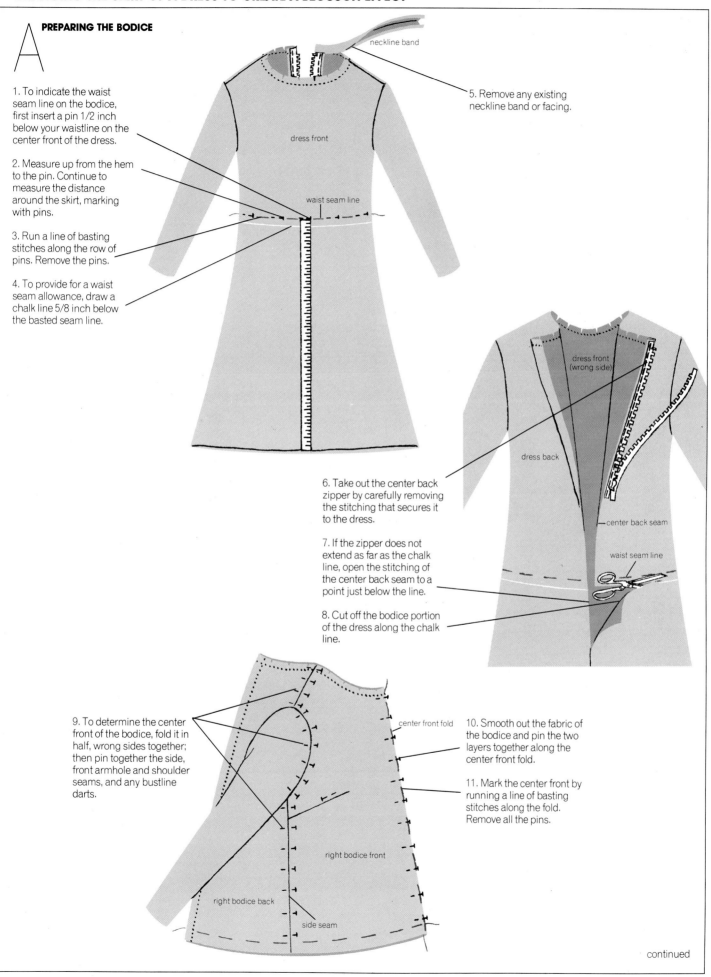

A PREPARING THE BODICE

1. To indicate the waist seam line on the bodice, first insert a pin 1/2 inch below your waistline on the center front of the dress.

2. Measure up from the hem to the pin. Continue to measure the distance around the skirt, marking with pins.

3. Run a line of basting stitches along the row of pins. Remove the pins.

4. To provide for a waist seam allowance, draw a chalk line 5/8 inch below the basted seam line.

5. Remove any existing neckline band or facing.

neckline band

dress front

waist seam line

dress front (wrong side)

dress back

center back seam

waist seam line

6. Take out the center back zipper by carefully removing the stitching that secures it to the dress.

7. If the zipper does not extend as far as the chalk line, open the stitching of the center back seam to a point just below the line.

8. Cut off the bodice portion of the dress along the chalk line.

9. To determine the center front of the bodice, fold it in half, wrong sides together; then pin together the side, front armhole and shoulder seams, and any bustline darts.

center front fold

right bodice front

right bodice back

side seam

10. Smooth out the fabric of the bodice and pin the two layers together along the center front fold.

11. Mark the center front by running a line of basting stitches along the fold. Remove all the pins.

continued

B PREPARING THE NEW BODICE CLOSURE

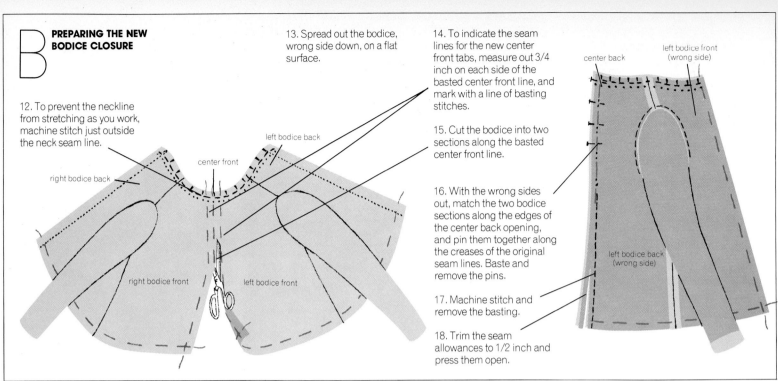

12. To prevent the neckline from stretching as you work, machine stitch just outside the neck seam line.

13. Spread out the bodice, wrong side down, on a flat surface.

14. To indicate the seam lines for the new center front tabs, measure out 3/4 inch on each side of the basted center front line, and mark with a line of basting stitches.

15. Cut the bodice into two sections along the basted center front line.

16. With the wrong sides out, match the two bodice sections along the edges of the center back opening, and pin them together along the creases of the original seam lines. Baste and remove the pins.

17. Machine stitch and remove the basting.

18. Trim the seam allowances to 1/2 inch and press them open.

right bodice back

left bodice back

center front

right bodice front

left bodice front

center back

left bodice front (wrong side)

left bodice back (wrong side)

C CONSTRUCTING THE SKIRT

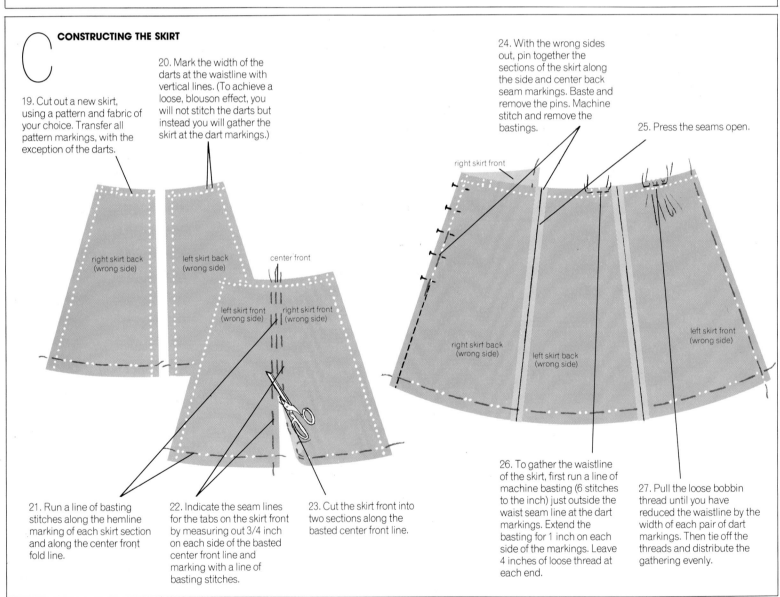

19. Cut out a new skirt, using a pattern and fabric of your choice. Transfer all pattern markings, with the exception of the darts.

20. Mark the width of the darts at the waistline with vertical lines. (To achieve a loose, blouson effect, you will not stitch the darts but instead you will gather the skirt at the dart markings.)

24. With the wrong sides out, pin together the sections of the skirt along the side and center back seam markings. Baste and remove the pins. Machine stitch and remove the bastings.

25. Press the seams open.

right skirt back (wrong side)

left skirt back (wrong side)

center front

left skirt front (wrong side)

right skirt front (wrong side)

right skirt front

right skirt back (wrong side)

left skirt back (wrong side)

left skirt front (wrong side)

21. Run a line of basting stitches along the hemline marking of each skirt section and along the center front fold line.

22. Indicate the seam lines for the tabs on the skirt front by measuring out 3/4 inch on each side of the basted center front line and marking with a line of basting stitches.

23. Cut the skirt front into two sections along the basted center front line.

26. To gather the waistline of the skirt, first run a line of machine basting (6 stitches to the inch) just outside the waist seam line at the dart markings. Extend the basting for 1 inch on each side of the markings. Leave 4 inches of loose thread at each end.

27. Pull the loose bobbin thread until you have reduced the waistline by the width of each pair of dart markings. Then tie off the threads and distribute the gathering evenly.

D | ATTACHING THE BODICE TO THE SKIRT

28. Make two parallel rows of machine basting (6 stitches to the inch) on each bodice front section—one just outside the waist seam line, the second 1/4 inch outside the first. Begin 1 inch in from the basted seam line for the tab; end 1 inch from the side seam. Leave 4 inches of loose thread at the ends.

29. Repeat Step 28 across both bodice back sections, beginning and ending each line of machine basting 1 inch from the side seam.

30. Gently pull the loose bobbin threads until each bodice section is approximately the same length as its corresponding skirt section.

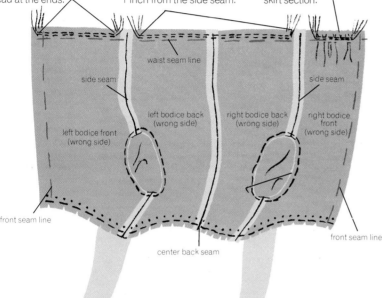

waist seam line

side seam

left bodice back (wrong side)

right bodice back (wrong side)

side seam

right bodice front (wrong side)

left bodice front (wrong side)

front seam line

center back seam

front seam line

31. Place the bodice over the skirt, with the wrong sides facing out, and align the waist seam lines. Match and pin first at the intersections of the basted seam markings for the front tabs, then pin at the intersections of the side and center back seams.

32. Adjust the machine basting on the bodice and continue to pin along the waist seam line, distributing the gathers evenly. Baste and remove the pins. Machine stitch along the waist seam line. Remove the hand bastings and trim the ends of the machine basting threads.

33. Trim the seam allowance of the bodice to 1/4 inch and the seam allowance of the skirt to 3/8 inch. Press the seam allowances toward the bodice.

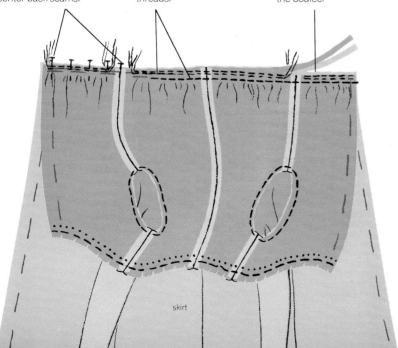

skirt

E | PREPARING THE FRONT TABS

34. To determine the length of the tabs, measure the front opening of the dress from the marking for the neck seam to the hemline basting. The width of the tab sections should be 3 inches.

35. Straighten the grain of the fabric you have selected for the tabs (page 34), and mark rectangles for the two front tabs on the wrong side of the fabric. Use the length and width measurements determined in Step 34, making sure to draw the long sides parallel to the selvages.

36. Mark a center fold line and 1/2-inch seam allowances around all four sides of each rectangle.

37. Cut out the rectangles along the outer chalk lines.

38. Run a line of basting stitches along the center fold lines of each rectangle.

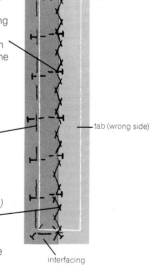

center fold line

selvage

center fold line

selvage

tab

tab

fabric (wrong side)

39. Mark and cut an interfacing rectangle the same size as one of the tabs. Cut the interfacing rectangle into two sections along the center line.

40. Pin one interfacing onto the wrong side of one front tab section, matching the seam markings and aligning the long unmarked inner edge of the interfacing with the basted center line on the tab.

41. Baste outside the long and the two short seam lines. Remove the pins.

tab (wrong side)

42. Catch stitch (Appendix) the interfacing to the tab along the center fold line, using thread of the same color as the fabric. Remove the pins.

interfacing

43. Repeat Steps 40-42 to attach the interfacing to the other front tab.

F ATTACHING THE FRONT TABS

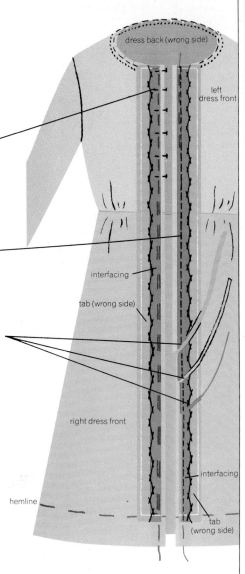

44. Pin the tabs, wrong sides out, to the dress fronts, matching the seam lines on the tab interfacings with the basted front seam lines on the dress. Pin first at the neck seam line, next at the waistline and then at the hemline intersections. Add pins at 1-inch intervals between. Baste and remove the pins.

45. Machine stitch from the neck edge to the hemline markings. Remove the bastings.

46. Trim the seam allowances of the interfacings down to the stitching lines. Trim the seam allowances of the tabs to 1/8 inch, and trim the seam allowances of the dress to 1/4 inch.

47. Press the seam allowances of the front seams toward the tabs.

48. Turn the dress wrong side out and extend the tabs away from the dress.

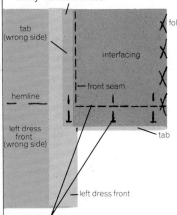

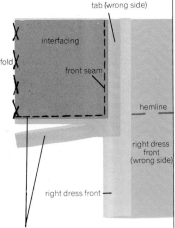

49. Fold each tab in half, wrong side out, and pin the layers together along the short hem seam line. Machine stitch, sewing from the intersection of the front seam to the folded edge. Remove the pins.

50. Trim the interfacing to the stitching line; trim the seam allowances of the tabs to 1/4 inch.

G FINISHING THE FRONT TABS

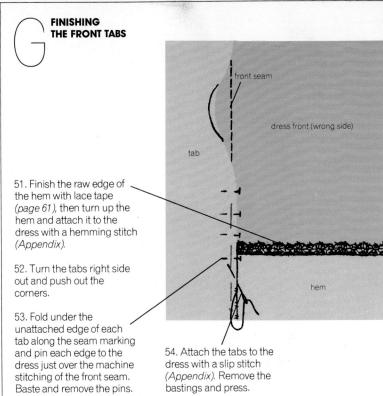

51. Finish the raw edge of the hem with lace tape (*page 61*), then turn up the hem and attach it to the dress with a hemming stitch (*Appendix*).

52. Turn the tabs right side out and push out the corners.

53. Fold under the unattached edge of each tab along the seam marking and pin each edge to the dress just over the machine stitching of the front seam. Baste and remove the pins.

54. Attach the tabs to the dress with a slip stitch (*Appendix*). Remove the bastings and press.

H CONSTRUCTING THE BIAS NECKLINE BAND

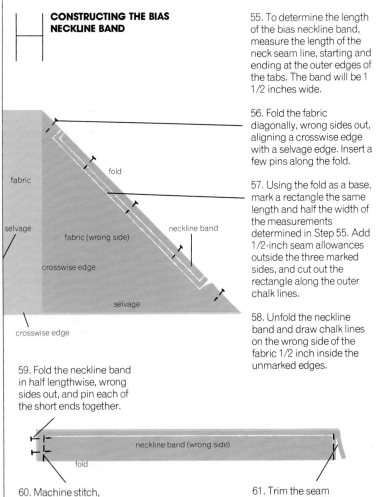

55. To determine the length of the bias neckline band, measure the length of the neck seam line, starting and ending at the outer edges of the tabs. The band will be 1 1/2 inches wide.

56. Fold the fabric diagonally, wrong sides out, aligning a crosswise edge with a selvage edge. Insert a few pins along the fold.

57. Using the fold as a base, mark a rectangle the same length and half the width of the measurements determined in Step 55. Add 1/2-inch seam allowances outside the three marked sides, and cut out the rectangle along the outer chalk lines.

58. Unfold the neckline band and draw chalk lines on the wrong side of the fabric 1/2 inch inside the unmarked edges.

59. Fold the neckline band in half lengthwise, wrong sides out, and pin each of the short ends together.

60. Machine stitch, beginning at the intersections of the seam lines rather than at the edges of the fabric. Remove the pins.

61. Trim the seam allowances to 1/8 inch.

62. Turn the neckline band right side out and push out the corners.

ATTACHING THE NECKLINE BAND

63. Pin one long side of the neckline band, wrong side out, to the dress along the neck seam lines. Match the stitched ends of the band with the edges of the tabs. Baste and remove the pins.

64. Machine stitch and remove the bastings.

65. Clip the front corners diagonally; trim the seam allowance of the band to 1/8 inch and of the dress to 1/4 inch.

67. Turn the unattached edge of the band to the inside of the dress. Using the seam marking as a guide, fold under the edge and pin it to the dress just over the machine stitching of the neck seam. Baste and remove the pins.

68. Attach the edge of the band to the dress with a slip stitch (*Appendix*). Remove the basting and press.

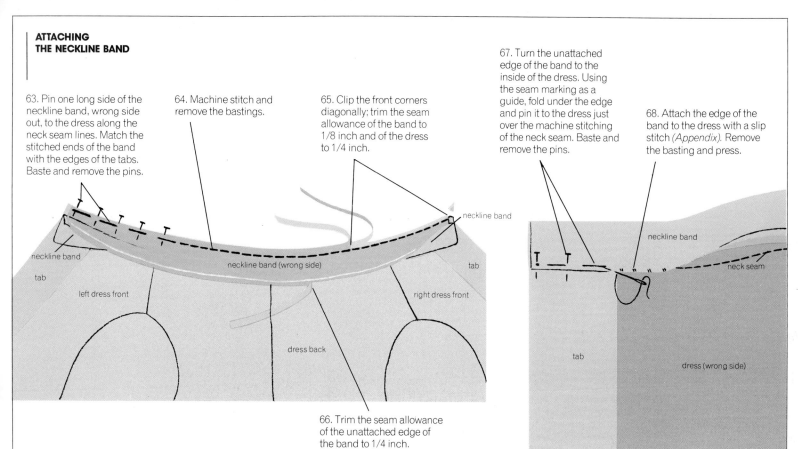

neckline band

neckline band

neckline band (wrong side)

tab

tab

left dress front

right dress front

dress back

neckline band

neck seam

tab

dress (wrong side)

66. Trim the seam allowance of the unattached edge of the band to 1/4 inch.

MAKING A SASH AND BUTTONHOLES

69. To make a sash, first cut a piece of fabric equal to the length desired and double the width, adding 1/2 inch to both measurements for seam allowances. Fold it in half lengthwise, wrong sides out, and pin the three open sides together. Next, machine stitch 1/4 inch from the pinned edges, leaving a 2-inch opening at the middle of the long side. Remove the pins. To reduce bulk, trim off the seam allowances diagonally at the two stitched corners. Then turn the sash right side out by pulling the fabric through the opening, and press. Pin the opening and sew it with a slip stitch.

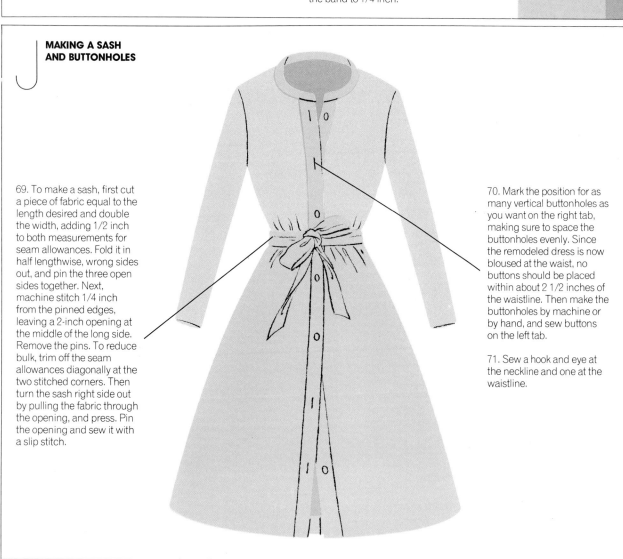

70. Mark the position for as many vertical buttonholes as you want on the right tab, making sure to space the buttonholes evenly. Since the remodeled dress is now bloused at the waist, no buttons should be placed within about 2 1/2 inches of the waistline. Then make the buttonholes by machine or by hand, and sew buttons on the left tab.

71. Sew a hook and eye at the neckline and one at the waistline.

Improvising
with shirts

That wardrobe staple, the tailored shirt, can provide the basic ingredient for a whole closetful of varied and personalized shirt styles. The classic convertible-collar shirt at near right, for example, can be remodeled into the cardigan shown beside it. For this alteration, the collar has been removed, the neckline cut into a V, and both the neck and button closures trimmed with strips of bias-cut fabric.

The next variation, the belted blouse, uses a man-tailored shirt as its starting point. A new collar and band of contrasting fabric have replaced the original ones. The shirttails have been replaced by a tie belt; the sleeves have been cut short and sporty new cuffs added.

Either type of shirt—convertible-collared or man-tailored—can be modified into the trim overblouse at far right, wherein a jaunty stock tie becomes a substitute for the old collar. Directions for doing this—and for making the other two transformations suggested here—appear on the following pages.

ADDING A STOCK TIE TO A SHIRT

A PREPARING THE SHIRT

1. Remove the original collar from the shirt, using a seam ripper and working from the center back of the collar toward the center front.

2. Fold the shirt in half, aligning the shoulder seams. Mark the center back of the shirt at the fold line with a few running stitches (*Appendix*).

3. Turn both front facings wrong side out along the original fold lines.

4. Measure in 1 to 1 1/2 inches from the front fold line along the neckline edge and mark with a pin.

5. Baste the facings to the shirt from the folded edge to the pin marker. Remove the pins.

6. Machine stitch the facings to the shirt, carefully following the original stitching line. Remove the basting.

7. At the end of the line of stitching, clip into the seam allowances of the facings and the shirt, cutting up to —but not into—the stitching.

8. Turn the shirt wrong side out. Then turn the facings to the inside of the shirt and push out the corners with blunt scissors. Press.

9. Pin and baste the free edges of the facings to the shirt along the neck seam line. Remove the pins.

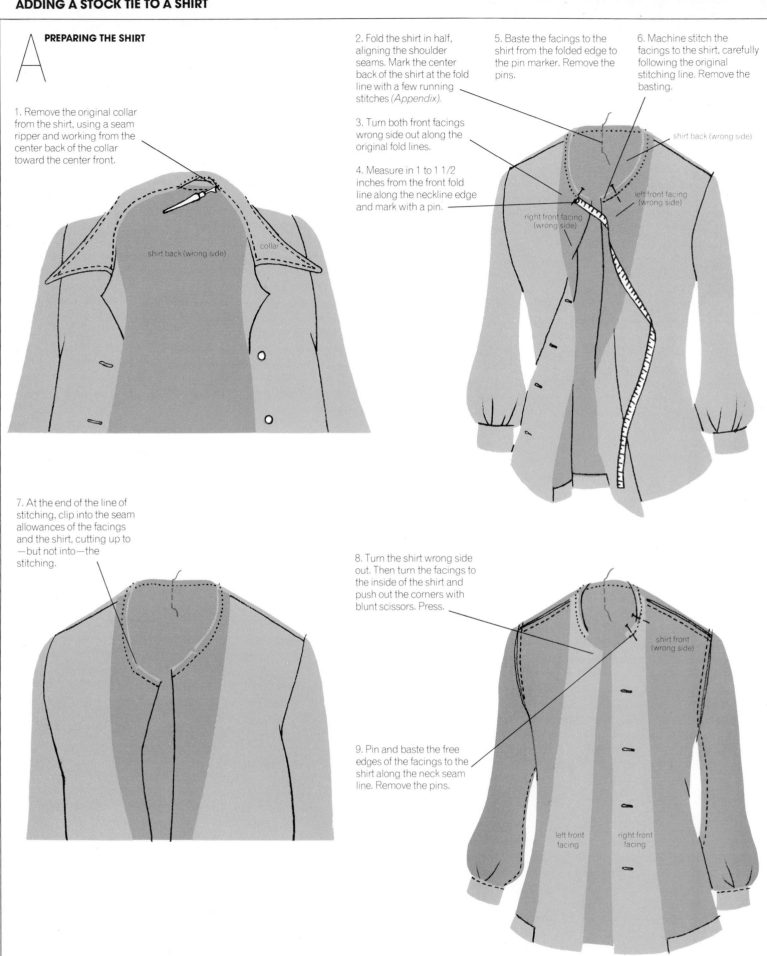

shirt back (wrong side)

collar

shirt back (wrong side)

left front facing (wrong side)

right front facing (wrong side)

shirt front (wrong side)

left front facing

right front facing

**PREPARING
THE STOCK TIE**

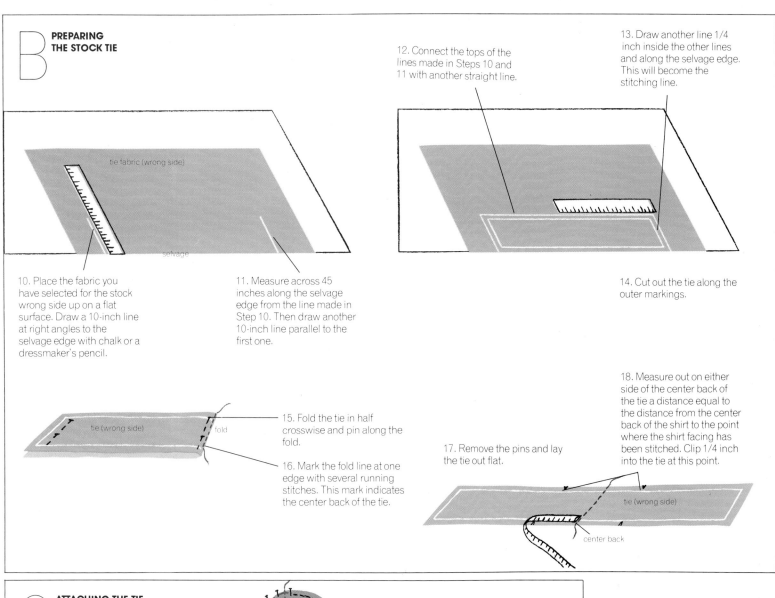

12. Connect the tops of the lines made in Steps 10 and 11 with another straight line.

13. Draw another line 1/4 inch inside the other lines and along the selvage edge. This will become the stitching line.

tie fabric (wrong side)

selvage

10. Place the fabric you have selected for the stock wrong side up on a flat surface. Draw a 10-inch line at right angles to the selvage edge with chalk or a dressmaker's pencil.

11. Measure across 45 inches along the selvage edge from the line made in Step 10. Then draw another 10-inch line parallel to the first one.

14. Cut out the tie along the outer markings.

tie (wrong side)

fold

15. Fold the tie in half crosswise and pin along the fold.

16. Mark the fold line at one edge with several running stitches. This mark indicates the center back of the tie.

17. Remove the pins and lay the tie out flat.

18. Measure out on either side of the center back of the tie a distance equal to the distance from the center back of the shirt to the point where the shirt facing has been stitched. Clip 1/4 inch into the tie at this point.

tie (wrong side)

center back

C **ATTACHING THE TIE
TO THE SHIRT**

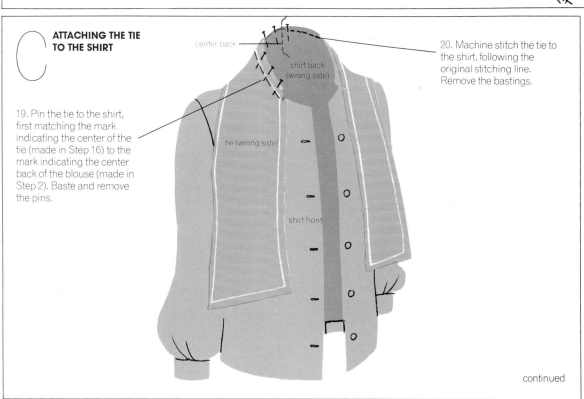

center back

shirt back (wrong side)

tie (wrong side)

shirt front

19. Pin the tie to the shirt, first matching the mark indicating the center of the tie (made in Step 16) to the mark indicating the center back of the blouse (made in Step 2). Baste and remove the pins.

20. Machine stitch the tie to the shirt, following the original stitching line. Remove the bastings.

continued

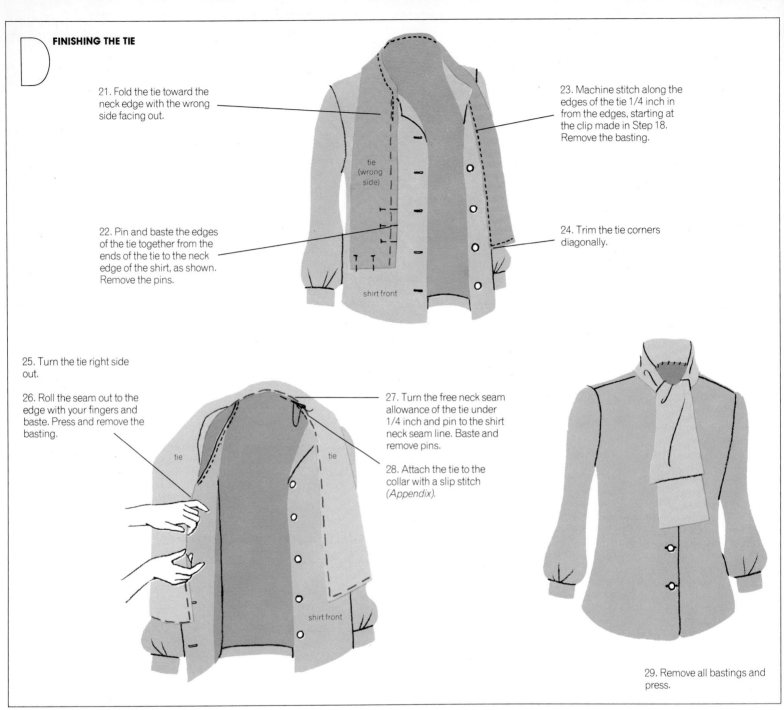

D FINISHING THE TIE

21. Fold the tie toward the neck edge with the wrong side facing out.

tie (wrong side)

23. Machine stitch along the edges of the tie 1/4 inch in from the edges, starting at the clip made in Step 18. Remove the basting.

22. Pin and baste the edges of the tie together from the ends of the tie to the neck edge of the shirt, as shown. Remove the pins.

24. Trim the tie corners diagonally.

shirt front

25. Turn the tie right side out.

26. Roll the seam out to the edge with your fingers and baste. Press and remove the basting.

27. Turn the free neck seam allowance of the tie under 1/4 inch and pin to the shirt neck seam line. Baste and remove pins.

28. Attach the tie to the collar with a slip stitch (Appendix).

tie

tie

shirt front

29. Remove all bastings and press.

CHANGING A SHIRT TO A CARDIGAN

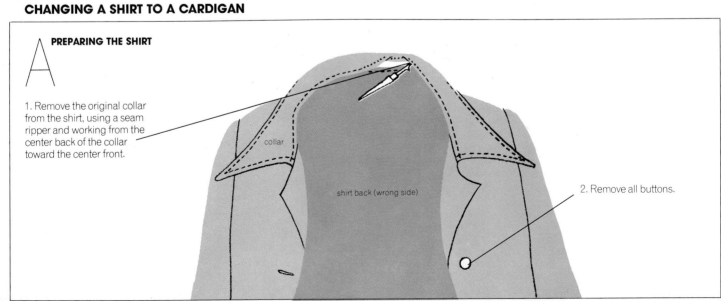

A PREPARING THE SHIRT

1. Remove the original collar from the shirt, using a seam ripper and working from the center back of the collar toward the center front.

collar

shirt back (wrong side)

2. Remove all buttons.

3. Fold under the front edge of the shirt from the neck edge to a point 5 to 7 inches down from the shoulder seam. Pin. Try on and adjust for fit.

4. Mark the fold line with a line of basting stitches, making sure these stitches run into the original stitching line at the neck edge. Remove the pins.

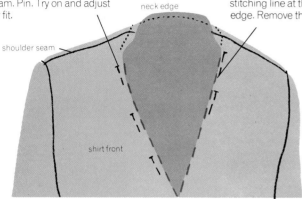

5. Pull out the edges of the shirt front that were folded under in Step 3.

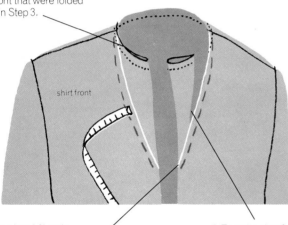

6. Draw a line 1/4 inch outside the lines of basting made in Step 4 to indicate a new front-edge cutting line.

7. Trim the shirt front along the new cutting line.

8. Fold the entire neckline edge toward the outside of the shirt, following the lines of basting made in Step 4 and the original stitching line around the back of the neck. Baste and press flat.

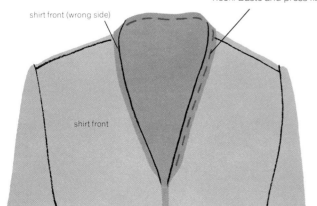

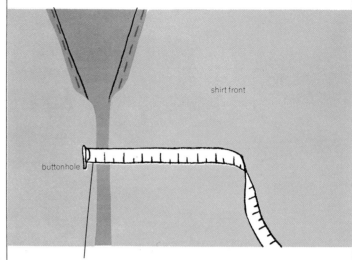

9. To determine the proper width for the cardigan band, measure the distance from the buttonhole to the outer edge of the shirt and multiply by two. Then add 1/2 inch for seam allowance.

10. To determine the proper length for the cardigan band, measure the entire length of the front and neck opening, beginning at one front hem edge and ending at the other. Then add 1/2 inch for seam allowance.

11. Cut out the band on the bias (page 35), using a fabric that has some stretch —such as a lightweight knit or jersey. If it is necessary to cut the band in two pieces, make sure the seam will fall along the back neckline.

continued

D ▶ ATTACHING THE BAND TO THE SHIRT

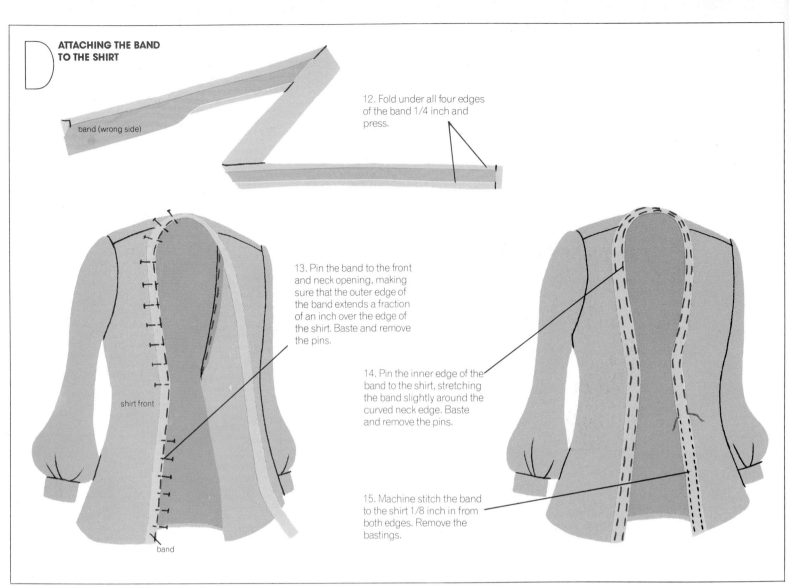

band (wrong side)

12. Fold under all four edges of the band 1/4 inch and press.

13. Pin the band to the front and neck opening, making sure that the outer edge of the band extends a fraction of an inch over the edge of the shirt. Baste and remove the pins.

shirt front

band

14. Pin the inner edge of the band to the shirt, stretching the band slightly around the curved neck edge. Baste and remove the pins.

15. Machine stitch the band to the shirt 1/8 inch in from both edges. Remove the bastings.

E ▶ FINISHING THE CARDIGAN

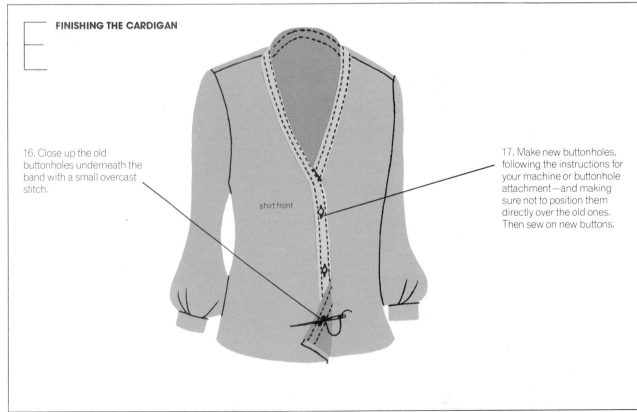

16. Close up the old buttonholes underneath the band with a small overcast stitch.

shirt front

17. Make new buttonholes, following the instructions for your machine or buttonhole attachment—and making sure not to position them directly over the old ones. Then sew on new buttons.

A PREPARING THE SHIRT

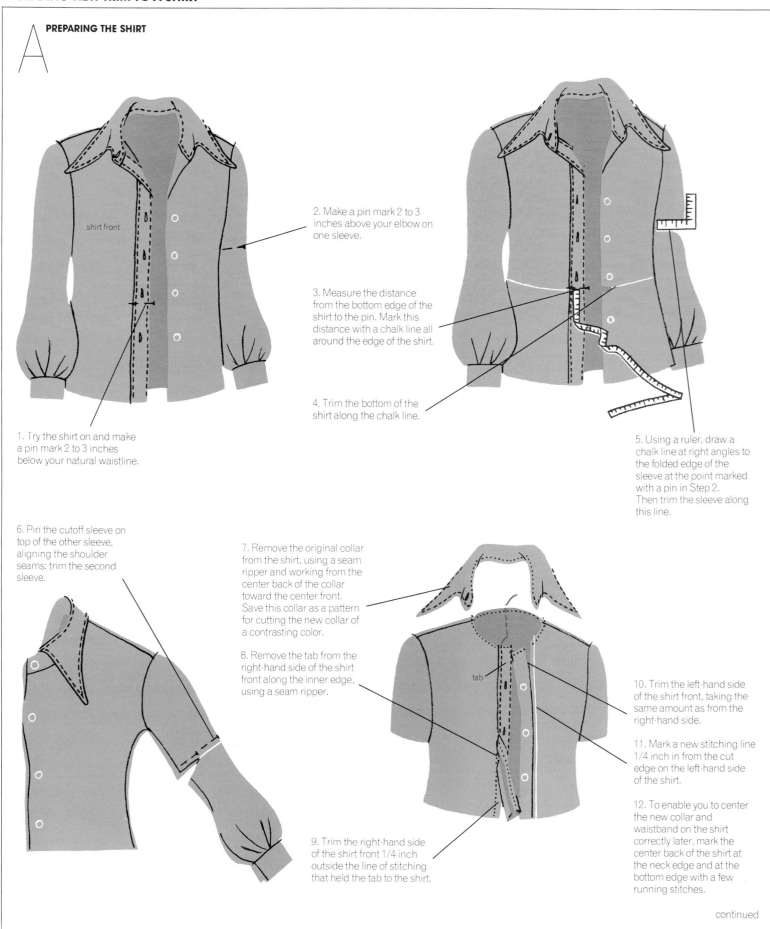

2. Make a pin mark 2 to 3 inches above your elbow on one sleeve.

3. Measure the distance from the bottom edge of the shirt to the pin. Mark this distance with a chalk line all around the edge of the shirt.

4. Trim the bottom of the shirt along the chalk line.

shirt front

1. Try the shirt on and make a pin mark 2 to 3 inches below your natural waistline.

5. Using a ruler, draw a chalk line at right angles to the folded edge of the sleeve at the point marked with a pin in Step 2. Then trim the sleeve along this line.

6. Pin the cutoff sleeve on top of the other sleeve, aligning the shoulder seams; trim the second sleeve.

7. Remove the original collar from the shirt, using a seam ripper and working from the center back of the collar toward the center front. Save this collar as a pattern for cutting the new collar of a contrasting color.

8. Remove the tab from the right-hand side of the shirt front along the inner edge, using a seam ripper.

tab

9. Trim the right-hand side of the shirt front 1/4-inch outside the line of stitching that held the tab to the shirt.

10. Trim the left-hand side of the shirt front, taking the same amount as from the right-hand side.

11. Mark a new stitching line 1/4 inch in from the cut edge on the left-hand side of the shirt.

12. To enable you to center the new collar and waistband on the shirt correctly later, mark the center back of the shirt at the neck edge and at the bottom edge with a few running stitches.

continued

B CUTTING OUT A NEW WAISTBAND, CUFF, TAB AND COLLAR

13. Fold the new fabric in half, lengthwise.

14. To cut out the new waistband and tie, first measure parallel to the selvage edge and then mark with chalk a length equal to one half your waist measurement—plus 2 inches (for wearing ease). Add 16 inches for the tie ends, then measure and mark with chalk a width equal to twice the width of the old tab.

15. Draw a cutting line 1/4 inch outside all four edges.

16. To cut out the new cuffs, measure and mark a rectangle with a bottom edge equal to the circumference of the raw edge of the cut sleeve. Then measure and mark a top edge equal to the circumference of the sleeve 2 or 2 1/2 inches above the cut edge.

21. Draw a cutting line 1/4 inch outside the edges of the collar.

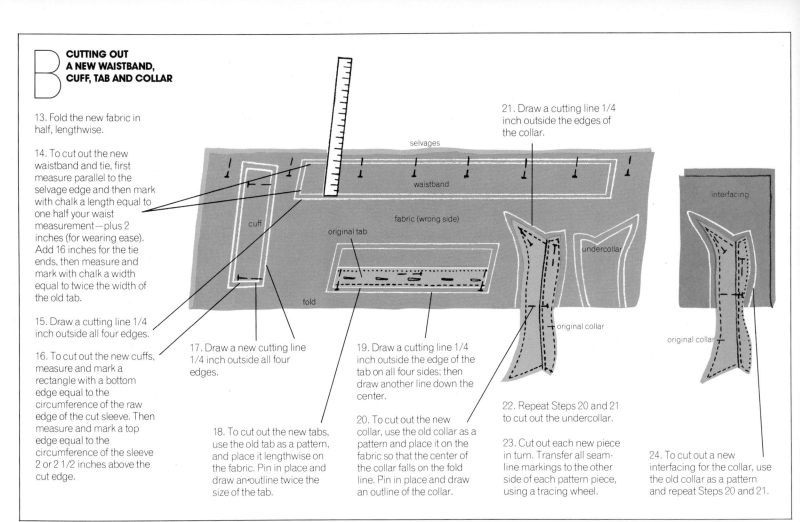

17. Draw a new cutting line 1/4 inch outside all four edges.

18. To cut out the new tabs, use the old tab as a pattern, and place it lengthwise on the fabric. Pin in place and draw an outline twice the size of the tab.

19. Draw a cutting line 1/4 inch outside the edge of the tab on all four sides; then draw another line down the center.

20. To cut out the new collar, use the old collar as a pattern and place it on the fabric so that the center of the collar falls on the fold line. Pin in place and draw an outline of the collar.

22. Repeat Steps 20 and 21 to cut out the undercollar.

23. Cut out each new piece in turn. Transfer all seam-line markings to the other side of each pattern piece, using a tracing wheel.

24. To cut out a new interfacing for the collar, use the old collar as a pattern and repeat Steps 20 and 21.

C ATTACHING THE TAB TO THE SHIRT

25. Turn the shirt wrong side out.

26. Pin the new tabs, wrong side up, to both shirt fronts. Baste, and remove the pins.

27. Machine stitch, and remove the basting.

28. Fold over the raw edge of the tab 1/4 inch and press.

29. Turn the shirt right side out. Press the seam allowances of both shirt and tab toward the tab.

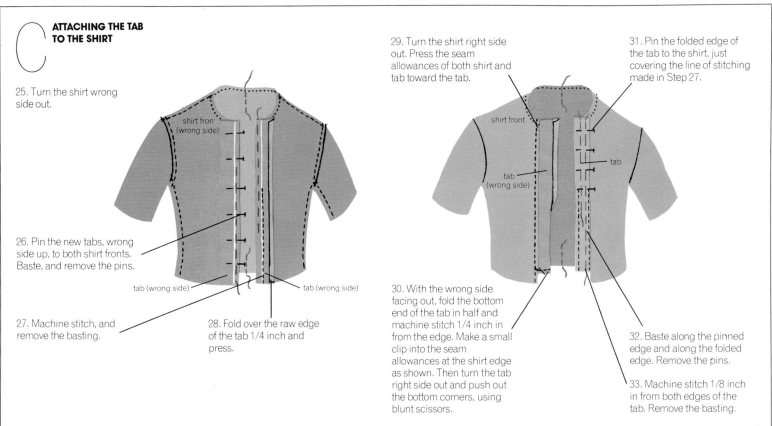

30. With the wrong side facing out, fold the bottom end of the tab in half and machine stitch 1/4 inch in from the edge. Make a small clip into the seam allowances at the shirt edge as shown. Then turn the tab right side out and push out the bottom corners, using blunt scissors.

31. Pin the folded edge of the tab to the shirt, just covering the line of stitching made in Step 27.

32. Baste along the pinned edge and along the folded edge. Remove the pins.

33. Machine stitch 1/8 inch in from both edges of the tab. Remove the basting.

D MAKING THE NEW COLLAR

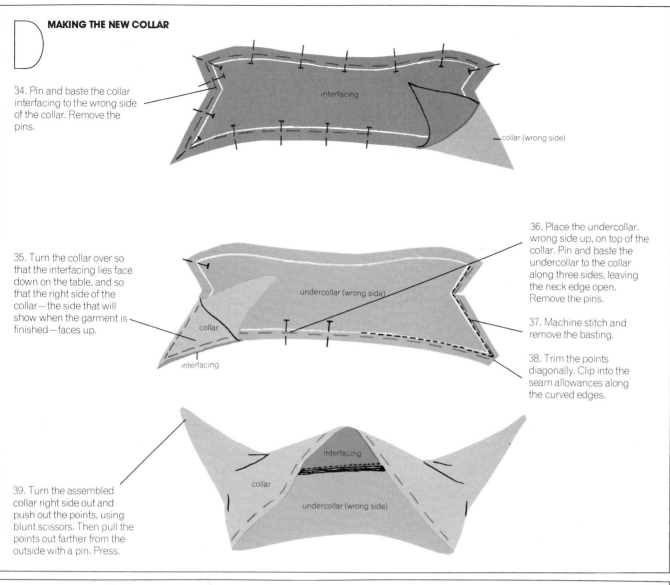

34. Pin and baste the collar interfacing to the wrong side of the collar. Remove the pins.

interfacing

collar (wrong side)

35. Turn the collar over so that the interfacing lies face down on the table, and so that the right side of the collar—the side that will show when the garment is finished—faces up.

undercollar (wrong side)

collar

interfacing

36. Place the undercollar, wrong side up, on top of the collar. Pin and baste the undercollar to the collar along three sides, leaving the neck edge open. Remove the pins.

37. Machine stitch and remove the basting.

38. Trim the points diagonally. Clip into the seam allowances along the curved edges.

39. Turn the assembled collar right side out and push out the points, using blunt scissors. Then pull the points out farther from the outside with a pin. Press.

interfacing

collar

undercollar (wrong side)

E ATTACHING THE COLLAR TO THE SHIRT

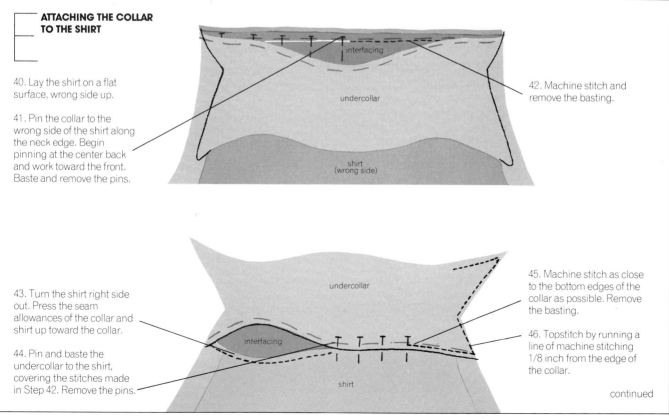

40. Lay the shirt on a flat surface, wrong side up.

41. Pin the collar to the wrong side of the shirt along the neck edge. Begin pinning at the center back and work toward the front. Baste and remove the pins.

interfacing

undercollar

shirt (wrong side)

42. Machine stitch and remove the basting.

43. Turn the shirt right side out. Press the seam allowances of the collar and shirt up toward the collar.

44. Pin and baste the undercollar to the shirt, covering the stitches made in Step 42. Remove the pins.

undercollar

interfacing

shirt

45. Machine stitch as close to the bottom edges of the collar as possible. Remove the basting.

46. Topstitch by running a line of machine stitching 1/8 inch from the edge of the collar.

continued

F MAKING THE CUFFS

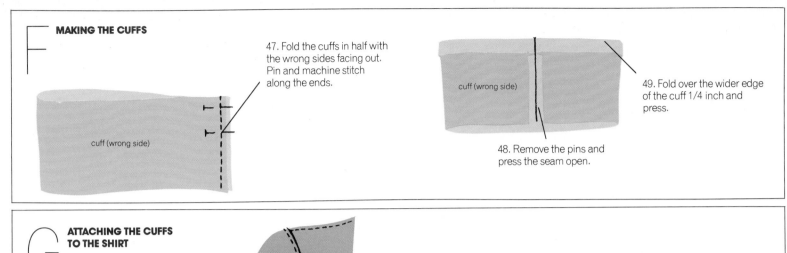

47. Fold the cuffs in half with the wrong sides facing out. Pin and machine stitch along the ends.

cuff (wrong side)

cuff (wrong side)

49. Fold over the wider edge of the cuff 1/4 inch and press.

48. Remove the pins and press the seam open.

G ATTACHING THE CUFFS TO THE SHIRT

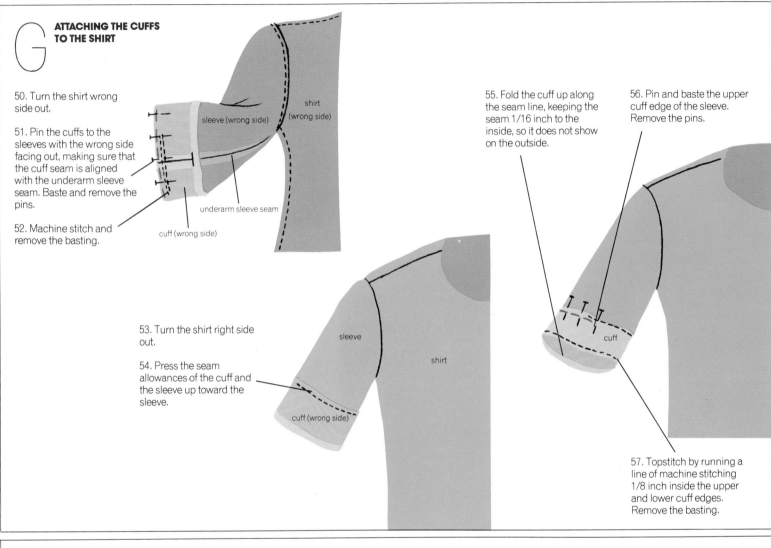

50. Turn the shirt wrong side out.

51. Pin the cuffs to the sleeves with the wrong side facing out, making sure that the cuff seam is aligned with the underarm sleeve seam. Baste and remove the pins.

52. Machine stitch and remove the basting.

sleeve (wrong side)

shirt (wrong side)

underarm sleeve seam

cuff (wrong side)

53. Turn the shirt right side out.

54. Press the seam allowances of the cuff and the sleeve up toward the sleeve.

sleeve

shirt

cuff (wrong side)

55. Fold the cuff up along the seam line, keeping the seam 1/16 inch to the inside, so it does not show on the outside.

56. Pin and baste the upper cuff edge of the sleeve. Remove the pins.

cuff

57. Topstitch by running a line of machine stitching 1/8 inch inside the upper and lower cuff edges. Remove the basting.

H MAKING THE WAISTBAND

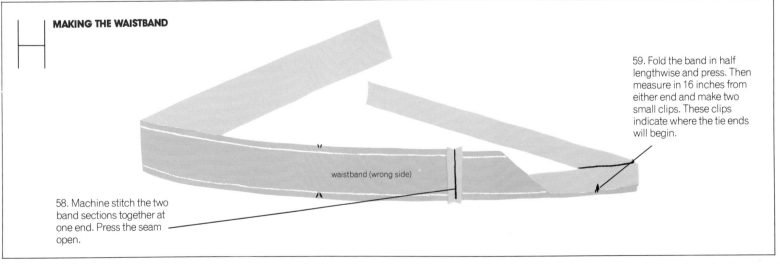

59. Fold the band in half lengthwise and press. Then measure in 16 inches from either end and make two small clips. These clips indicate where the tie ends will begin.

waistband (wrong side)

58. Machine stitch the two band sections together at one end. Press the seam open.

ATTACHING THE WAISTBAND

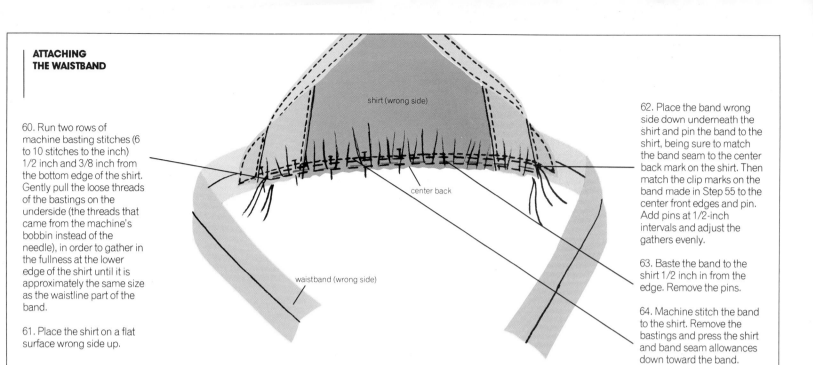

60. Run two rows of machine basting stitches (6 to 10 stitches to the inch) 1/2 inch and 3/8 inch from the bottom edge of the shirt. Gently pull the loose threads of the bastings on the underside (the threads that came from the machine's bobbin instead of the needle), in order to gather in the fullness at the lower edge of the shirt until it is approximately the same size as the waistline part of the band.

61. Place the shirt on a flat surface wrong side up.

shirt (wrong side)

center back

waistband (wrong side)

62. Place the band wrong side down underneath the shirt and pin the band to the shirt, being sure to match the band seam to the center back mark on the shirt. Then match the clip marks on the band made in Step 55 to the center front edges and pin. Add pins at 1/2-inch intervals and adjust the gathers evenly.

63. Baste the band to the shirt 1/2 inch in from the edge. Remove the pins.

64. Machine stitch the band to the shirt. Remove the bastings and press the shirt and band seam allowances down toward the band.

J FINISHING THE WAISTBAND

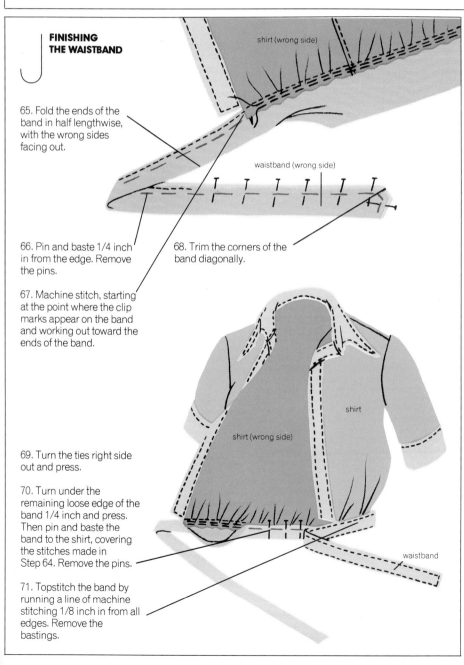

shirt (wrong side)

waistband (wrong side)

65. Fold the ends of the band in half lengthwise, with the wrong sides facing out.

66. Pin and baste 1/4 inch in from the edge. Remove the pins.

67. Machine stitch, starting at the point where the clip marks appear on the band and working out toward the ends of the band.

68. Trim the corners of the band diagonally.

69. Turn the ties right side out and press.

70. Turn under the remaining loose edge of the band 1/4 inch and press. Then pin and baste the band to the shirt, covering the stitches made in Step 64. Remove the pins.

71. Topstitch the band by running a line of machine stitching 1/8 inch in from all edges. Remove the bastings.

shirt

shirt (wrong side)

waistband

K ADDING BUTTONHOLES AND BUTTONS

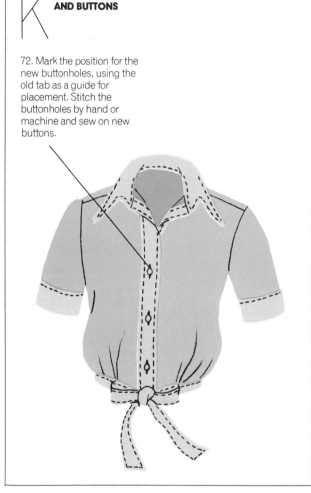

72. Mark the position for the new buttonholes, using the old tab as a guide for placement. Stitch the buttonholes by hand or machine and sew on new buttons.

Clever guises for old pants

Old pants—especially ones that are too narrow or too short—can be cleverly revived as knickers, flares or shorts. The particular reincarnation you choose for them will depend on the style and condition of the originals. Neatly tailored knickers, like the ones shown here, do not emerge from pants that are too baggy to start with, or that are made from extra-heavy fabric. Nor can pants be converted into flares unless the original creases can be removed. The reason is that flaring consists of adding inserts of new fabric in the outer side seams—as a result of which the crease lines will change.

Shorts provide the handiest solution for pants with knees that have worn thin, and patch pockets can be fashioned from the cutoff portions.

Methods for effecting all of these changes can be found on the following pages. As you work, try on the pants; walk around and sit down in them. This will prevent such mishaps as shorts that ride up too far on the thigh, or knickers that bind at the knee because the band is too tight.

PANTS REMODELED INTO KNICKERS

A CUTTING AND MARKING THE PANTS LEG

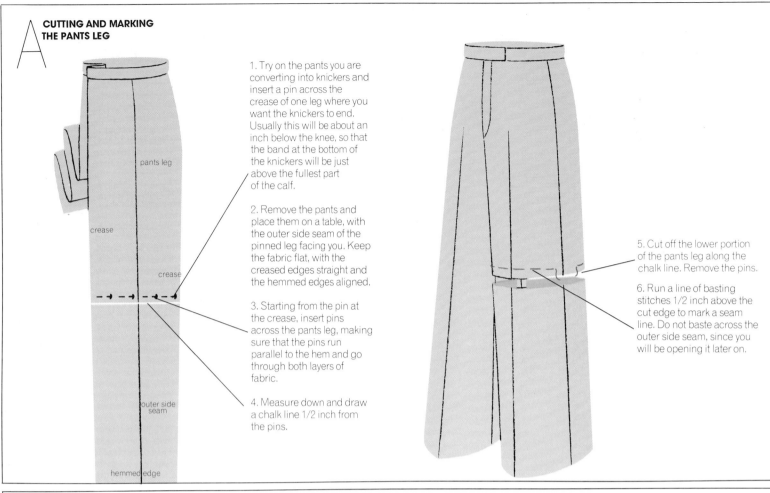

1. Try on the pants you are converting into knickers and insert a pin across the crease of one leg where you want the knickers to end. Usually this will be about an inch below the knee, so that the band at the bottom of the knickers will be just above the fullest part of the calf.

2. Remove the pants and place them on a table, with the outer side seam of the pinned leg facing you. Keep the fabric flat, with the creased edges straight and the hemmed edges aligned.

3. Starting from the pin at the crease, insert pins across the pants leg, making sure that the pins run parallel to the hem and go through both layers of fabric.

4. Measure down and draw a chalk line 1/2 inch from the pins.

5. Cut off the lower portion of the pants leg along the chalk line. Remove the pins.

6. Run a line of basting stitches 1/2 inch above the cut edge to mark a seam line. Do not baste across the outer side seam, since you will be opening it later on.

B MAKING THE PLACKET OPENING

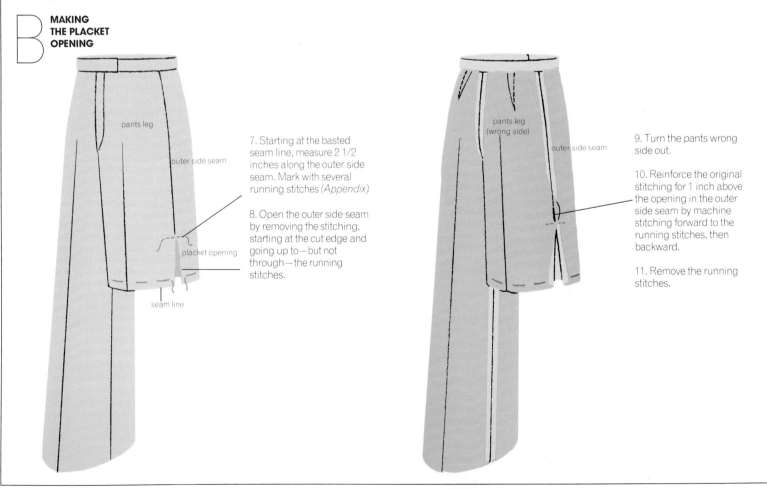

7. Starting at the basted seam line, measure 2 1/2 inches along the outer side seam. Mark with several running stitches (*Appendix*).

8. Open the outer side seam by removing the stitching, starting at the cut edge and going up to—but not through—the running stitches.

9. Turn the pants wrong side out.

10. Reinforce the original stitching for 1 inch above the opening in the outer side seam by machine stitching forward to the running stitches, then backward.

11. Remove the running stitches.

C CUTTING OUT THE BAND FOR THE BOTTOM OF THE KNICKERS

12. Measure around the top of your calf, at the point where the band will go. The tape measure should be snug when your knee is bent and slightly loose (but not so loose that it can slide down over the calf) when you stand erect.

13. Add 2 inches to the measurement (1 inch for an overlapping buttonhole tab and 1/2 inch each for seam allowances at both ends of the band).

14. Place the cutoff lower portion of the pants leg on a table. Keep the fabric flat, with the creased edges straight and the cut edges and hemmed edges aligned.

15. Starting at the cut edge, measure the distance you determined in Step 13 along one of the creases, and mark with a chalk line at a right angle to the crease.

16. Decide how wide you want the finished band to be and add 1/2 inch for seam allowance.

17. Measure in from the crease the distance you determined in Step 16, then draw a chalk line parallel to the crease from the cut edge to the chalk line made in Step 15.

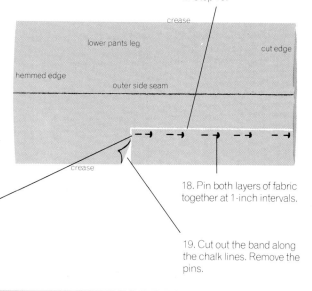

18. Pin both layers of fabric together at 1-inch intervals.

19. Cut out the band along the chalk lines. Remove the pins.

D MARKING THE BAND

20. Open the cutout band so that the wrong side is up.

21. Using a ruler and chalk, draw seam lines 1/2 inch in from—and parallel to—all four cut edges.

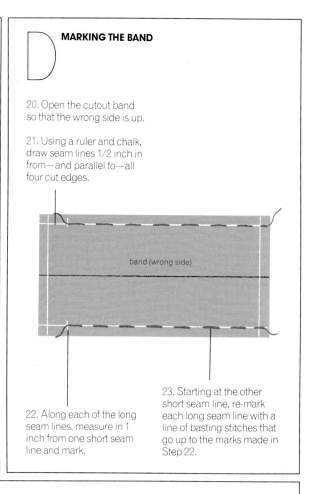

22. Along each of the long seam lines, measure in 1 inch from one short seam line and mark.

23. Starting at the other short seam line, re-mark each long seam line with a line of basting stitches that go up to the marks made in Step 22.

E CLOSING THE ENDS OF THE BAND

24. Fold the band in half along the original crease so that the wrong sides are out and the seam lines are aligned.

25. Pin the band together at 1/2-inch intervals along the short seam lines and along the unbasted portion of the long seam line.

26. Baste just outside the pinned seam lines. Remove the pins.

27. Machine stitch along the short seam lines, starting at the folded edges. On the end nearest the mark made in Step 22, pivot (Appendix) and stitch along the long seam line up to the mark. Remove the bastings.

28. Make a diagonal cut into the seam allowance, as shown, going up to—but not through—the end of the stitching on the long seam line.

29. Trim the seam allowances to 1/8 inch at both ends and along the long seam line, up to the diagonal cut.

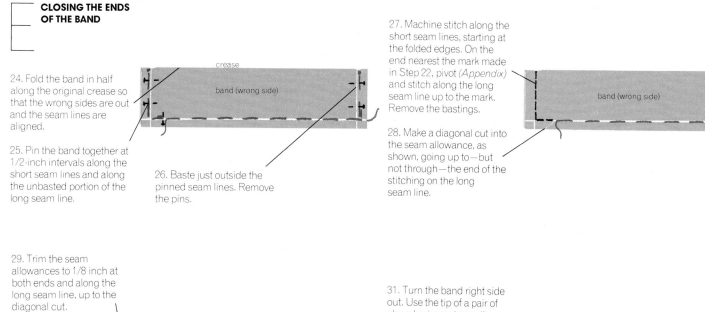

30. Trim the corner diagonally.

31. Turn the band right side out. Use the tip of a pair of closed scissors to gently push out the buttonhole tab.

32. Press the band.

continued

F | GATHERING THE LEG OF THE KNICKERS

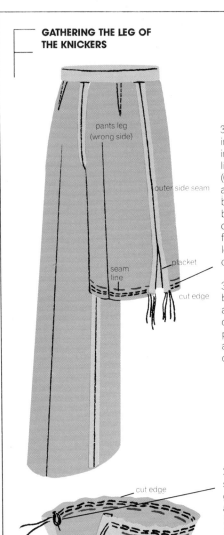

33. Starting and ending 1 inch from the placket made in Box B, run two parallel lines of machine basting (6 stitches to the inch) around the leg. Make one basting line just outside the basted seam line and the other 1/8 inch outside the first line. Leave 4 inches of loose thread at both ends of each line.

34. Gently pull the loose bobbin basting threads, first at one end, then at the other, gathering the cut pants edge until it is approximately the size of the opening in the band.

35. Turn the pants leg right side out. Working on the gathered bottom end, insert a pin at one end of the basting lines and secure the loose threads by looping them around the pin.

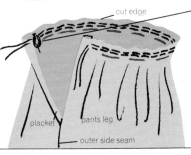

G | ATTACHING THE BAND TO THE LEG

36. Place the band around the gathered edge of the leg and align the basted seam lines. Make sure the buttonhole tab is pointing toward the back of the pants.

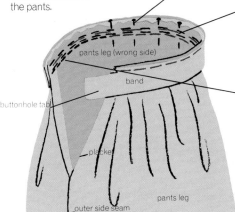

37. Spread open the band and, while holding it open, pin the leg to one side of the band at one end, and then at 1/2-inch intervals.

38. Adjust the gathers so they are evenly distributed.

39. Baste the band to the pants leg between the lines of machine basting.

40. Remove the pins, including the pin inserted in Step 35.

41. Working inside the leg with the gathered side up, machine stitch the band to the pants leg along the basted seam line. Begin and end the stitching at the edges of the placket. As you sew, pull the gathers straight to keep them from bunching—and be careful to keep the band open so that you will not sew through the other side.

42. Remove all the hand bastings except for the basted seam line on the unattached edge of the band.

43. Trim the attached band seam allowance to 1/8 inch.

44. Trim the gathered seam allowance to 1/4 inch.

45. Press the trimmed seam allowances toward the band.

H | FINISHING THE BAND

46. Trim the unattached band seam allowance to 1/4 inch.

47. Turn the band out away from the leg.

48. Turn under the unattached seam allowance of the band and pin it over the stitching line of the pants leg at 1/2-inch intervals.

49. Baste and remove the pins.

50. Attach the edge of the band to the leg with a slip stitch (Appendix). Sew through the threads of the machine stitching rather than through the garment fabric so that your stitches will not be visible on the outside of the leg.

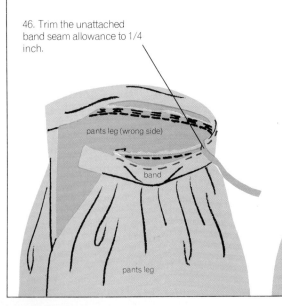

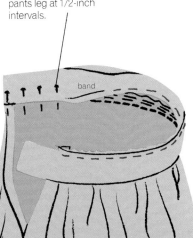

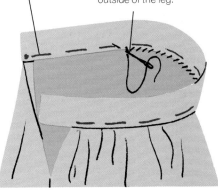

51. Remove the bastings and press, being careful not to press the gathers.

MAKING THE BUTTONHOLE IN THE TAB

52. To determine the center placement line for your buttonhole, measure the width of the tab and find the middle. Mark with several horizontal running stitches.

53. To determine the outer placement line for your buttonhole, measure in from the outer edge of the tab a distance equal to one half the diameter of the button plus 1/4 inch if the button is small or 1/2 inch if the button is large. Mark with several vertical running stitches.

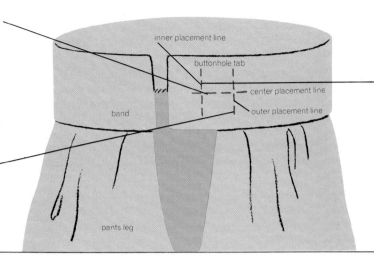

54. To determine the inner placement line for your buttonhole, measure in from the outside placement line a distance equal to the diameter of your button plus 1/8 inch if it is flat or 1/4 inch if it is thicker. Mark with several vertical running stitches.

55. Using the placement lines as a guide, make a horizontal buttonhole by machine or by hand.

PLACING THE BUTTON

56. Pin the tab over the other end of the band, matching the lower edges of the band and lining up the edges of the placket.

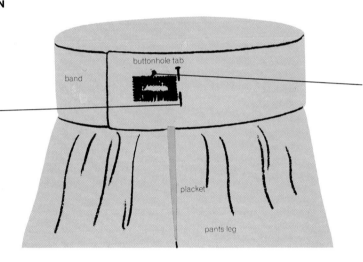

57. To determine the position of the button, insert a pin through the buttonhole at the outer end.

58. Lift up the tab and mark the position for the center of the button with two crossed pins. Remove other pins.

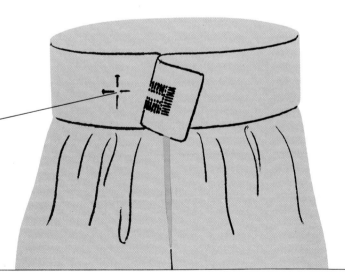

59. Sew the button on by hand. Remove the pins after the first stitch.

60. Repeat on the other leg.

PANTS REMODELED INTO CUFFED SHORTS WITH PATCH POCKETS

A CUTTING AND MARKING THE PANTS LEGS

1. Try on the pants you want to convert into shorts and insert a pin across the crease of one leg where you want the lower edge of the cuff to be.

2. Remove the pants and place them on a table with the outer side seam of the pinned leg facing you. Keep the fabric flat, with the creased edges straight and the hemmed edges aligned.

3. Starting from the pin at the crease, insert pins across the pants leg, making sure the pins run parallel to the hem and that they go through both layers of fabric.

4. Measure down and draw a chalk line 1/2 inch from the pins.

5. Cut off the lower portion of the pants leg along the chalk line. Remove the pins.

6. Run a line of basting stitches 1/2 inch above the cut edge to mark a seam line.

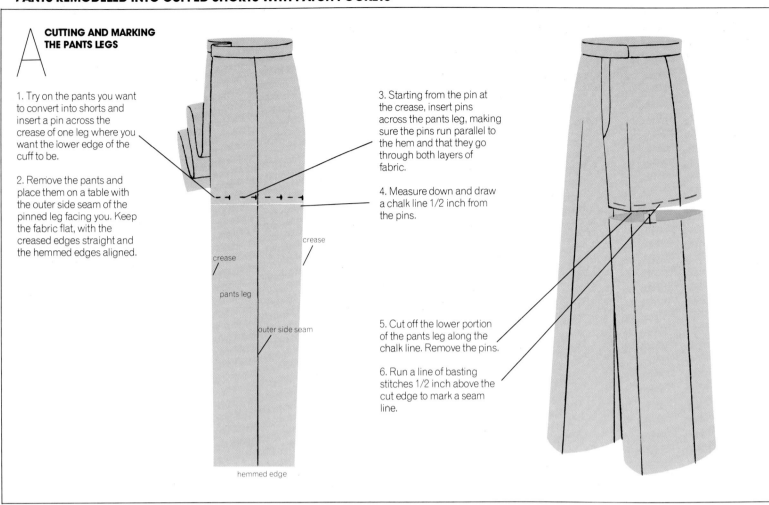

B CUTTING OUT THE CUFF

7. To determine how long the cuff should be, measure around the pants leg along the basted seam line and add 1 inch for seam allowances.

8. Place the cutoff lower portion of the pants leg on a table. Keep the fabric flat, with the creased edges straight and the cut edges and the hemmed edges aligned.

9. Starting at the cut edge, measure the distance you determined in Step 7 along one of the creases and mark with a chalk line at a right angle to the crease.

10. Decide how wide you want the finished cuff to be and add 1/2 inch for seam allowance.

11. Measure in from the crease the same distance you determined in Step 10 and draw a chalk line parallel to the crease, from the cut edge to the chalk line made in Step 9.

12. Pin both layers of fabric together at 1-inch intervals.

13. Cut the cuff out along the chalk lines. Remove the pins.

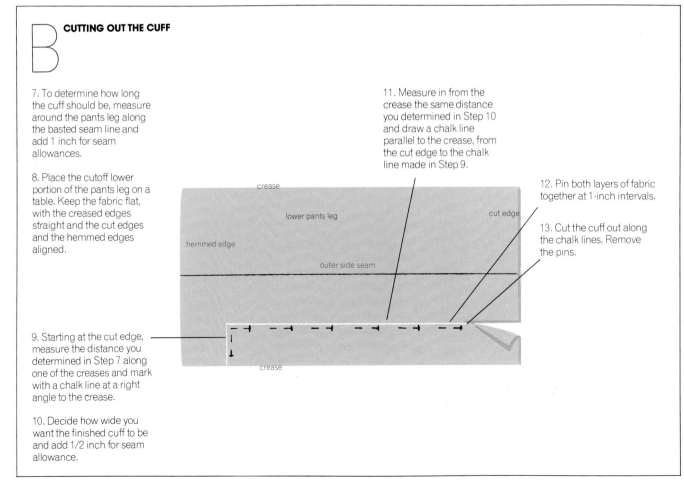

C | PREPARING THE CUFF

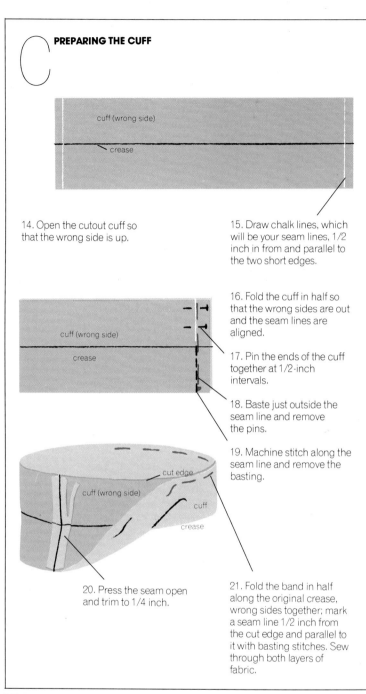

14. Open the cutout cuff so that the wrong side is up.

15. Draw chalk lines, which will be your seam lines, 1/2 inch in from and parallel to the two short edges.

16. Fold the cuff in half so that the wrong sides are out and the seam lines are aligned.

17. Pin the ends of the cuff together at 1/2-inch intervals.

18. Baste just outside the seam line and remove the pins.

19. Machine stitch along the seam line and remove the basting.

20. Press the seam open and trim to 1/4 inch.

21. Fold the band in half along the original crease, wrong sides together; mark a seam line 1/2 inch from the cut edge and parallel to it with basting stitches. Sew through both layers of fabric.

D | ATTACHING THE CUFF TO THE PANTS LEG

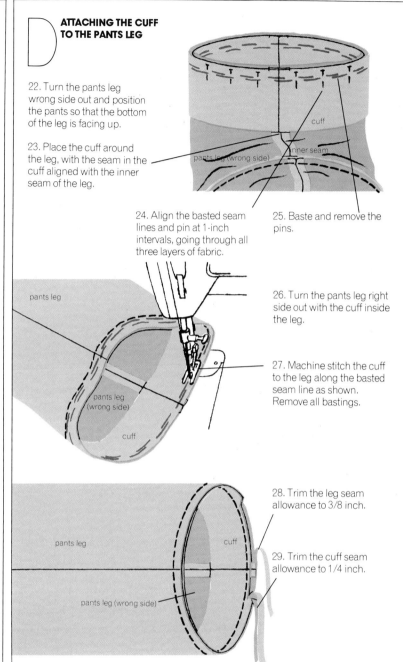

22. Turn the pants leg wrong side out and position the pants so that the bottom of the leg is facing up.

23. Place the cuff around the leg, with the seam in the cuff aligned with the inner seam of the leg.

24. Align the basted seam lines and pin at 1-inch intervals, going through all three layers of fabric.

25. Baste and remove the pins.

26. Turn the pants leg right side out with the cuff inside the leg.

27. Machine stitch the cuff to the leg along the basted seam line as shown. Remove all bastings.

28. Trim the leg seam allowance to 3/8 inch.

29. Trim the cuff seam allowance to 1/4 inch.

E | FINISHING THE CUFF

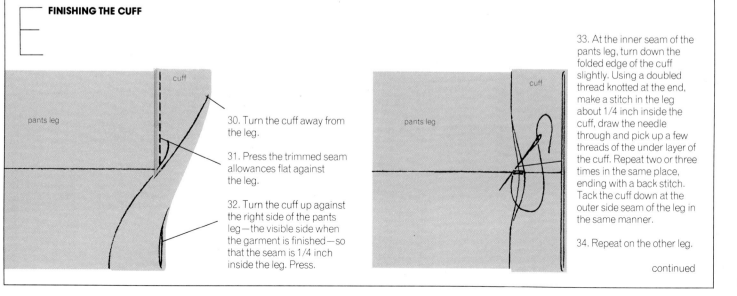

30. Turn the cuff away from the leg.

31. Press the trimmed seam allowances flat against the leg.

32. Turn the cuff up against the right side of the pants leg—the visible side when the garment is finished—so that the seam is 1/4 inch inside the leg. Press.

33. At the inner seam of the pants leg, turn down the folded edge of the cuff slightly. Using a doubled thread knotted at the end, make a stitch in the leg about 1/4 inch inside the cuff, draw the needle through and pick up a few threads of the under layer of the cuff. Repeat two or three times in the same place, ending with a back stitch. Tack the cuff down at the outer side seam of the leg in the same manner.

34. Repeat on the other leg.

continued

93

CUTTING OUT THE PATCH POCKET

35. Remove the stitching from one of the seams of the remaining portion of the pants leg from which you cut the cuff.

36. With the fabric wrong side up, press it to remove the crease. If the crease is still visible, try to cut out the pocket so that the crease will not be visible.

37. Decide how deep you want the pocket to be and add 1 3/4 inches for hem and seam allowances.

38. Measure in from the cut edge the distance you determined and draw a chalk line across the fabric parallel to the cut edge.

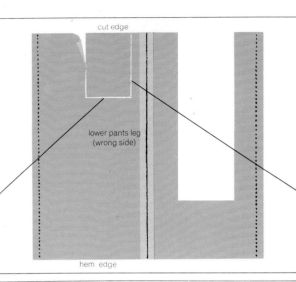

39. Decide how wide you want the pocket to be and add 1 inch for seam allowances.

40. Draw two chalk lines, separated by the distance you determined in Step 39, at right angles to the cut edge and going from the cut edge to the chalk line you drew in Step 38.

41. Cut out the pocket along the chalk lines.

PREPARING THE POCKET

42. With the pocket wrong side up, measure in 1 1/4 inches from—and parallel to—the original cut edge, and draw a chalk line. This will be your hem fold line.

43. Draw chalk lines, which will be your seam lines, 1/2 inch in from—and parallel to—the other three cut edges.

44. Re-mark the seam lines and the hem fold line with lines of basting stitches.

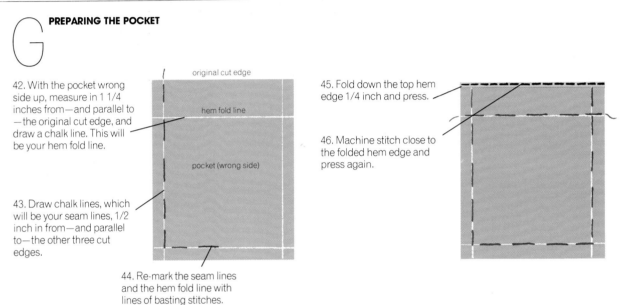

45. Fold down the top hem edge 1/4 inch and press.

46. Machine stitch close to the folded hem edge and press again.

HEMMING THE POCKET

47. Turn the pocket wrong side down and fold the fabric along the hem fold line.

48. Pin the hem to the pocket along the basted seam lines, then baste just outside the basted seam lines and remove the pins.

49. Machine stitch along the three seam lines just outside the basted markings. Begin at the fold and stitch down the side seam; pivot (Appendix) and stitch across the bottom of the pocket. Pivot again, then stitch up the other side seam to the fold. Remove all bastings.

50. Trim the two corners of the hem edge diagonally.

51. Trim both side seam allowances of the hem only to 1/4 inch.

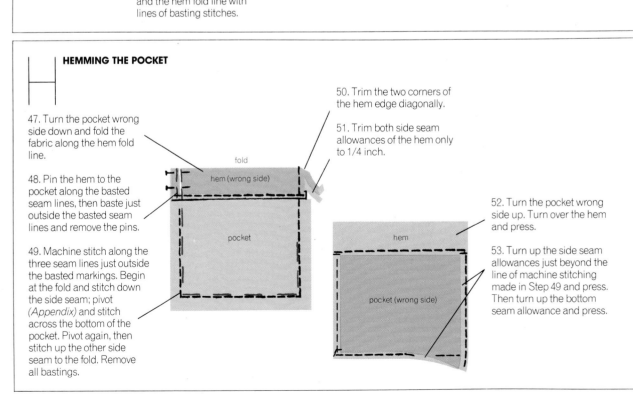

52. Turn the pocket wrong side up. Turn over the hem and press.

53. Turn up the side seam allowances just beyond the line of machine stitching made in Step 49 and press. Then turn up the bottom seam allowance and press.

ATTACHING THE POCKET TO THE SHORTS

54. Try on the shorts and place the pocket, wrong side down, in the position you want. Pin the pocket to the shorts at each corner.

55. Place the shorts on a table and check to see if the top of the pocket is parallel to the waistline of the shorts. Adjust its position if necessary. Then pin the pocket to the shorts at 1-inch intervals.

56. Baste along the side and bottom edges of the pocket 1/4 inch in from the edges. Remove the pins.

57. Machine stitch the pocket to the shorts close to the edge. Remove the bastings.

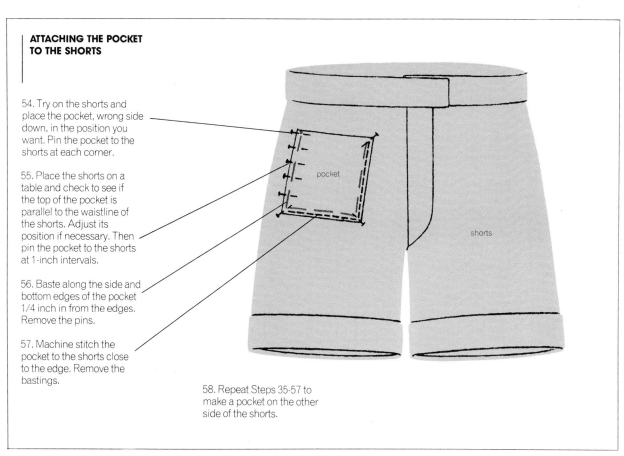

58. Repeat Steps 35-57 to make a pocket on the other side of the shorts.

PANTS REMODELED INTO FLARED-LEGS WITH BORDERS

A PREPARING THE PANTS

1. To widen the legs on a pair of pants by adding inserts of contrasting fabric, begin by trying on the pants and inserting a pin in the outer side seam where you want the top of the triangular insert to go.

2. Remove the pants, mark the pinned spot with several running stitches and remove the pin.

3. Let down the hem around the bottom of the pants leg and trim the hem allowance to 1/2 inch.

4. Open the outer side seam by removing the stitching, starting at the trimmed hem edge and going up to—but not through—the running stitches.

5. Turn the pants wrong side out.

6. Reinforce the original stitching for 1 inch above the opening made in the outer side seam by machine stitching forward to the running stitches, then backward.

7. Lightly press the opened seam allowances and hem allowance to flatten the fold lines without removing the lines completely, since they will be used for seam lines.

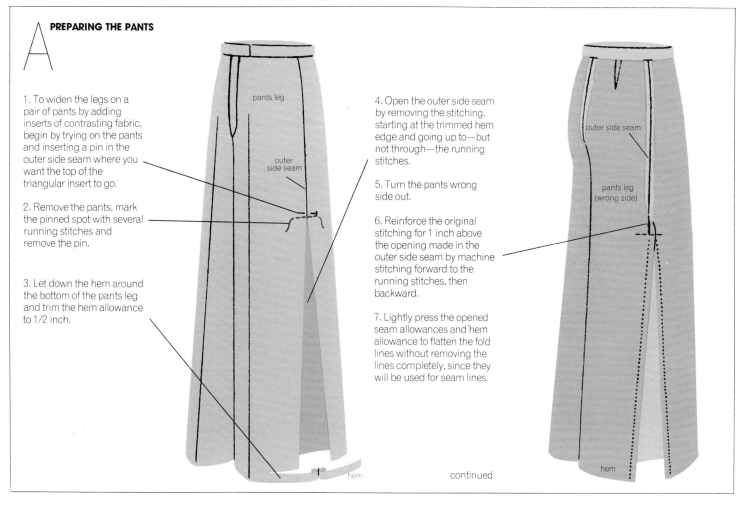

continued

B CUTTING OUT THE INSERT AND ATTACHING IT TO THE PANTS

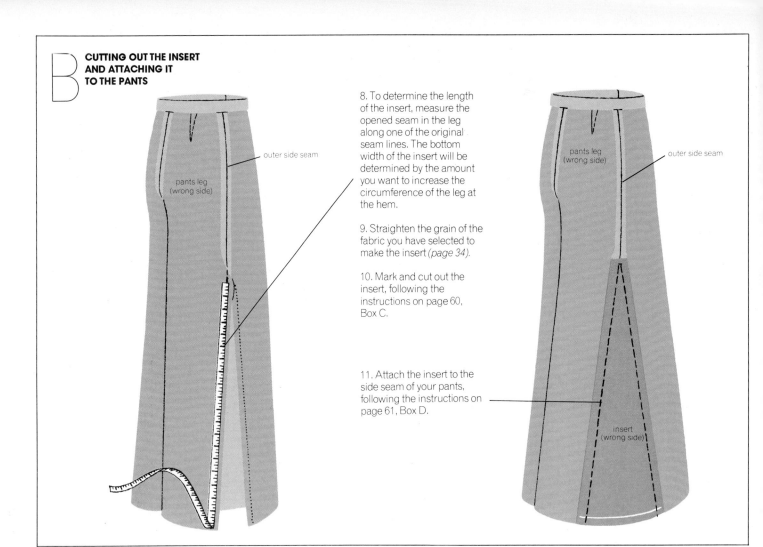

8. To determine the length of the insert, measure the opened seam in the leg along one of the original seam lines. The bottom width of the insert will be determined by the amount you want to increase the circumference of the leg at the hem.

9. Straighten the grain of the fabric you have selected to make the insert *(page 34)*.

10. Mark and cut out the insert, following the instructions on page 60, Box C.

11. Attach the insert to the side seam of your pants, following the instructions on page 61, Box D.

C CUTTING OUT THE BORDER

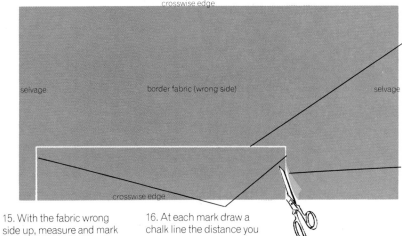

12. To determine the length of the border, measure around the leg along the lower seam line formed by the original hem fold line and the curved seam line of the insert. Add 1 inch for seam allowances.

13. Try on the pants to see how much to add to the length of the leg below the lower seam line. Double the measurement and add 1 inch for seam allowances. Remove the pants.

14. Straighten the grain of the fabric you have selected to make the border for the pants hem *(page 34)*.

15. With the fabric wrong side up, measure and mark the length of the border on one crosswise edge.

16. At each mark draw a chalk line the distance you determined in Step 13 at a right angle to the crosswise edge.

17. Draw a chalk line connecting the tops of the lines made in Step 16.

18. Cut out the border along the chalk lines.

D PREPARING THE BORDER

19. With the cutout border wrong side up, draw chalk lines—which will be your seam lines—1/2 inch in from and parallel to all four cut edges.

20. Fold the border in half lengthwise so that the wrong sides are together and the seam lines are aligned. Press the fold.

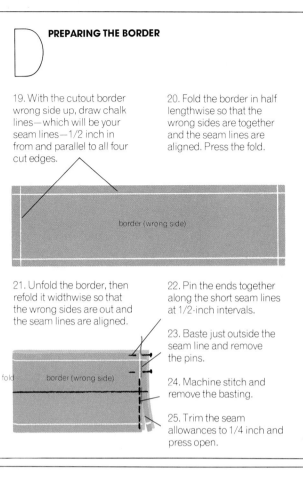

21. Unfold the border, then refold it widthwise so that the wrong sides are out and the seam lines are aligned.

22. Pin the ends together along the short seam lines at 1/2-inch intervals.

23. Baste just outside the seam line and remove the pins.

24. Machine stitch and remove the basting.

25. Trim the seam allowances to 1/4 inch and press open.

E ATTACHING THE BORDER

26. Turn the pants so that the bottom of the leg is facing upward. Position the border, wrong side out, around the pants leg so that the seam in the border matches the inner seam of the leg.

27. Align one long seam line on the border with the lower seam line on the leg as shown, and pin the border to the leg at 1-inch intervals.

28. Baste just outside the seam line and remove the pins.

29. Machine stitch along the seam line and remove the basting.

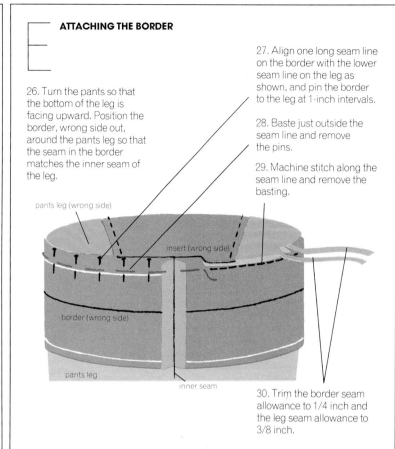

30. Trim the border seam allowance to 1/4 inch and the leg seam allowance to 3/8 inch.

F FINISHING THE BORDER

31. Turn the leg wrong side out.

32. Turn the unattached edge of the border away from the leg and press under the seam allowance.

33. Press the trimmed seam allowances flat against the border.

34. Fold the border in half along the pressed fold line so that the wrong sides are together.

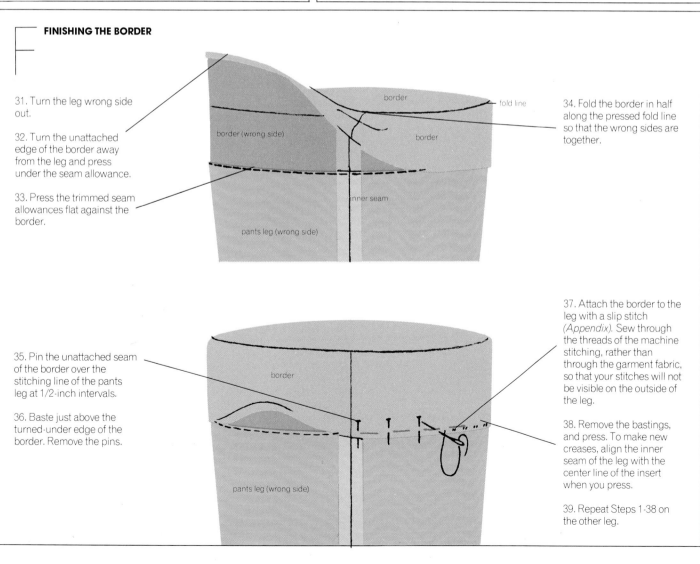

35. Pin the unattached seam of the border over the stitching line of the pants leg at 1/2-inch intervals.

36. Baste just above the turned-under edge of the border. Remove the pins.

37. Attach the border to the leg with a slip stitch (Appendix). Sew through the threads of the machine stitching, rather than through the garment fabric, so that your stitches will not be visible on the outside of the leg.

38. Remove the bastings, and press. To make new creases, align the inner seam of the leg with the center line of the insert when you press.

39. Repeat Steps 1-38 on the other leg.

Long life for a short skirt

Skirts are a little like haircuts; you can easily trim them shorter, but it takes a bit of time—and creative artifice—to make them attractively longer. But even a skirt as brief as the A-line mini at right can, by the grafting on of new material, be changed in shape and character to styles as varied as those shown here.

In the first example, the original has been pared down on the bias and extended with diagonal stripes of a new fabric *(pages 102-104).*

The second transformation was worked by cutting the original skirt into panels that now alternate with panels of another cloth and are set off by a decorative border *(pages 105-109).* This kind of alteration is tricky, and cannot be done at all if the darts on the mini were slashed during its manufacture, or if the hem crease will not steam out.

Far easier to accomplish is the elegant creation at far right, which has sprouted a succession of new borders *(pages 100-101).* It works best in light fabric, such as cotton or silk, since each border is gathered slightly at the seam.

LENGTHENING A SHORT SKIRT BY ADDING RUFFLES

A PREPARING THE SKIRT

1. Decide how long you want the finished skirt to be.

2. Insert a pin at the place on the skirt where the first ruffle will be attached.

3. Measure up from the hem to the pin. Continue to measure the distance around the skirt, marking with pins.

4. Run a line of basting stitches along the row of pins. Remove the pins.

5. Draw a chalk line around the skirt 1/2 inch below the basting.

6. Cut off the skirt along the chalk line.

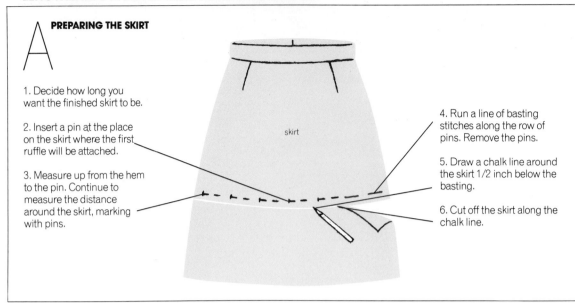

B CUTTING OUT THE FABRIC FOR THE FIRST RUFFLE

7. To determine the length for the front ruffle piece, first measure the row of basting stitches on the skirt front. Multiply the measurement by 1 1/2 and add 1 inch for seam allowances.

8. Decide how wide you want the ruffle to be and add 1 inch for seam allowances.

9. Straighten the grain of the fabric you have selected for the ruffle (page 34).

10. Mark a rectangle on the wrong side of the fabric, using the length measurement determined in Step 7 and the width determined in Step 8. Make sure to draw the width sides parallel to the selvages.

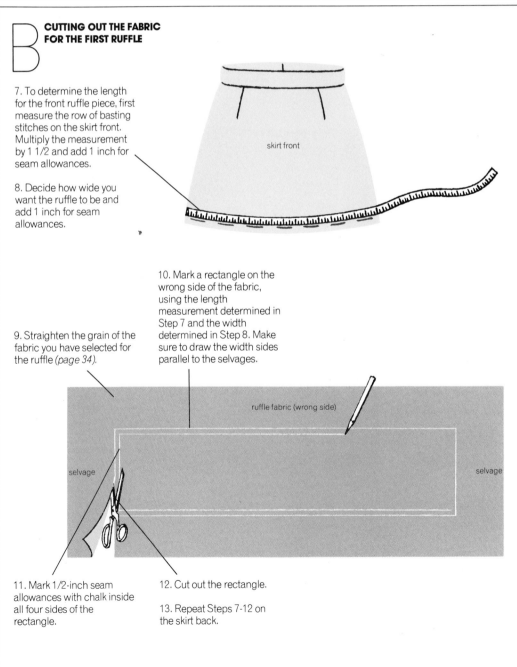

11. Mark 1/2-inch seam allowances with chalk inside all four sides of the rectangle.

12. Cut out the rectangle.

13. Repeat Steps 7-12 on the skirt back.

C MAKING THE RUFFLE TIER

14. Place the two rectangles together with the wrong sides facing out.

15. Pin the rectangles together along the side seam lines.

16. Baste and remove the pins.

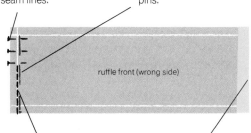

ruffle front (wrong side)

17. Machine stitch and remove the bastings.

19. Press the side seams open.

18. Repeat Steps 14-17 on the other side seam.

20. On the ruffle front, run a line of machine basting (six stitches to the inch) 1/2 inch below the top edge. Then run a second line 1/4 inch outside the first. Leave about 4 inches of loose thread at the end of each of the stitching lines.

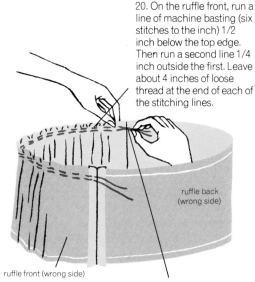

ruffle back (wrong side)

ruffle front (wrong side)

21. Pull the loose bobbin threads until the ruffle front is approximately the desired length.

22. Insert a pin at one end of the basting lines and secure the loose threads by looping them around the pin.

23. Distribute the gathers of the ruffle evenly.

24. Repeat Steps 20-23 on the ruffle back.

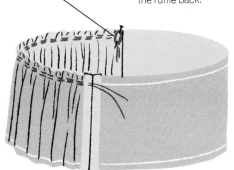

D ATTACHING THE RUFFLE TIER TO THE SKIRT

25. Place the ruffle, wrong side out, on the side of the skirt that will show when the garment is completed. Align the gathered edges of the ruffle with the bottom edge of the skirt.

26. Match the side seams of the ruffle to those of the skirt, and pin the ruffle to the skirt at 2-inch intervals, adjusting the gathers evenly.

27. Baste between the two lines of existing basting on the ruffle. Remove the pins.

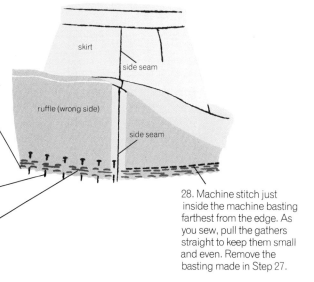

skirt

side seam

ruffle (wrong side)

side seam

28. Machine stitch just inside the machine basting farthest from the edge. As you sew, pull the gathers straight to keep them small and even. Remove the basting made in Step 27.

29. Turn the skirt wrong side out and turn the ruffle away from the skirt.

30. Trim off the long loose ends of the gathering threads.

31. Trim the skirt seam allowance to 1/4 inch.

skirt (wrong side)

ruffle (wrong side)

32. Turn the skirt and ruffle right side out. Press the seam flat, using the tip of the iron to avoid pressing the gathers of the ruffle. Make sure to turn the seam allowances inside toward the skirt.

33. If any gathering threads are visible, remove them with a seam ripper.

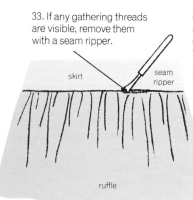

skirt

seam ripper

ruffle

34. To determine the length of the remaining ruffles, multiply the length of the last ruffle attached by 1 1/2 and add 1 inch for seam allowances. Now make and attach the ruffles—except for the bottom one, which must be hemmed before it is attached.

E HEMMING THE BOTTOM RUFFLE TIER

35. With the ruffle wrong side out, turn up one of the long edges 1/4 inch and press flat.

36. Turn up the edge again 1/4 inch. Pin at 2-inch intervals.

37. Baste and remove the pins.

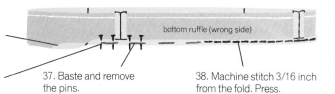

bottom ruffle (wrong side)

38. Machine stitch 3/16 inch from the fold. Press.

39. Repeat Steps 20-33 on the bottom ruffle.

A PLANNING THE SKIRT

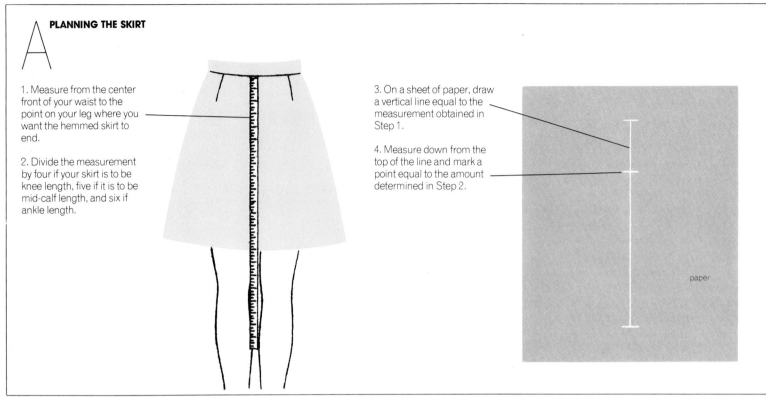

1. Measure from the center front of your waist to the point on your leg where you want the hemmed skirt to end.

2. Divide the measurement by four if your skirt is to be knee length, five if it is to be mid-calf length, and six if ankle length.

3. On a sheet of paper, draw a vertical line equal to the measurement obtained in Step 1.

4. Measure down from the top of the line and mark a point equal to the amount determined in Step 2.

paper

B PREPARING THE SKIRT

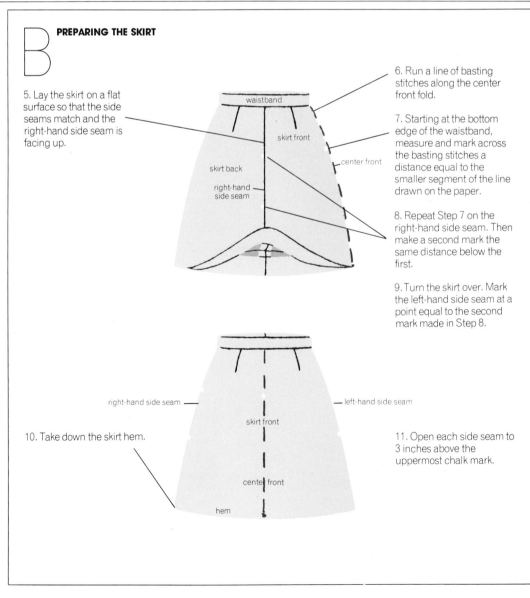

5. Lay the skirt on a flat surface so that the side seams match and the right-hand side seam is facing up.

waistband

skirt front

skirt back

center front

right-hand side seam

6. Run a line of basting stitches along the center front fold.

7. Starting at the bottom edge of the waistband, measure and mark across the basting stitches a distance equal to the smaller segment of the line drawn on the paper.

8. Repeat Step 7 on the right-hand side seam. Then make a second mark the same distance below the first.

9. Turn the skirt over. Mark the left-hand side seam at a point equal to the second mark made in Step 8.

right-hand side seam

left-hand side seam

skirt front

10. Take down the skirt hem.

center front

hem

11. Open each side seam to 3 inches above the uppermost chalk mark.

12. Position the skirt, front facing up, on the paper, matching the line of basting with the vertical line drawn on the paper.

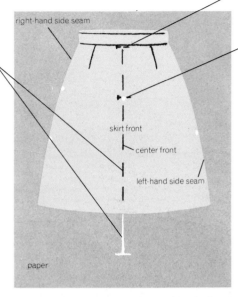

right-hand side seam

skirt front

center front

left-hand side seam

paper

13. Pin the skirt to the paper at the point where the top of the line of basting matches the top of the vertical line.

14. Pin again where the chalk mark on the line of basting matches the dividing mark on the vertical line.

15. Smooth the skirt fabric on the left side of the basting—turning down the sides of the waistband if necessary—so that the fabric lies flat against the paper.

16. Pin the skirt to the paper between the two chalk marks on the right-hand side seam crease.

17. Trace the contour of the skirt between the chalk marks onto the paper.

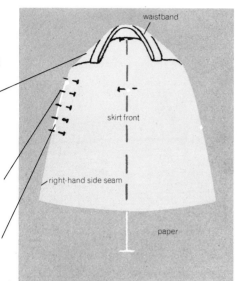

waistband

skirt front

right-hand side seam

paper

18. Remove the skirt from the paper.

19. Measure the lower segment of the vertical line.

20. Extend the side line made in Step 17 until it equals the measurement made in Step 19.

21. Connect the mark on the vertical line with the top of the side line.

22. Make dots between the bottoms of the vertical and side lines by measuring from the line drawn in Step 21 a distance equal to the length of the side line.

23. Connect the dots to form a slightly curved line.

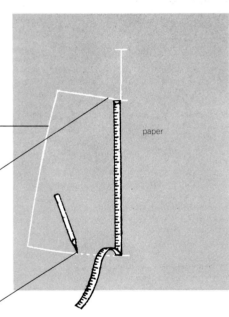

paper

24. Fold the paper along the vertical line and pin the two layers together around the edges of the drawing.

25. Cut along the drawn lines, remove the pins and unfold the pattern.

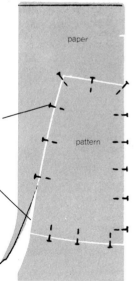

paper

pattern

26. Divide the left-hand side line of the pattern (in the finished skirt this will be the right-hand side) into as many equal portions as you intend to have stripes—i.e., three for knee length, four for mid-calf, five for ankle.

27. Repeat Step 26 on the right-hand side of the pattern.

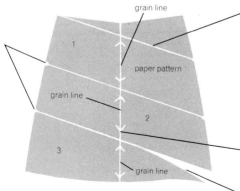

grain line

1

paper pattern

grain line

2

3

grain line

28. Draw a diagonal line connecting the top of the left-hand side of the pattern to the first mark on the right-hand side. Continue to draw diagonal lines until you reach the bottom of the right-hand side of the pattern.

29. Draw straight-grain arrows on the center line of all but the top stripe. Number each stripe except the top one.

30. Cut the bias stripes apart and discard the top one.

continued

D MAKING A SEAM LINE FOR THE FIRST BIAS STRIPE

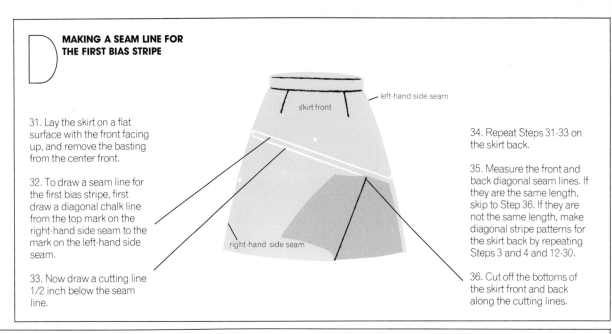

31. Lay the skirt on a flat surface with the front facing up, and remove the basting from the center front.

32. To draw a seam line for the first bias stripe, first draw a diagonal chalk line from the top mark on the right-hand side seam to the mark on the left-hand side seam.

33. Now draw a cutting line 1/2 inch below the seam line.

34. Repeat Steps 31-33 on the skirt back.

35. Measure the front and back diagonal seam lines. If they are the same length, skip to Step 36. If they are not the same length, make diagonal stripe patterns for the skirt back by repeating Steps 3 and 4 and 12-30.

36. Cut off the bottoms of the skirt front and back along the cutting lines.

E CUTTING OUT THE BIAS STRIPES

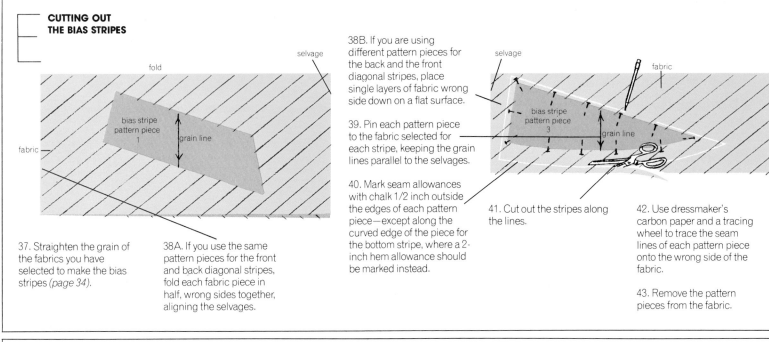

37. Straighten the grain of the fabrics you have selected to make the bias stripes (page 34).

38A. If you use the same pattern pieces for the front and back diagonal stripes, fold each fabric piece in half, wrong sides together, aligning the selvages.

38B. If you are using different pattern pieces for the back and the front diagonal stripes, place single layers of fabric wrong side down on a flat surface.

39. Pin each pattern piece to the fabric selected for each stripe, keeping the grain lines parallel to the selvages.

40. Mark seam allowances with chalk 1/2 inch outside the edges of each pattern piece—except along the curved edge of the piece for the bottom stripe, where a 2-inch hem allowance should be marked instead.

41. Cut out the stripes along the lines.

42. Use dressmaker's carbon paper and a tracing wheel to trace the seam lines of each pattern piece onto the wrong side of the fabric.

43. Remove the pattern pieces from the fabric.

F RECONSTRUCTING THE GARMENT

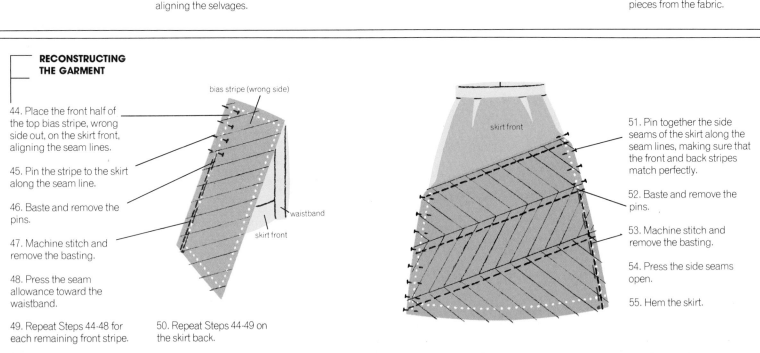

44. Place the front half of the top bias stripe, wrong side out, on the skirt front, aligning the seam lines.

45. Pin the stripe to the skirt along the seam line.

46. Baste and remove the pins.

47. Machine stitch and remove the basting.

48. Press the seam allowance toward the waistband.

49. Repeat Steps 44-48 for each remaining front stripe.

50. Repeat Steps 44-49 on the skirt back.

51. Pin together the side seams of the skirt along the seam lines, making sure that the front and back stripes match perfectly.

52. Baste and remove the pins.

53. Machine stitch and remove the basting.

54. Press the side seams open.

55. Hem the skirt.

A PREPARING THE SKIRT

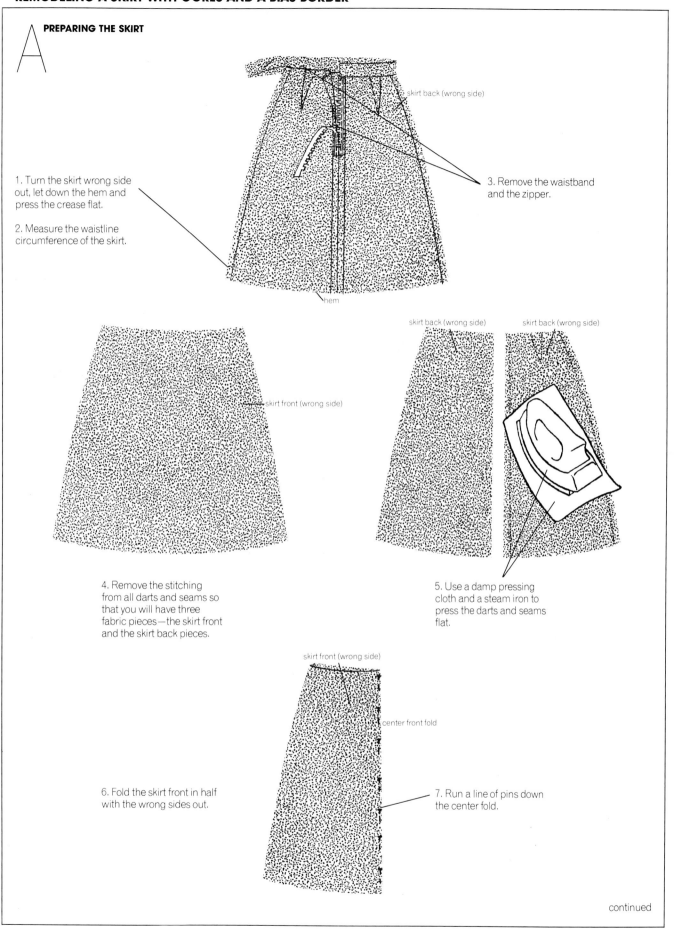

1. Turn the skirt wrong side out, let down the hem and press the crease flat.

2. Measure the waistline circumference of the skirt.

skirt back (wrong side)

3. Remove the waistband and the zipper.

hem

skirt front (wrong side)

skirt back (wrong side)   skirt back (wrong side)

4. Remove the stitching from all darts and seams so that you will have three fabric pieces—the skirt front and the skirt back pieces.

5. Use a damp pressing cloth and a steam iron to press the darts and seams flat.

skirt front (wrong side)

center front fold

6. Fold the skirt front in half with the wrong sides out.

7. Run a line of pins down the center fold.

continued

B ESTABLISHING THE LENGTH OF THE GORES

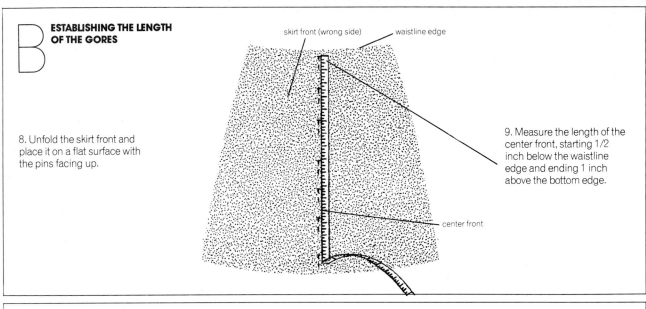

skirt front (wrong side)   waistline edge

center front

8. Unfold the skirt front and place it on a flat surface with the pins facing up.

9. Measure the length of the center front, starting 1/2 inch below the waistline edge and ending 1 inch above the bottom edge.

C MAKING A PATTERN FOR THE GORES

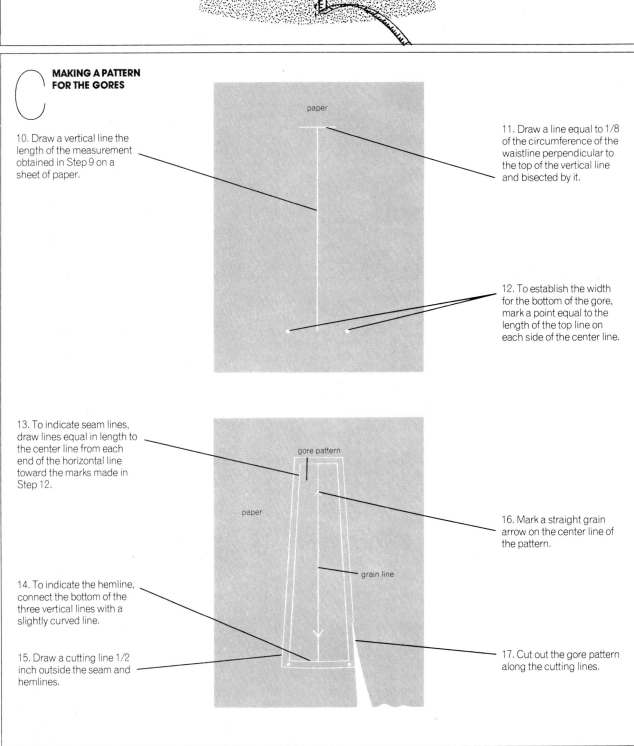

paper

gore pattern

paper

grain line

10. Draw a vertical line the length of the measurement obtained in Step 9 on a sheet of paper.

11. Draw a line equal to 1/8 of the circumference of the waistline perpendicular to the top of the vertical line and bisected by it.

12. To establish the width for the bottom of the gore, mark a point equal to the length of the top line on each side of the center line.

13. To indicate seam lines, draw lines equal in length to the center line from each end of the horizontal line toward the marks made in Step 12.

16. Mark a straight grain arrow on the center line of the pattern.

14. To indicate the hemline, connect the bottom of the three vertical lines with a slightly curved line.

15. Draw a cutting line 1/2 inch outside the seam and hemlines.

17. Cut out the gore pattern along the cutting lines.

D CUTTING OUT THE GORES

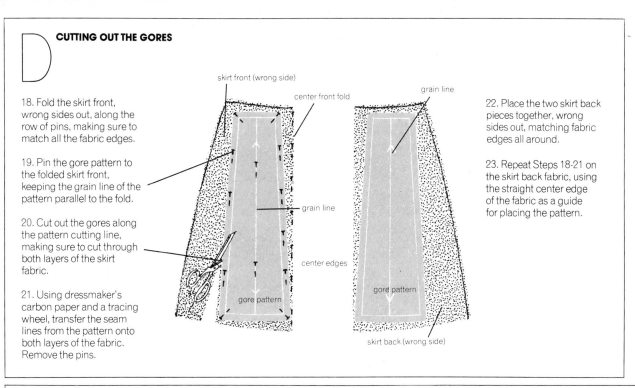

18. Fold the skirt front, wrong sides out, along the row of pins, making sure to match all the fabric edges.

19. Pin the gore pattern to the folded skirt front, keeping the grain line of the pattern parallel to the fold.

20. Cut out the gores along the pattern cutting line, making sure to cut through both layers of the skirt fabric.

21. Using dressmaker's carbon paper and a tracing wheel, transfer the seam lines from the pattern onto both layers of the fabric. Remove the pins.

skirt front (wrong side)

center front fold

grain line

grain line

center edges

gore pattern

gore pattern

skirt back (wrong side)

22. Place the two skirt back pieces together, wrong sides out, matching fabric edges all around.

23. Repeat Steps 18-21 on the skirt back fabric, using the straight center edge of the fabric as a guide for placing the pattern.

E MAKING THE BIAS HEM BAND PATTERN

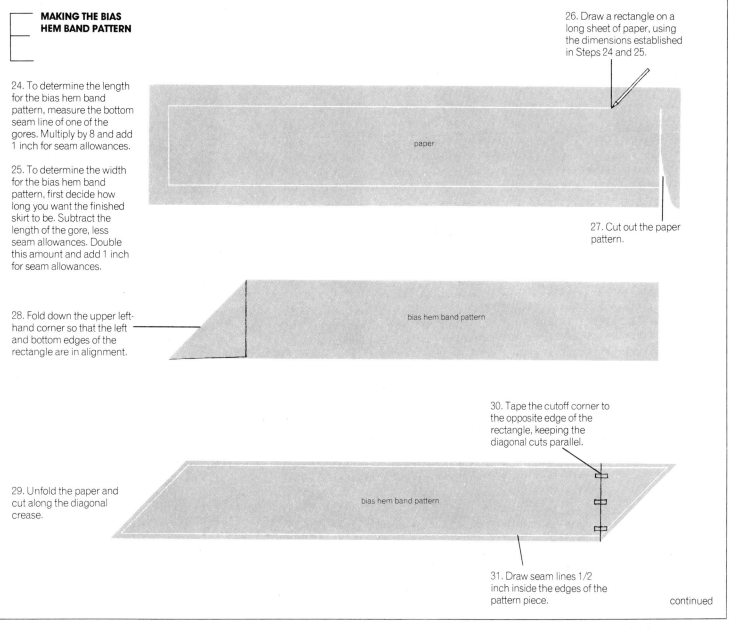

24. To determine the length for the bias hem band pattern, measure the bottom seam line of one of the gores. Multiply by 8 and add 1 inch for seam allowances.

25. To determine the width for the bias hem band pattern, first decide how long you want the finished skirt to be. Subtract the length of the gore, less seam allowances. Double this amount and add 1 inch for seam allowances.

26. Draw a rectangle on a long sheet of paper, using the dimensions established in Steps 24 and 25.

paper

27. Cut out the paper pattern.

28. Fold down the upper left-hand corner so that the left and bottom edges of the rectangle are in alignment.

bias hem band pattern

30. Tape the cutoff corner to the opposite edge of the rectangle, keeping the diagonal cuts parallel.

29. Unfold the paper and cut along the diagonal crease.

bias hem band pattern

31. Draw seam lines 1/2 inch inside the edges of the pattern piece.

continued

F

DETERMINING THE AMOUNT OF ADDITIONAL FABRIC NEEDED

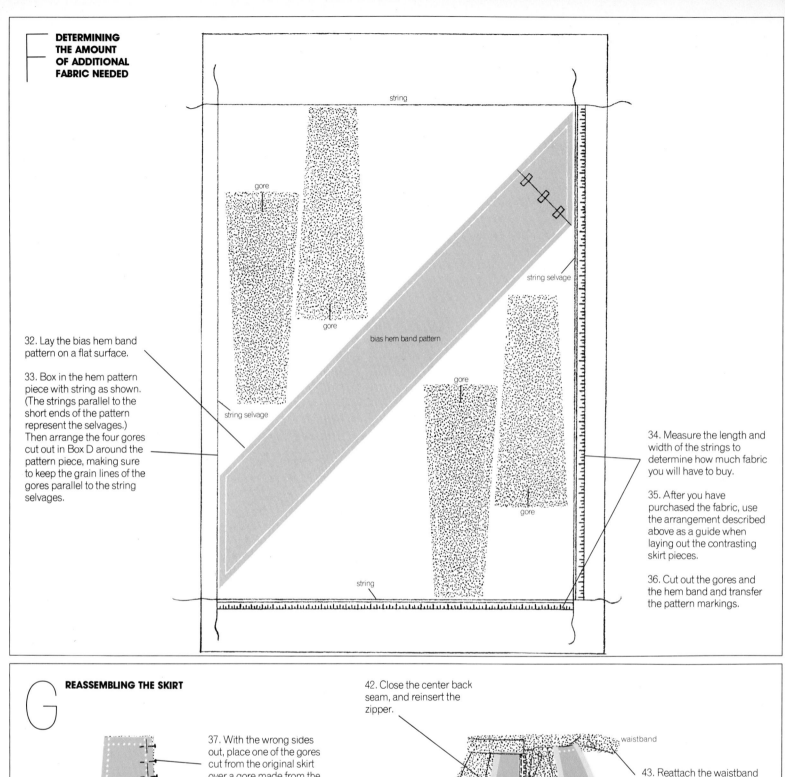

string

gore

gore

gore

bias hem band pattern

string selvage

string selvage

gore

gore

string

32. Lay the bias hem band pattern on a flat surface.

33. Box in the hem pattern piece with string as shown. (The strings parallel to the short ends of the pattern represent the selvages.) Then arrange the four gores cut out in Box D around the pattern piece, making sure to keep the grain lines of the gores parallel to the string selvages.

34. Measure the length and width of the strings to determine how much fabric you will have to buy.

35. After you have purchased the fabric, use the arrangement described above as a guide when laying out the contrasting skirt pieces.

36. Cut out the gores and the hem band and transfer the pattern markings.

G

REASSEMBLING THE SKIRT

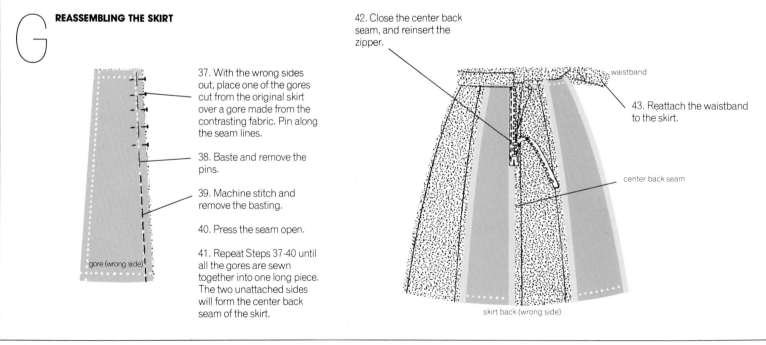

gore (wrong side)

waistband

center back seam

skirt back (wrong side)

37. With the wrong sides out, place one of the gores cut from the original skirt over a gore made from the contrasting fabric. Pin along the seam lines.

38. Baste and remove the pins.

39. Machine stitch and remove the basting.

40. Press the seam open.

41. Repeat Steps 37-40 until all the gores are sewn together into one long piece. The two unattached sides will form the center back seam of the skirt.

42. Close the center back seam, and reinsert the zipper.

43. Reattach the waistband to the skirt.

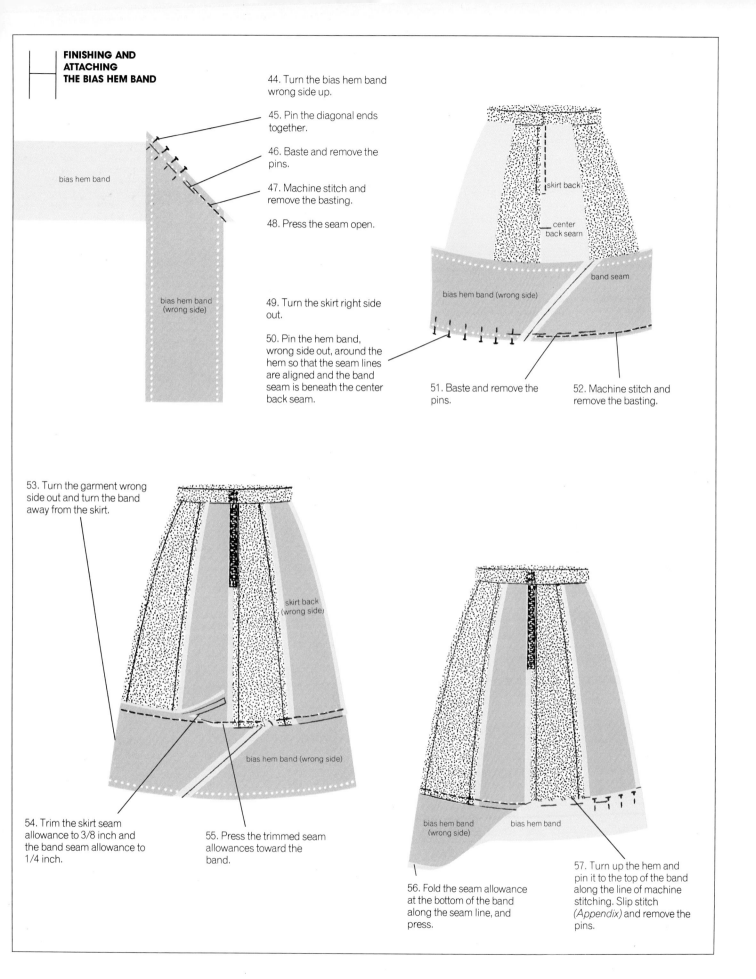

FINISHING AND ATTACHING THE BIAS HEM BAND

44. Turn the bias hem band wrong side up.

45. Pin the diagonal ends together.

46. Baste and remove the pins.

47. Machine stitch and remove the basting.

48. Press the seam open.

bias hem band

bias hem band (wrong side)

49. Turn the skirt right side out.

50. Pin the hem band, wrong side out, around the hem so that the seam lines are aligned and the band seam is beneath the center back seam.

skirt back

center back seam

band seam

bias hem band (wrong side)

51. Baste and remove the pins.

52. Machine stitch and remove the basting.

53. Turn the garment wrong side out and turn the band away from the skirt.

skirt back (wrong side)

bias hem band (wrong side)

54. Trim the skirt seam allowance to 3/8 inch and the band seam allowance to 1/4 inch.

55. Press the trimmed seam allowances toward the band.

56. Fold the seam allowance at the bottom of the band along the seam line, and press.

bias hem band (wrong side)

bias hem band

57. Turn up the hem and pin it to the top of the band along the line of machine stitching. Slip stitch (*Appendix*) and remove the pins.

Flourishes on skirts

New style can be brought to a neatly tailored skirt by fancying it up with extra fabric. The straight hemline of the six-gored skirt at near right—so called for its six separate panels —can be transformed by adding a zigzag border as shown in the skirt next to it. Or the skirt can be given whole new panels of pleats, as in the other two garments. In one, the pleats hang straight along the original lines of the skirt; in the other, they flare outward in lavish triangular panels called godets.

All of these variations, as demonstrated on the following pages, are simple to perform, since none require changing the waist, zipper or hip sections of the original. But pay particular attention to the weight of the new fabric. In adding the zigzag border or a plain godet, choose fabric of the same weight as the original. But in the pleated versions, to avoid unsightly bulkiness, use a lighter fabric, and finish the hem with lace seam tape. Also be careful to avoid permanent-press fabrics that refuse to hold creases.

RESTYLING THE SKIRT WITH A PLAIN OR PLEATED GODET

A PREPARING THE SKIRT

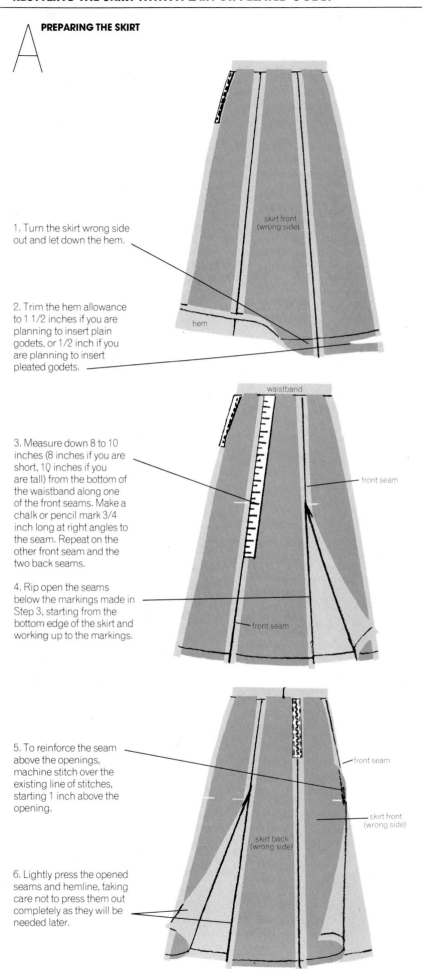

1. Turn the skirt wrong side out and let down the hem.

2. Trim the hem allowance to 1 1/2 inches if you are planning to insert plain godets, or 1/2 inch if you are planning to insert pleated godets.

skirt front (wrong side).

hem

3. Measure down 8 to 10 inches (8 inches if you are short, 10 inches if you are tall) from the bottom of the waistband along one of the front seams. Make a chalk or pencil mark 3/4 inch long at right angles to the seam. Repeat on the other front seam and the two back seams.

waistband

front seam

front seam

4. Rip open the seams below the markings made in Step 3, starting from the bottom edge of the skirt and working up to the markings.

5. To reinforce the seam above the openings, machine stitch over the existing line of stitches, starting 1 inch above the opening.

6. Lightly press the opened seams and hemline, taking care not to press them out completely as they will be needed later.

front seam

skirt front (wrong side)

skirt back (wrong side)

B CUTTING OUT THE PLAIN AND PLEATED GODETS

7A. For the plain godet, you will need 3/4 yard of fabric, 36, 45 or 54 inches wide, in a weight similar to that of the skirt.

7B. For the sunburst pleated godet, you will need 3/4 yard of fabric, 36, 45 or 54 inches wide, in a light weight that creases well.

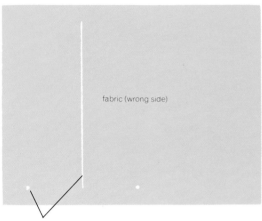

fabric (wrong side)

8A. To make the plain godet, place your fabric wrong side up on a flat surface and draw a vertical line equal in length to the length of the opened seam all the way to the bottom edge of the skirt. Make a dot on either side of the bottom of the vertical line 4 to 5 inches (4 inches if you are short, 5 inches if you are tall) from the line.

8B. To make the sunburst pleated godet, draw a vertical line equal in length to the length of the opened seam all the way to the bottom edge of the skirt —plus 1 1/2 inches. Then make a dot on either side of the bottom of the vertical line 6 to 7 inches (6 inches if you are short, 7 inches if you are tall) from the line.

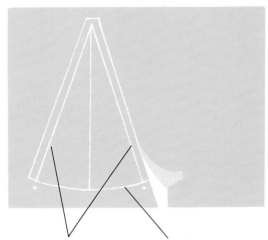

9. Draw two straight lines equal in length to the vertical line, running diagonally from the top of the vertical line toward the dots. These will become the stitching lines. Then draw another line 1/2 inch outside these lines, as shown, to provide for seam allowances.

10. Connect the bottom ends of the triangle with a curved line and cut out the godet.

11. Repeat Steps 8-10 to cut out three more godets. If you are making a plain godet, skip to Box D. If you are making a pleated godet, continue with the instructions in Box C.

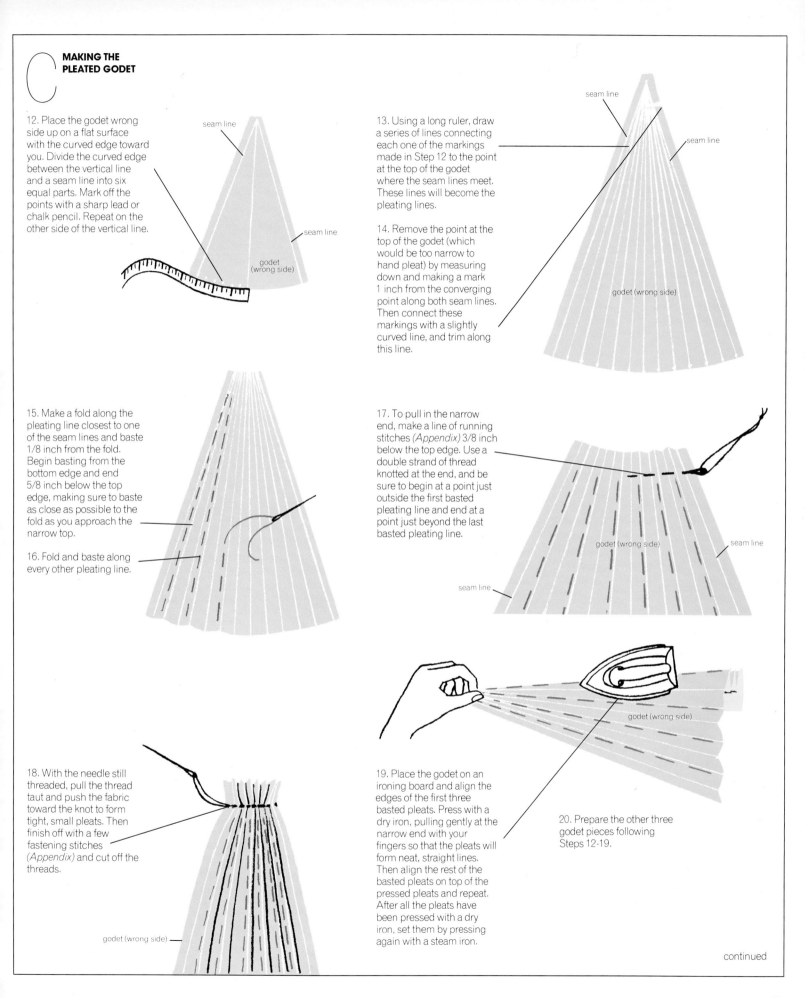

C MAKING THE PLEATED GODET

12. Place the godet wrong side up on a flat surface with the curved edge toward you. Divide the curved edge between the vertical line and a seam line into six equal parts. Mark off the points with a sharp lead or chalk pencil. Repeat on the other side of the vertical line.

seam line

seam line

godet (wrong side)

13. Using a long ruler, draw a series of lines connecting each one of the markings made in Step 12 to the point at the top of the godet where the seam lines meet. These lines will become the pleating lines.

14. Remove the point at the top of the godet (which would be too narrow to hand pleat) by measuring down and making a mark 1 inch from the converging point along both seam lines. Then connect these markings with a slightly curved line, and trim along this line.

seam line

seam line

godet (wrong side)

15. Make a fold along the pleating line closest to one of the seam lines and baste 1/8 inch from the fold. Begin basting from the bottom edge and end 5/8 inch below the top edge, making sure to baste as close as possible to the fold as you approach the narrow top.

16. Fold and baste along every other pleating line.

17. To pull in the narrow end, make a line of running stitches (Appendix) 3/8 inch below the top edge. Use a double strand of thread knotted at the end, and be sure to begin at a point just outside the first basted pleating line and end at a point just beyond the last basted pleating line.

godet (wrong side)

seam line

seam line

18. With the needle still threaded, pull the thread taut and push the fabric toward the knot to form tight, small pleats. Then finish off with a few fastening stitches (Appendix) and cut off the threads.

godet (wrong side)

19. Place the godet on an ironing board and align the edges of the first three basted pleats. Press with a dry iron, pulling gently at the narrow end with your fingers so that the pleats will form neat, straight lines. Then align the rest of the basted pleats on top of the pressed pleats and repeat. After all the pleats have been pressed with a dry iron, set them by pressing again with a steam iron.

godet (wrong side)

20. Prepare the other three godet pieces following Steps 12-19.

continued

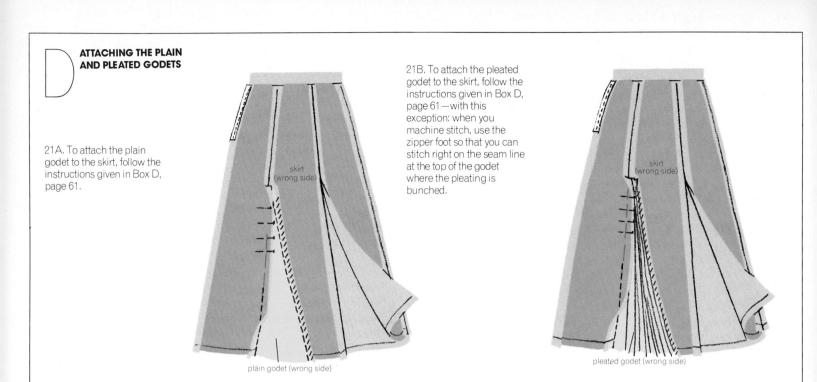

D ATTACHING THE PLAIN AND PLEATED GODETS

21A. To attach the plain godet to the skirt, follow the instructions given in Box D, page 61.

plain godet (wrong side)

21B. To attach the pleated godet to the skirt, follow the instructions given in Box D, page 61—with this exception: when you machine stitch, use the zipper foot so that you can stitch right on the seam line at the top of the godet where the pleating is bunched.

pleated godet (wrong side)

E HEMMING THE SKIRT

22. Turn the skirt right side out.

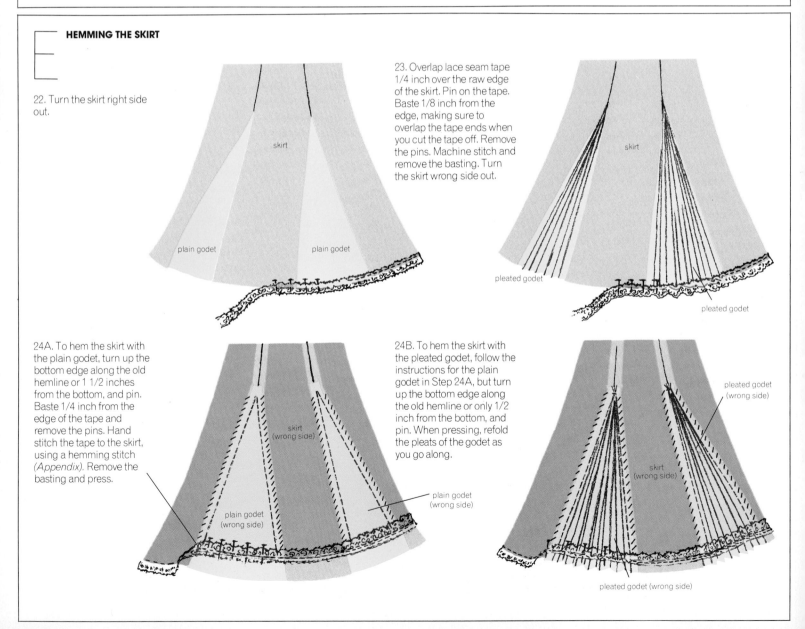

skirt

plain godet

plain godet

23. Overlap lace seam tape 1/4 inch over the raw edge of the skirt. Pin on the tape. Baste 1/8 inch from the edge, making sure to overlap the tape ends when you cut the tape off. Remove the pins. Machine stitch and remove the basting. Turn the skirt wrong side out.

skirt

pleated godet

pleated godet

24A. To hem the skirt with the plain godet, turn up the bottom edge along the old hemline or 1 1/2 inches from the bottom, and pin. Baste 1/4 inch from the edge of the tape and remove the pins. Hand stitch the tape to the skirt, using a hemming stitch (Appendix). Remove the basting and press.

skirt (wrong side)

plain godet (wrong side)

plain godet (wrong side)

24B. To hem the skirt with the pleated godet, follow the instructions for the plain godet in Step 24A, but turn up the bottom edge along the old hemline or only 1/2 inch from the bottom, and pin. When pressing, refold the pleats of the godet as you go along.

pleated godet (wrong side)

skirt (wrong side)

pleated godet (wrong side)

RESTYLING THE SKIRT WITH PLEATED SIDE INSETS

A PREPARING THE SKIRT

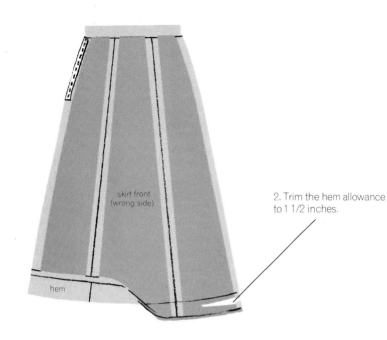

1. Turn the skirt wrong side out and let down the hem.

2. Trim the hem allowance to 1 1/2 inches.

skirt front
(wrong side)

hem

3. Measure down 8 to 10 inches (1 inch below the standard 7- or 9-inch skirt zipper) from the bottom of the waistband, along one of the front seams. Make a chalk or pencil mark. Repeat and make a similar mark on the adjacent side seam, and at a point midway between the two seams.

4. Draw a line connecting the markings made in Step 3 and extend it across the seam allowance at both ends. This will become the seam line when the inset is attached.

5. Draw another line 1/2 inch below the seam line. This will become the cutting line when the bottom part of the present skirt panel is removed.

6. Repeat Steps 3-5 on the other front side panel.

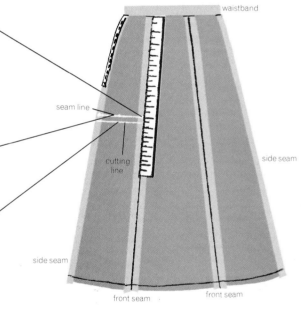

waistband

seam line

cutting line

side seam

side seam

front seam

front seam

7. Rip open the front and side seams, beginning from the bottom edge of the skirt and working up to a point 1/2 inch above the seam lines.

8. Lightly press the opened seams and the hemline, taking care not to press them out completely as they will be needed later.

9. Write in "right" and "left" on the respective panels below the drawn lines.

10. Cut along the cutting lines drawn in Step 5, taking care not to cut into adjacent panels.

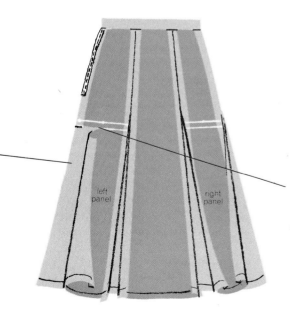

left panel

right panel

continued

B ▶ PREPARING THE INSET FABRIC FOR PLEATING

11. For the two pleated side insets you will need 3/4 yard of fabric, 54 or 60 inches wide, in a weight similar to or lighter than that of the skirt.

12. Before marking the inset fabric for pleating, measure along the seam line (drawn in Step 4) where the inset will be attached. Then see how many 1-inch pleats will fit between the side seam and the front seam lines. (Disregard fractions; if the seam line measures 6 1/2 inches, for example, plan on six pleats.)

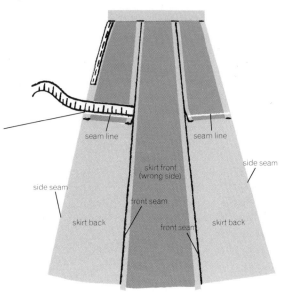

13. Place the fabric wrong side up on a flat surface, with the selvage edges in a vertical position and the raw edges in a horizontal position, as shown.

14. Using a yardstick, measure in 4 inches from one selvage edge and make a dot along the raw top edge. Then make dots at 1-inch intervals along the raw edge until you have three dots for each pleat you plan to make. (For example, if you need six pleats, make 18 dots in all.)

15. Move the yardstick one third of the way down the fabric and repeat Step 14. Then move the yardstick two thirds of the way down, and make another row of dots. Make a final row of dots along the bottom raw edge.

C ▶ PLEATING THE INSET FABRIC

16. Fold the fabric along the first row of dots nearest the selvage, and place the folded edge against the third row of dots. Press with a dry iron, holding down the fold with your free hand or with pins. If your fabric does not fold easily, draw a line connecting the first row of dots. Fold along the line; baste, press, and then place the folded edge against the third row of dots. Press once more.

17. Fold along the next row of dots, and place the folded edge against the third row of dots from that fold. Press.

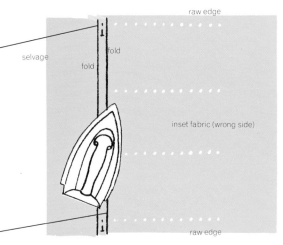

18. Repeat Step 17, until the required number of rows are pleated and pressed with a dry iron. Then set the pleats by pressing them again with a steam iron.

19. To hold the pleats in place while you are cutting and sewing the inset, run a few lines of basting stitches through all layers, as shown.

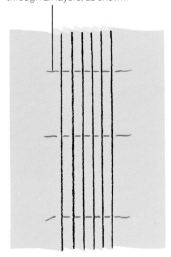

D CUTTING OUT THE INSET

20. Turn the pleated fabric wrong side down so that the selvage edge that was on the left while the fabric was being pleated is now on the right.

21. Place the left skirt panel —the one you cut off in Step 10—wrong side down on top of the pleated inset fabric. Make sure that the wider end of the skirt panel is closest to you; this will ensure that the pleats will fall toward the left in the finished skirt. Leave at least a 1 1/4-inch space between the narrow end of the panel and the raw edge of the pleated fabric.

22. Before pinning the skirt panel to the pleated inset fabric, align the panel as follows: make sure that all pleats, including the folds underneath, are contained within the seam lines (the old stitching lines) on either side of the narrow end of the panel. Also make sure that the outer edges of the pleats are almost equidistant from the seam lines on either side of the wider end of the panel. Then pin the panel in place.

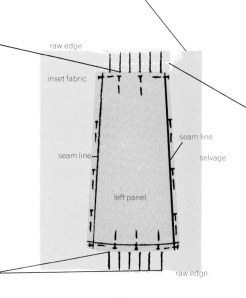

raw edge

inset fabric

seam line

seam line

selvage

left panel

raw edge

23. Draw a 1-inch extension of the panel at the narrow end to provide a seam allowance. Cut along this line and along the side and bottom edges of the panel. Remove the pins.

24. Cut out the right inset by repeating Steps 20-23, keeping the narrow end of the panel closest to you; this will ensure that the pleats will fall toward the right in the finished skirt.

E ATTACHING THE INSET

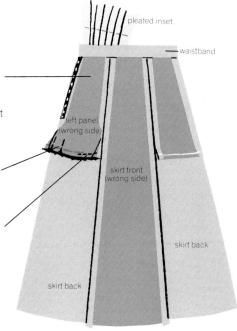

pleated inset

waistband

left panel (wrong side)

skirt front (wrong side)

skirt back

skirt back

25. Turn the skirt wrong side out.

26. Insert the pleated left inset into the skirt, wrong side down and narrow end first, as shown. Pin the narrow end of the inset to the cut edge of the left panel of the skirt. Baste just outside the seam line and remove the pins.

27. Machine stitch along the seam line drawn in Step 4. Remove the basting.

28. Press the seam allowances toward the waistband.

29. Pin the inset to the skirt along the side seam and the front seam. Baste just outside the old seam line. Remove the pins.

30. Machine stitch along the old seam line, beginning at the bottom edge of the skirt and continuing 1/2 inch beyond the top of the inset.

31. Press the seams open.

32. Remove the bastings made in Step 19, holding the pleats in place.

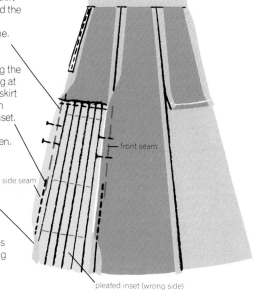

front seam

side seam

pleated inset (wrong side)

continued

HEMMING THE SKIRT

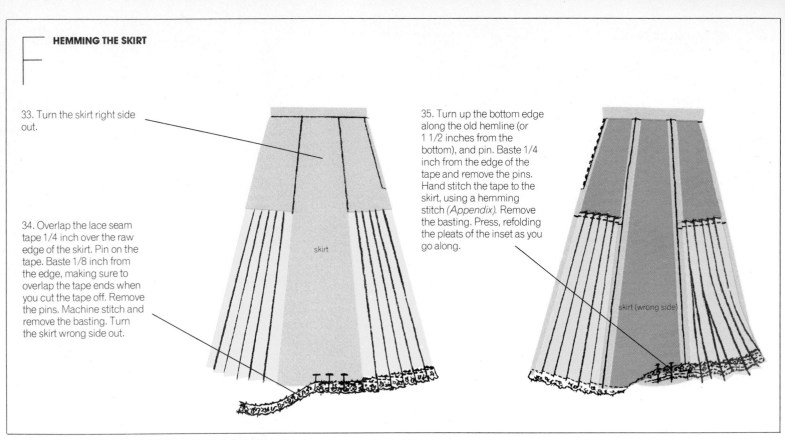

33. Turn the skirt right side out.

34. Overlap the lace seam tape 1/4 inch over the raw edge of the skirt. Pin on the tape. Baste 1/8 inch from the edge, making sure to overlap the tape ends when you cut the tape off. Remove the pins. Machine stitch and remove the basting. Turn the skirt wrong side out.

35. Turn up the bottom edge along the old hemline (or 1 1/2 inches from the bottom), and pin. Baste 1/4 inch from the edge of the tape and remove the pins. Hand stitch the tape to the skirt, using a hemming stitch (Appendix). Remove the basting. Press, refolding the pleats of the inset as you go along.

RESTYLING THE SKIRT WITH A ZIGZAG BORDER

A PREPARING THE SKIRT

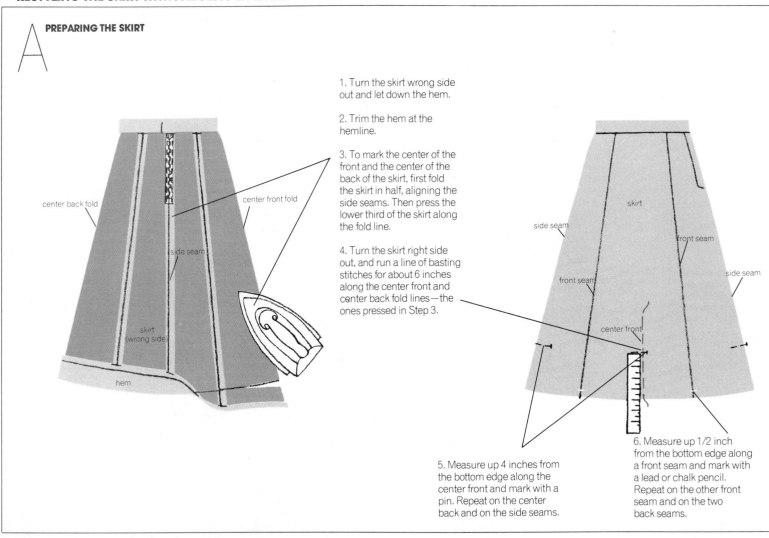

1. Turn the skirt wrong side out and let down the hem.

2. Trim the hem at the hemline.

3. To mark the center of the front and the center of the back of the skirt, first fold the skirt in half, aligning the side seams. Then press the lower third of the skirt along the fold line.

4. Turn the skirt right side out, and run a line of basting stitches for about 6 inches along the center front and center back fold lines—the ones pressed in Step 3.

5. Measure up 4 inches from the bottom edge along the center front and mark with a pin. Repeat on the center back and on the side seams.

6. Measure up 1/2 inch from the bottom edge along a front seam and mark with a lead or chalk pencil. Repeat on the other front seam and on the two back seams.

B | MAKING A PATTERN FOR THE BORDER

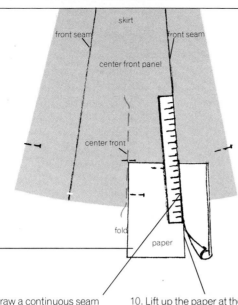

7. To make the pattern for the center front panel, take a piece of paper 2 inches longer than the width of the center front panel of the skirt at the hemline, and 11 inches wide. Fold it in half, crosswise.

8. Place the folded edge of the paper against the center front basting, and the top corner against the pin marking made in Step 5. Pin the paper in place.

9. Draw a continuous seam line down the length of the paper by placing one edge of a long ruler against the front seam above the paper. Put aside the ruler.

10. Lift up the paper at the bottom. Cut through both thicknesses of the paper along the drawn line, taking care not to cut into the skirt.

11. Draw a diagonal line on the paper, connecting the top corner of the paper fold at the center front with the 1/2-inch marking on the front seam line made in Step 6.

12. Measure down 5 to 7 inches from the ends of the drawn line along both edges of the paper. Mark and draw another diagonal line.

13. Remove the pins holding down the paper to the skirt, and cut along the diagonal lines through both thicknesses of the paper. Clip a V-shaped notch on the bottom diagonal line 1 inch from the fold.

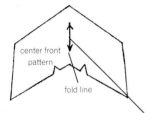

14. Open the paper pattern and write "center front" on it. Then draw an arrow along the fold line. This arrow will enable you to position the pattern correctly in relation to the grain of the fabric when you cut out the border.

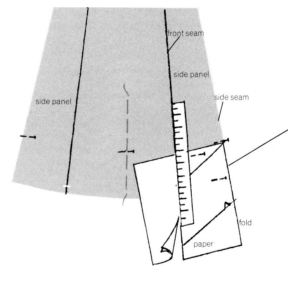

15. Make the pattern for the side front panels in the same way, following Steps 7-13; but this time place the fold of the paper against the side seam.

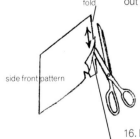

16. Draw an arrow on each side of the fold line. Then separate the two side front patterns by cutting through the fold.

17. Write "side front" on both halves of the paper pattern.

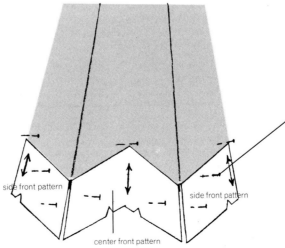

18. Arrange and pin the patterns in place on the skirt, and hold it against you in front of a mirror. If the position of the border is too low, or the width of the border too wide or narrow, make the necessary adjustment. However, if the position is satisfactory, make the patterns for the back panels in the same way, following Steps 7-17 with this exception: make double V-notches to distinguish the back from the front.

continued

C TRIMMING THE SKIRT

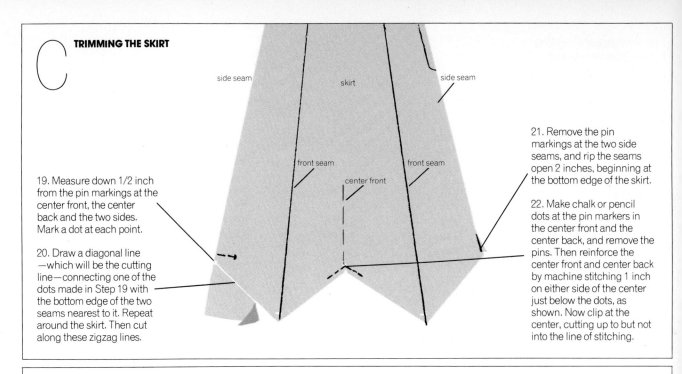

side seam | skirt | side seam

front seam | front seam

center front

19. Measure down 1/2 inch from the pin markings at the center front, the center back and the two sides. Mark a dot at each point.

20. Draw a diagonal line —which will be the cutting line—connecting one of the dots made in Step 19 with the bottom edge of the two seams nearest to it. Repeat around the skirt. Then cut along these zigzag lines.

21. Remove the pin markings at the two side seams, and rip the seams open 2 inches, beginning at the bottom edge of the skirt.

22. Make chalk or pencil dots at the pin markers in the center front and the center back, and remove the pins. Then reinforce the center front and center back by machine stitching 1 inch on either side of the center just below the dots, as shown. Now clip at the center, cutting up to but not into the line of stitching.

D CUTTING OUT THE BORDER

23. To make the zigzag border, you will need 1/2 yard of the border and of the facing fabrics, each measuring 36, 45 or 54 inches wide. However, if you want the border and the facing to be of the same fabric, you will need 3/4 yard of fabric 36, 45 or 54 inches wide.

24. Place the fabric for the border wrong side up on a flat surface. Position all the patterns on it, making sure that the V notches made in Steps 13 and 18 are all pointing in one direction. Also be sure that the grain arrows marked in Step 18 are parallel to the selvage edge, and that there is enough space around each pattern to provide for a 1/2-inch seam allowance. Pin the patterns in place.

25. Trace around each pattern piece with a lead or chalk pencil. This line will be the seam line.

26. Draw another line 1/2 inch away from the seam line. This line will be the cutting line.

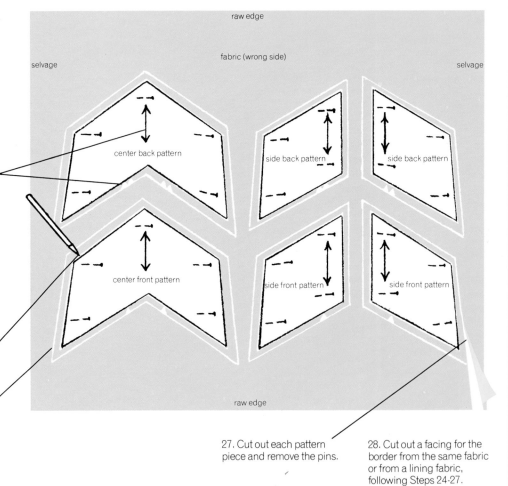

raw edge

fabric (wrong side)

selvage | selvage

center back pattern | side back pattern | side back pattern

center front pattern | side front pattern | side front pattern

raw edge

27. Cut out each pattern piece and remove the pins.

28. Cut out a facing for the border from the same fabric or from a lining fabric, following Steps 24-27.

MAKING THE BORDER

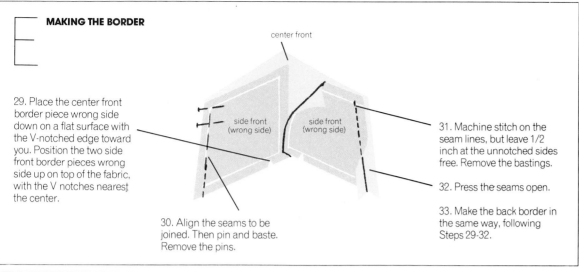

center front

29. Place the center front border piece wrong side down on a flat surface with the V-notched edge toward you. Position the two side front border pieces wrong side up on top of the fabric, with the V notches nearest the center.

side front (wrong side)

side front (wrong side)

30. Align the seams to be joined. Then pin and baste. Remove the pins.

31. Machine stitch on the seam lines, but leave 1/2 inch at the unnotched sides free. Remove the bastings.

32. Press the seams open.

33. Make the back border in the same way, following Steps 29-32.

BASTING THE BORDER TO THE SKIRT

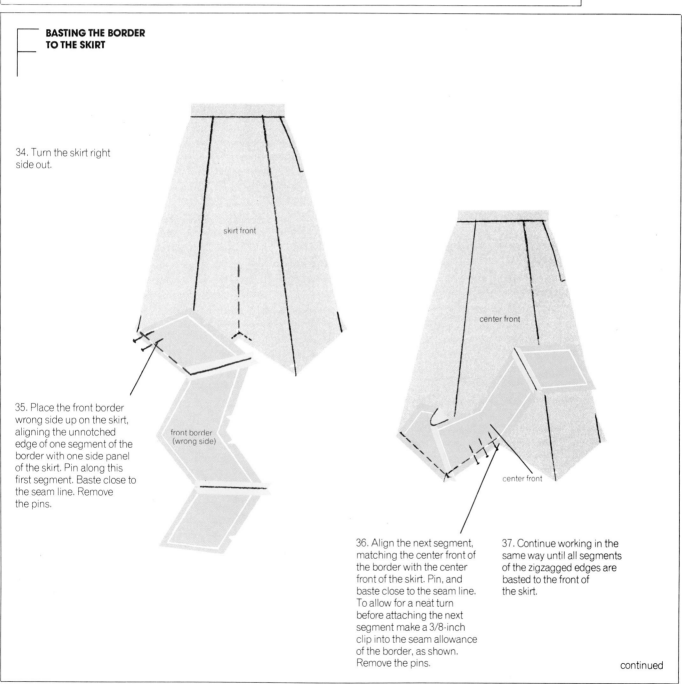

skirt front

front border (wrong side)

center front

center front

34. Turn the skirt right side out.

35. Place the front border wrong side up on the skirt, aligning the unnotched edge of one segment of the border with one side panel of the skirt. Pin along this first segment. Baste close to the seam line. Remove the pins.

36. Align the next segment, matching the center front of the border with the center front of the skirt. Pin, and baste close to the seam line. To allow for a neat turn before attaching the next segment make a 3/8-inch clip into the seam allowance of the border, as shown. Remove the pins.

37. Continue working in the same way until all segments of the zigzagged edges are basted to the front of the skirt.

continued

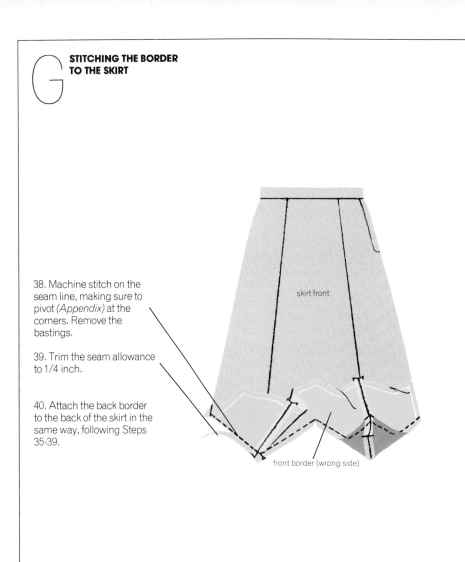

38. Machine stitch on the seam line, making sure to pivot *(Appendix)* at the corners. Remove the bastings.

39. Trim the seam allowance to 1/4 inch.

40. Attach the back border to the back of the skirt in the same way, following Steps 35-39.

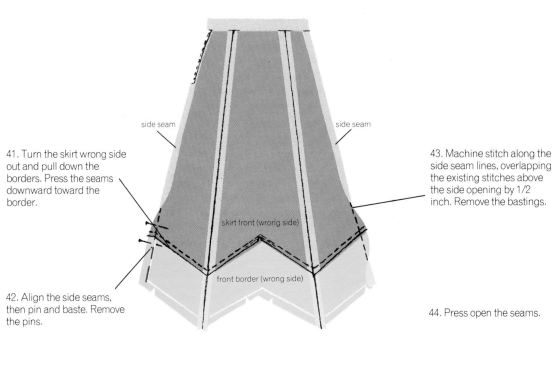

41. Turn the skirt wrong side out and pull down the borders. Press the seams downward toward the border.

42. Align the side seams, then pin and baste. Remove the pins.

43. Machine stitch along the side seam lines, overlapping the existing stitches above the side opening by 1/2 inch. Remove the bastings.

44. Press open the seams.

**MAKING AND ATTACHING
THE BORDER FACING**

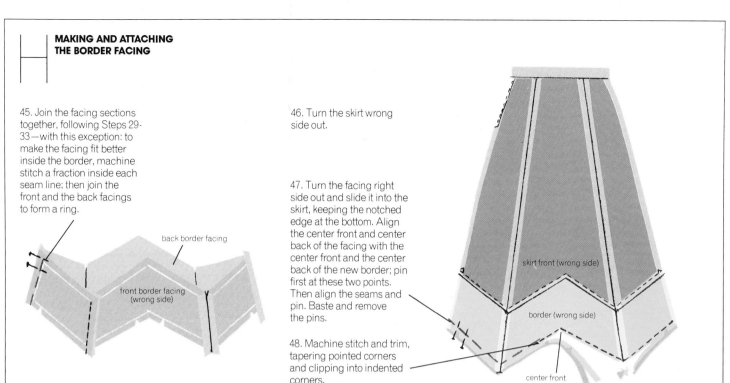

45. Join the facing sections together, following Steps 29-33—with this exception: to make the facing fit better inside the border, machine stitch a fraction inside each seam line; then join the front and the back facings to form a ring.

back border facing

front border facing (wrong side)

46. Turn the skirt wrong side out.

47. Turn the facing right side out and slide it into the skirt, keeping the notched edge at the bottom. Align the center front and center back of the facing with the center front and the center back of the new border; pin first at these two points. Then align the seams and pin. Baste and remove the pins.

48. Machine stitch and trim, tapering pointed corners and clipping into indented corners.

skirt front (wrong side)

border (wrong side)

center front

FINISHING THE BORDER

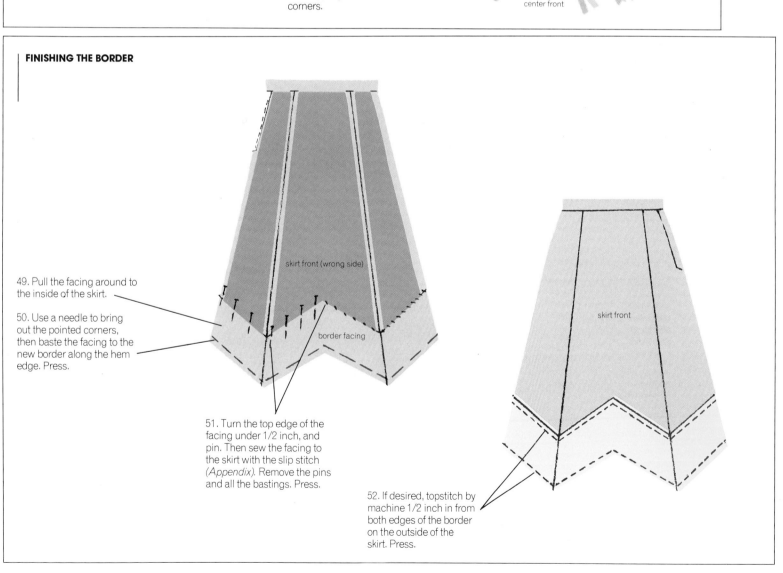

49. Pull the facing around to the inside of the skirt.

50. Use a needle to bring out the pointed corners, then baste the facing to the new border along the hem edge. Press.

skirt front (wrong side)

border facing

skirt front

51. Turn the top edge of the facing under 1/2 inch, and pin. Then sew the facing to the skirt with the slip stitch (*Appendix*). Remove the pins and all the bastings. Press.

52. If desired, topstitch by machine 1/2 inch in from both edges of the border on the outside of the skirt. Press.

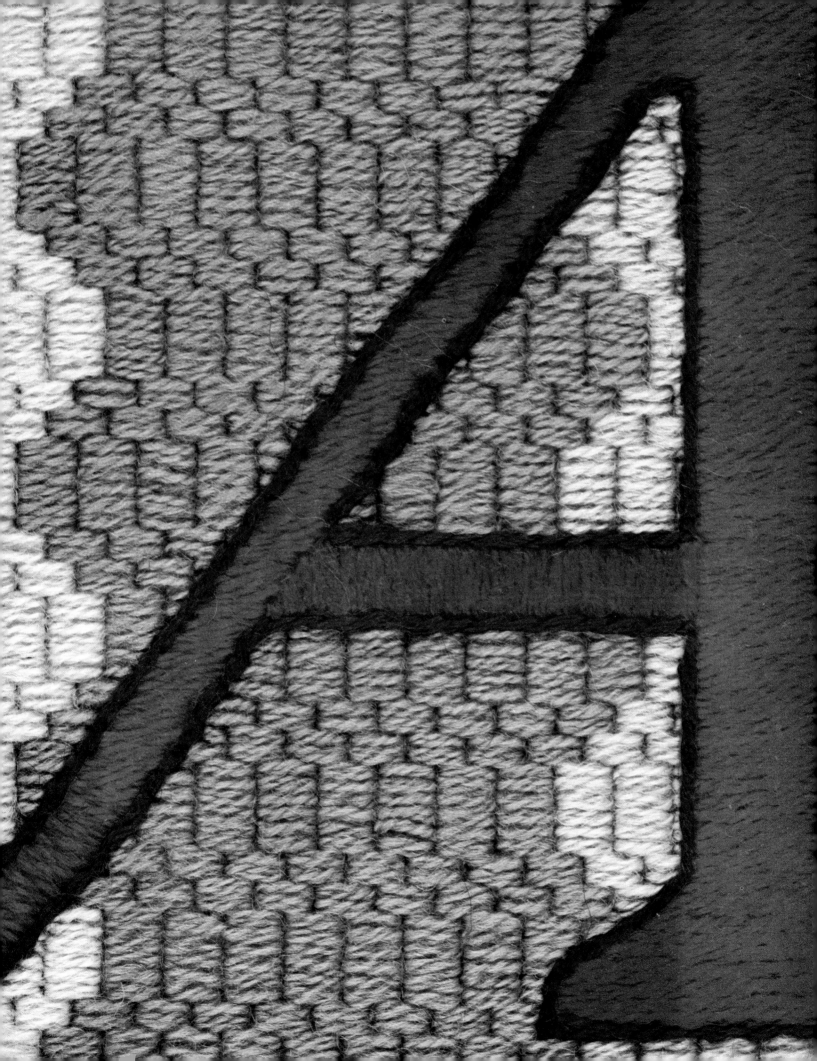

Attending a gala opening of the Metropolitan Opera, New Yorker Ethel Scull, wife of a local taxi magnate, arrived in a simple black dress emblazoned with the emblem of her husband's taxi fleet. The design showed a smiling cherub holding a telephone in one hand and a microphone in the other. Below was the legend, "Scull's Angels, Two-Way Radio." With this imaginative creation, Mrs. Scull upstaged every

THE LASTING FASCINATION OF HERALDRY

other woman in the audience—not to mention a number of high-ranking couturiers who sell dresses with their own names prominently featured in the patterns of the material. "Instead of advertising some designer's name, I'm advertising myself," the taxi queen proclaimed.

Few women know how to flaunt themselves with the same splash and daring as Mrs. Scull. But the impulse among Americans to proclaim their individuality—and do it with a flourish—has never been stronger. In today's fashion world, where standard dresses spin out of factories in a cascade of machine-made look-alikes, there is a special satisfaction in putting one's own stamp on things. And as more and more people are discovering, among the most creative and versatile ways of doing this are the traditional arts of embroidery and needlepoint.

Another case in point is Lyn Revson, who expresses herself in needlework with considerable inventiveness. She took up the craft in 1965, and began presenting her husband, Charles, head of Revlon Inc., with needlepoint cushions, each one adorned with a personal reference to Revson himself. One of them displayed 13 sets of his initials, each in a different style of lettering. Another featured a portrait of Revson's eyes and eyebrows. Even more unusual were pillows inscribed with characteristic Revson sayings. They ranged from a circumspect "In My Considered Opinion" to others far more pungent and colloquial.

Such fanciful personal emblems are part of an ancient—and immensely practical—tradition. On the battlefields of the early Middle Ages, soldiers often lost sight of their leaders. As charges and countercharges demolished battle lines, friend would sometimes find himself hacking at friend. At the Battle of Hastings, for example, the action became so confused that William the Conqueror had to remove his helmet so his bewildered troops could see he was indeed still alive and fighting.

Finally some brilliant—though anonymous—knight came up with a solution. He had his lady embroider a tunic in bright, recognizable colors and symbols that he could wear over his armor. And thus the coat of arms was born. No one knows whether this inventive knight lived through his next battle, but his tunic won an instant success. Noblemen all over Europe began designing telltale coats of arms to be embroidered on their battle dress.

Each aristocrat searched his imagination and his heritage to find symbols unique to himself. Visual puns on family names became a fecund source of such emblems. Thus the name Hope was turned into a dove with an olive branch; a man named Bridge chose a three-arched span and the Ramsey family adopted a ram. Churchmen picked up the fad, and an Abbot Islip worked up an emblem that consisted of a human eye, a small slip of a tree and—to compound the pun—a human figure falling from another tree.

Such colorful coats of arms proliferated from tunics on to helmets, banners and even horse trappings. When there were no real battles, noblemen showed off their colors at jousting tournaments. It was at such pageants that the term heraldry originated as a generic name for the study of coats of arms. In order to keep track of the participants, the master of ceremonies—the herald—had to act as a walking encyclopedia of who was who. Eventually the heralds became the king's experts and arbitrators on disputed uses of armorial symbols. The office has persisted into the present century. In 1954, the English convoked a Court of Chivalry to settle a complaint about a usurped coat of arms.

By the 14th Century, the coat of arms had been adapted to all sorts of nonviolent finery. Lords and ladies who would never dream of going into battles took to having their individual marks embroidered on everything from book covers to bedclothes. Monograms, mottoes, even whole names were added to the original heraldic devices. They were lavishly executed not only in embroidery, but also in a new technique called canvas work—known today as needlepoint.

One of the most skilled needlework artists in history was Mary Stuart, the ill-fated Queen of Scots, who spent much of her life either in prison or under house arrest. When not negotiating for her release—or plotting escape—Mary busied herself with embroidery and needlepoint. She made practical things such as dresses, cushions and wall hangings—the latter a functional device for cutting down drafts in cold stone castles.

Mary had an amazingly varied repertoire of personalizing techniques. She employed several forms of her monograms: "MA" for her first name, "MR" for Mary Regina, and an intertwined "RMAS" for her whole name and title. Moreover the intrigue and secrecy that consumed so much of her public life spilled over into her needlework. She delighted in using a cryptic, highly stylized form of monogram called a cipher. One of her favorites was the complex insignia in the corner of the panel shown on page 131.

The Queen often capped her initials with a crown; and she used regal emblems of her family, such as her mother's phoenix in flames and the three crescent moons of her father-in-law Henry II. Her most memorable symbols, however, reflected her feelings at the loss of her throne. In one, a royal ship drags a broken mast. In another, a bird cowers in its cage while a hawk, representing her captor, Elizabeth, flies overhead.

A contemporary of Mary's, Sir Ralph Neville, fourth Earl of Westmorland, not content with mere symbols, had his portrait and those of his wife, seven sons and 13 daughters embroidered in silk and silver threads onto an altar frontal.

Today, people use these same ancient devices—monograms, symbols, family emblems—to render their personal trademarks in needlework. Some, following the historical lead of the Earl of Westmorland, even commission family portraits. In the possession of the Rockefeller family, for example, is a 3-by-4-foot montage of the entire Rockefeller clan—including their various homes, pets and hobbies—all worked in brilliant wools. Theodore Roosevelt Jr., the son of the President, also found himself portrayed in yarn (page 133). His wife stitched him in hunting regalia, surrounded by the big game animals that he, like his father, enjoyed shooting. And for other people who want to stitch an exact likeness, there is a needlecraft company that will take a photograph, transfer it to needlepoint canvas, and mail it back with plenty of flesh-toned yarn.

If you have neither the taste nor time for elaborate needlepoint portraiture, you can still find commercially designed projects for rendering personal monograms and emblems in yarn. Any needlework catalogue offers intriguing kits that give designs and directions for working them. There are bridal and birth samplers; career plaques for doctors, teachers and stockbrokers; even pillow covers with golf clubs and a place for inserting your name.

But the most effective way to demonstrate your personal style is to dream up your own project, design your own monogram and invent your own unique emblem. You can stitch your initials into clothing, bath towels, pillowcases, luggage tags or even a tote bag *(pages 150-151)*. You can make monogrammed coasters with tennis rackets or sailboats on them, or table napkins with a picture of your house. Or you can take a design from an heirloom rug and transpose it into pillow covers or slip covers.

As you devise your own projects, you will discover that different styles of lettering used in monogramming have their own personalities. Some are as lean and straight as a Puritan elder, while others float in florid shapes like rococo angels. The three alphabets on pages 146-153 suggest a few possibilities. But others are all around you ready to be adapted—from signs, magazines, book covers and packages. The letters you choose proclaim your taste and style.

Even the techniques you use, the particular embroidery and needlepoint stitches, contribute to the individuality of your work —as indeed, does your choice of yarn and fabric. Directions for executing various common needlework stitches are given in the following section.

Two Flemish lords, decked out in their most lavish finery, have at each other in mock combat on the jousting field. In this 15th Century painting, the nobleman at the left sports a distinctive combination of colors and crosses that show he is the Seigneur de la Gruthuyse. His opponent, the Seigneur de Ghistelle, wears crimson battle regalia with an identifying white trim embroidered to look like ermine tails—his personal device.

Distinctive emblems in colorful yarn

Europe's nobility planted needlework emblems on everything from coronation robes to bedroom slippers. The examples shown here range in style from ostentatious to occult; in some cases both qualities were displayed by the same needleworker. Queen Mary Stuart stitched a proud needlepoint monogram into one panel *(right, bottom)* and encircled it with her motto in French: *Sa vertu m'atire* (Its strength draws me). By transposing some letters and dropping others the motto becomes a clever anagram of her name. On another piece *(opposite, top),* she hid her mark in a brain-teasing cipher that required two languages to decode. The cipher, the strange insignia near the right-hand edge, consists of an "M" and an "A" intertwined within a stylized octagonal Φ —the Greek "F"—which stood for Francis II, her first husband and king of France.

In egalitarian America, people usually chose more democratic emblems. Thus the embroidered ship of the Stevens family *(page 132)* recalls a longstanding involvement with merchant shipping, while on the facing page the sampler worked by Mrs. Theodore Roosevelt Jr. celebrates her husband's exploits as a big-game hunter like his President-father.

The arms of the Duke of Normandy, in 15th Century embroidery

A monogram of Queen Mary Stuart, 16th Century needlepoint

A needlepoint panel with Mary Stuart's cipher, 16th Century

Part of an altar frontal, embroidered for a Spanish noble in the 18th Century

The embroidered monogram of Napoleon III with Imperial bees, 19th Century

This emblem of the Stevens clan of New Jersey recalls the family's venerable history in the shipping business. When John Stevens came to America in 1699, he became a merchant sailor and made a fortune in the West Indies trade. Subsequent family members ran ferryboats from Hoboken to New York City, and in 1851 John Cox Stevens won the first yacht race for the America's Cup. Here the emblem, embroidered during the 1840s on a pillowcase, is accompanied by the monogram of its original owner, Mary Baird Stevens.

Behold he cometh leaping upon the mountains skipping upon the hills.

T from E 1934

Sporting a red beard and white pith helmet, Theodore Roosevelt Jr. strides across the mountaintops in quest of big game in this sampler created by his wife, Eleanor. Most of the figures were worked in needlepoint, but a few decorative touches, such as the rays of the sun, are executed in embroidery. The Biblical quotation comes from the Song of Solomon. While Eleanor did all the work, her husband supervised; each evening he sat down and gave copious advice on the coloring and shape of the animals that he had hunted around the world.

An arsenal of embroidery stitches

The embroidery stitches demonstrated on the following pages range in difficulty from the simple running stitch at right, to the more complex padded satin stitch, shown opposite. This latter stitch is really a composite of two different stitches. Beneath the visible surface of the plain satin stitch *(Appendix)* lies a layer of foundation stitching, which gives the finished work a padded effect.

For light padding, as shown, a foundation of running stitch is suggested; for medium padding, an outline, chain or split stitch; for heavy padding, the satin stitch itself.

Another versatile stitch is called couching, a technique in which lengths of thread are tied to the fabric with small auxiliary stitches. In the anchored couching stitch *(page 138)*, the main thread is stitched into the fabric, or anchored, at periodic intervals; it is then couched, or tied down, between the anchored ends with a second thread. In the unanchored version of this stitch *(page 139)*, the embroiderer anchors the main thread just at the beginning of the stitch, then holds it on the surface of the fabric while couching it with a second thread; at the end, both threads are anchored.

In making any of these stitches, use an embroidery hoop, taking care not to distort the fabric by pulling the thread too taut.

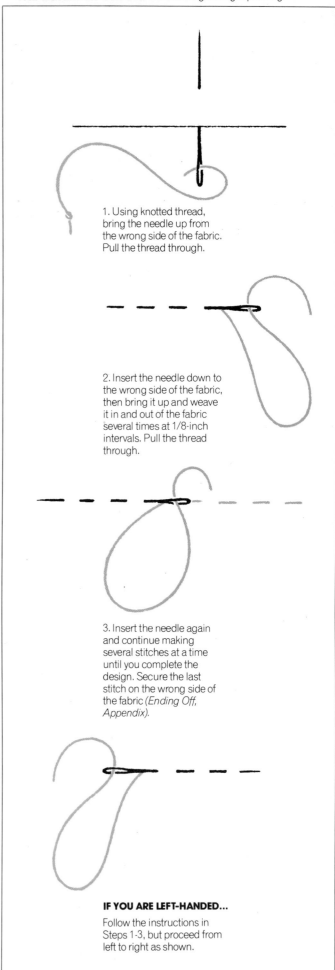

THE RUNNING STITCH: For outlining and light padding

1. Using knotted thread, bring the needle up from the wrong side of the fabric. Pull the thread through.

2. Insert the needle down to the wrong side of the fabric, then bring it up and weave it in and out of the fabric several times at 1/8-inch intervals. Pull the thread through.

3. Insert the needle again and continue making several stitches at a time until you complete the design. Secure the last stitch on the wrong side of the fabric *(Ending Off, Appendix)*.

IF YOU ARE LEFT-HANDED...
Follow the instructions in Steps 1-3, but proceed from left to right as shown.

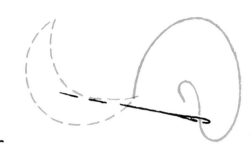

1. To make the padding for this stitch, select a heavyweight thread or use more strands of your regular thread, and knot the end. Then bring the needle up from the wrong side of the fabric just inside the guide line for the design; if the design is pointed, as in this example, start near the point at the lower right-hand end. Pull the thread through.

2. Make a row of running stitches *(opposite)* just inside the guide line until you reach the other end of the design.

3. Rotate the fabric 180° and make another line of running stitches about 1/8 inch away from the first line. Continue to make similar lines of running stitches until the design is filled. Then secure the last stitch on the wrong side of the fabric *(Ending Off, Appendix)*.

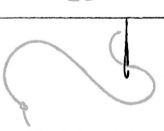

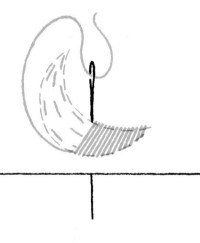

4. To make the covering for this stitch, knot a strand of regular thread and bring the needle up from the wrong side of the fabric below and slightly to the left of the hole made in Step 1.

5. Cover the lines of running stitches with the satin stitch *(Appendix)*, working at right angles to the running stitches. Secure the last stitch on the wrong side of the fabric *(Ending Off, Appendix)*.

IF YOU ARE LEFT-HANDED...

Follow Steps 1-5, but start the running stitches at the top point, as shown.

THE OUTLINE STITCH: For outlining designs

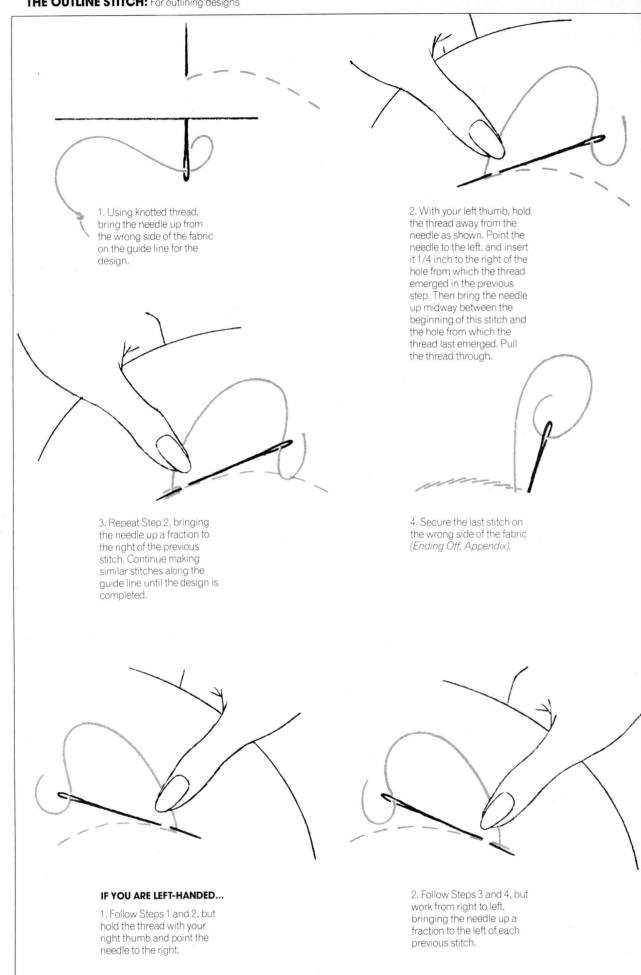

1. Using knotted thread, bring the needle up from the wrong side of the fabric on the guide line for the design.

2. With your left thumb, hold the thread away from the needle as shown. Point the needle to the left, and insert it 1/4 inch to the right of the hole from which the thread emerged in the previous step. Then bring the needle up midway between the beginning of this stitch and the hole from which the thread last emerged. Pull the thread through.

3. Repeat Step 2, bringing the needle up a fraction to the right of the previous stitch. Continue making similar stitches along the guide line until the design is completed.

4. Secure the last stitch on the wrong side of the fabric (*Ending Off, Appendix*).

IF YOU ARE LEFT-HANDED...

1. Follow Steps 1 and 2, but hold the thread with your right thumb and point the needle to the right.

2. Follow Steps 3 and 4, but work from right to left, bringing the needle up a fraction to the left of each previous stitch.

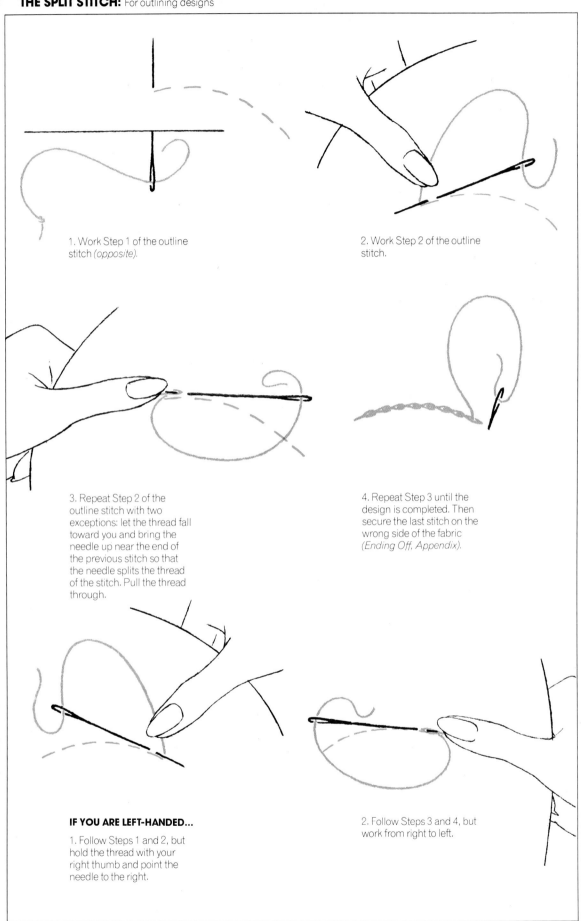

1. Work Step 1 of the outline stitch (opposite).

2. Work Step 2 of the outline stitch.

3. Repeat Step 2 of the outline stitch with two exceptions: let the thread fall toward you and bring the needle up near the end of the previous stitch so that the needle splits the thread of the stitch. Pull the thread through.

4. Repeat Step 3 until the design is completed. Then secure the last stitch on the wrong side of the fabric (Ending Off, Appendix).

IF YOU ARE LEFT-HANDED...

1. Follow Steps 1 and 2, but hold the thread with your right thumb and point the needle to the right.

2. Follow Steps 3 and 4, but work from right to left.

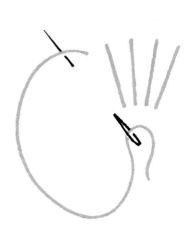

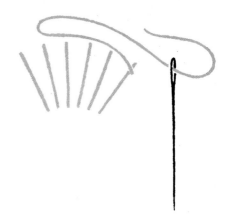

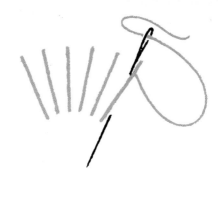

1. Using knotted thread, bring the needle up from the wrong side of the fabric and make a group of straight stitches in whatever arrangement your design requires. Secure the last stitch on the wrong side of the fabric (*Ending Off, Appendix*).

2. Using knotted thread of the same or a contrasting color, bring the needle up just to the right and close to the top of the first straight stitch.

3. Insert the needle down to the wrong side of the fabric just to the left of the straight stitch and directly opposite the hole from which the thread emerged in the previous step. Slant the needle downward and to the right, and bring it up just to the right of the straight stitch.

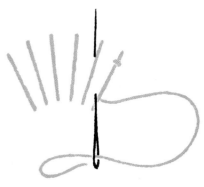

4. Insert the needle down to the wrong side of the fabric just to the left of the straight stitch and directly opposite the hole from which the thread emerged in the previous step. Slant the needle upward and bring it up just to the left of the next straight stitch.

5. Continue in this manner, repeating Steps 3 and 4, and staggering the stitches at random. Secure the last stitch on the wrong side of the fabric (*Ending Off, Appendix*).

IF YOU ARE LEFT-HANDED...
1. Follow Steps 1-5 but cross over the straight stitches from left to right, and insert the needle downward from right to left as shown. In Step 4, bring the needle up just to the right of the next stitch.

THE UNANCHORED COUCHING STITCH: For filling large areas

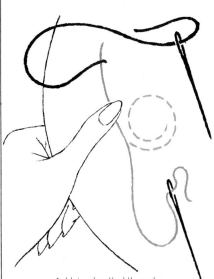

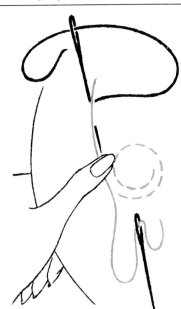

1. Using knotted thread, bring the needle up from the wrong side of the fabric at one end of the guide line of your design. Pull the thread through; then hold the thread down on the design with your left thumb.

2. Thread another needle with the same or a contrasting color, and knot the end. Bring the needle up from the wrong side of the fabric just to the right and about 1/4 inch from the end of the thread you are holding down. Pull the thread through.

3. Insert the needle down to the wrong side of the fabric just to the left of the thread being held down and directly opposite the hole from which the thread emerged in the previous step. Then slant the needle downward and bring it up just to the right of the thread being held down. Pull the thread through.

4. Continue making similar stitches along the entire length of the thread being held down. The distance between stitches is arbitrary but should remain constant throughout the design.

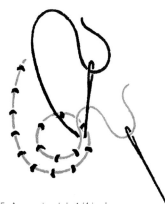

5. Approximately 1/4 inch from the end, secure the last stitch on the wrong side of the fabric (*Ending Off, Appendix*). Then secure the end of the thread being held down in the same way.

IF YOU ARE LEFT-HANDED...
Follow Steps 1-5, but hold the thread with your right thumb, and bring the needle up just to the left of the thread being held down. Then insert the needle just to the right of the thread being held down.

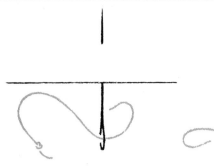

1. Using knotted thread, bring the needle up from the wrong side of the fabric. Pull the thread through.

2. Point the needle away from you and insert it down to the wrong side of the fabric at the desired distance from the hole from which the thread emerged in the previous step. Then bring the needle partially up in the same hole from which the thread last emerged; do not pull the needle or the thread all the way through.

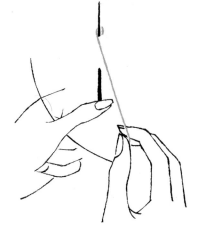

3. Hold the bottom of the needle firmly with your left thumb and wind the thread around the needle counterclockwise, as shown.

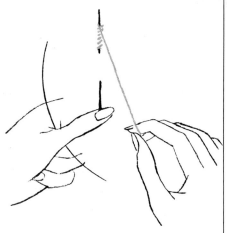

4. Continue to wind the thread around the needle until the length of the coil equals the distance between the two holes.

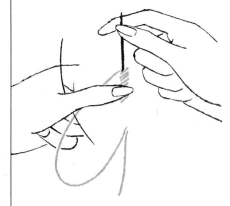

5. Hold the coiled thread with your left thumb and pull the needle out of the coil with your right thumb and forefinger.

6. Pull the thread gently toward you until the coil lies flat on the fabric.

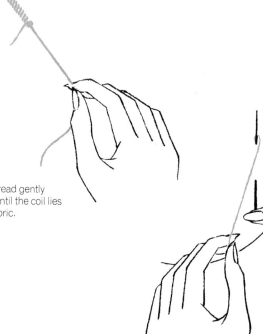

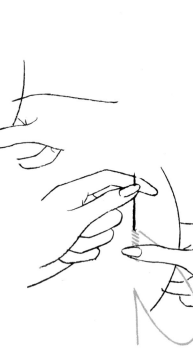

7. Insert the needle down to the wrong side of the fabric just to the right of the hole into which it was inserted in Step 2; then bring it partially up the desired distance away and repeat Steps 3-6.

8. Continue to make as many similar stitches as your design requires. Secure the last stitch on the wrong side of the fabric (*Ending Off, Appendix*).

IF YOU ARE LEFT-HANDED...

1. Follow Steps 1-3, but hold the bottom of the needle firmly with your right thumb, and wind the thread clockwise around the needle, as shown.

2. Follow Steps 4-9, but hold the coil with your right thumb; pull the needle with your left thumb and forefinger. Make the second stitch to the left of the first stitch, and continue from right to left.

THE TURKEY STITCH: For a tufted, fuzzy texture

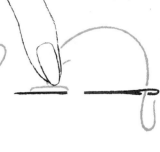

1. Using unknotted thread, insert the needle down to the wrong side of the fabric, then bring it up 1/8 inch to the left of the first hole.

2. Pull the thread only partially through, leaving about an inch of the unknotted end on top of the fabric.

3. Let the thread loop toward you, as shown. Then point the needle to the left, and insert it 1/4 inch to the right of the hole from which the thread emerged in the previous step. Bring the needle up in the same hole occupied by the unknotted end; this will lock the stitch.

4. Pull the thread through. Then, with your left thumb holding the thread away from you, point the needle to the left and insert it 1/4 inch to the right of the hole from which the thread emerged in the previous step; bring it up at the end of the previous stitch.

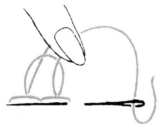

5. Pull the thread only partially through, leaving a loop about 1/2 inch high.

6. Repeat Step 3, bringing the needle up in the same hole occupied by the end of the just-completed loop.

7. Repeat Steps 4 and 5.

8. Repeat Step 6, then continue repeating Steps 4-6, making as many little loops as your design requires. End the row with Step 6 to lock the last stitch. Then cut the thread that emerges from the last stitch about an inch from the top of the fabric.

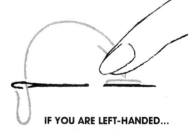

9. Work a new row, starting as close as possible to the first stitch made in Step 1.

10. Continue to make as many rows as your design requires.

11. When all the rows are completed, snip each loop at the top with a scissors and trim to the height desired.

12. For a more sheared look, cut across the massed top of loops.

IF YOU ARE LEFT-HANDED...
Follow Steps 1-12, but point the needle to the right and insert it 1/4 inch to the left of the hole from which the thread last emerged. In Step 4, hold the thread away from you with your right thumb, as shown.

Decorative needlepoint stitches

All the needlepoint stitchery in this section has a common ancestor: the straight Gobelin stitch described at right. Once started, it marches across the needlepoint canvas in neat vertical strokes, each stitch parallel to the one next to it, like ties on a railroad track.

The fun of straight Gobelin comes from elaborating the basic stitch into patterns: the neat masonry of the brick stitch, the flickering rise and fall of the flame stitch, the long-and-short alternations of the old Florentine stitch. Worked in different combinations of colored yarn, they may be used to create any number of striking needlepoint designs. They can also provide distinguished backgrounds for an embroidered motif, such as a monogram.

In making any of these stitches, use a Size 20 blunt tapestry needle. Avoid carrying the yarn over more than six holes in the canvas; a longer stitch would grow too slack. And make each stitch with a single stroke: push the needle through the canvas, and then out again, before pulling the yarn through.

THE STRAIGHT GOBELIN STITCH

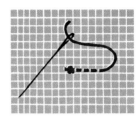

1. Anchor the yarn to the canvas four holes to the left of the hole in which you wish to begin, as shown in the instructions for starting a piece of yarn *(Appendix)*.

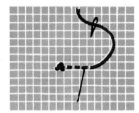

2. Insert the needle four holes above the hole from which the yarn emerged in the previous step. Slant the needle downward and bring it out one hole to the left of the hole from which the yarn last emerged. Pull the yarn through.

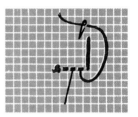

3. Repeat Step 2 as many times as your design requires to complete the row.

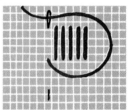

4. On the last stitch of the row, insert the needle four holes above the hole from which the yarn emerged in the previous step. Point the needle straight down and bring it out four holes below the hole from which the yarn last emerged. Pull the yarn through.

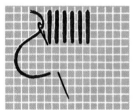

5. Keeping the yarn to the left of the stitches, insert the needle four holes above the hole from which the yarn emerged in the previous step (the same hole that was used in making the last stitch of the preceding row). Slant the needle downward and bring it out one hole to the right of the hole from which the yarn last emerged. Pull the yarn through.

6. Repeat Step 5 until the row is completed; then start a new row by repeating Step 4. Continue for as many rows as your design requires.

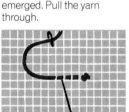

IF YOU ARE LEFT-HANDED...

1. Start at the top left-hand corner, slanting the needle downward and to the right as shown.

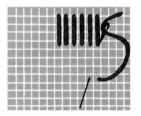

2. On the second row, insert the needle from right to left, keeping the yarn to the right of the stitches.

THE BRICK STITCH

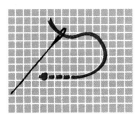

1. Anchor the yarn to the canvas four holes to the left of the hole in which you wish to begin, as shown in the instructions for starting a piece of yarn (*Appendix*).

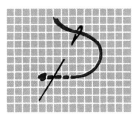

2. Insert the needle as for one straight Gobelin stitch, following the instructions on the opposite page. Slant the needle downward and bring it out two holes above and one hole to the left of the hole from which the yarn last emerged. Pull the yarn through.

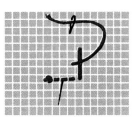

3. Insert the needle four holes above the hole from which the yarn emerged in the previous step. Slant the needle downward and bring it out two holes below and one hole to the left of the hole from which the yarn last emerged. Pull the yarn through.

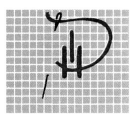

4. Repeat Steps 2 and 3 as many times as your design requires to complete the row.

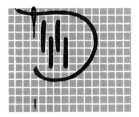

5. On the last stitch of the row, insert the needle four holes above the hole from which the yarn emerged in the previous step. Point the needle straight down and bring it out four holes below the hole from which the yarn last emerged. Pull the yarn through.

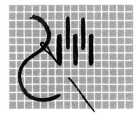

6. Keeping the yarn to the left of the stitches, insert the needle four holes above the hole from which the yarn emerged in the previous step (the same hole that was used in making the last stitch in the preceding row). Slant the needle downward and bring it out two holes above and one hole to the right of the hole from which the yarn last emerged. Pull the yarn through.

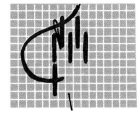

7. Insert the needle four holes above the hole from which the yarn emerged in the previous step (the same hole that was used in making the stitch directly above). Slant the needle downward and bring it out two holes below and one hole to the right of the hole from which the yarn last emerged. Pull the yarn through.

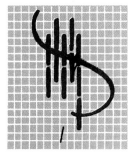

8. Repeat Steps 6 and 7 until the row is completed; then start a new row by repeating Step 5. Continue for as many rows as your design requires.

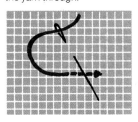

IF YOU ARE LEFT-HANDED...
1. Start at the top left-hand corner, slanting the needle downward and to the right as shown.

2. On the second row, insert the needle from right to left, keeping the yarn to the right of the stitches.

THE FLAME STITCH

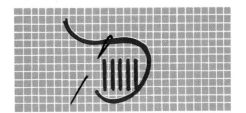

1. Make as many straight Gobelin stitches as your design requires (five in this example), following the directions on page 142.

2. On the next stitch, again insert the needle four holes above the hole from which the yarn emerged in the previous stitch. Slant the needle downward and bring it out two holes above and one hole to the left of the hole from which the yarn last emerged. Pull the yarn through.

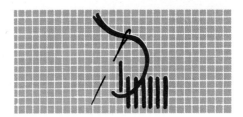

3. Make as many straight Gobelin stitches as your design requires (one in this example). Then repeat Step 2 and continue in this pattern until you reach the top of the design.

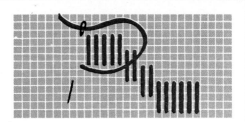

4. Repeat Step 1. On the next stitch, again insert the needle four holes above the hole from which the yarn emerged in the previous step. Slant the needle downward and bring it out two holes below and one hole to the left of the hole from which the yarn last emerged. Pull the yarn through.

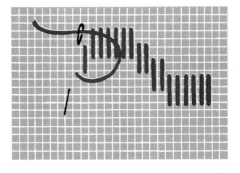

5. Repeat Step 4, making as many straight Gobelin stitches as your design requires (one in this example). Continue in this pattern until you reach the bottom of the design.

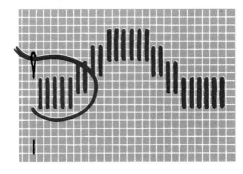

6. Repeat Steps 1 and 2 and continue the pattern to the end of the row.

7. On the next stitch, insert the needle four holes above the hole from which the yarn emerged in the previous step. Point the needle straight down and bring it out four holes below the hole from which the yarn last emerged. Pull the yarn through.

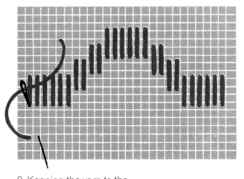

8. Keeping the yarn to the left of the stitches, insert the needle four holes above the hole from which the yarn emerged in the previous step (the same hole that was used in making the last stitch of the preceding row). Slant the needle downward and bring it out four holes below the next stitch. Pull the yarn through.

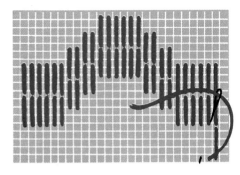

9. Repeat Step 8 until the row is completed; then repeat Step 7 to start a new row. Continue the pattern, ascending and descending as shown, for as many rows as your design requires.

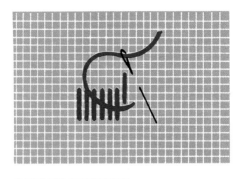

IF YOU ARE LEFT-HANDED...

1. Start at the top left-hand corner, slanting the needle downward and to the right as shown.

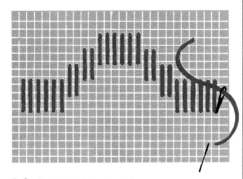

2. On the second row, insert the needle from right to left, keeping the yarn to the right of the stitches.

THE OLD FLORENTINE STITCH

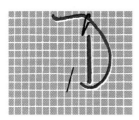

1. Make one straight Gobelin stitch, following the instructions on page 142, but inserting the needle six holes above the hole in which you begin.

2. On the second stitch, bring the needle out two holes above and one hole to the left of the hole from which the yarn last emerged. Pull the yarn through.

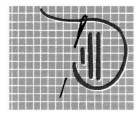

3. Insert the needle two holes above the hole from which the yarn emerged in the previous step and bring it out one hole to the left of the hole from which the yarn last emerged. Pull the yarn through.

4. On the second stitch, bring the needle out two holes below and one hole to the left of the hole from which the yarn last emerged. Pull the yarn through.

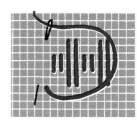

5. Repeat Steps 1-4 as many times as your design requires to complete the row.

6. On the last stitch of the row, point the needle straight down and bring it out two holes below the hole from which the yarn last emerged. Pull the yarn through.

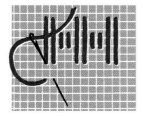

7. Keeping the yarn to the left of the stitches, insert the needle two holes above the hole from which the yarn emerged in the previous step (the same hole that was used in making the last stitch of the preceding row). Slant the needle downward and bring it out one hole to the right of the hole from which the yarn last emerged. Pull the yarn through.

8. Insert the needle two holes above the hole from which the yarn emerged in the previous step. Slant the needle downward and bring it out two holes below and one hole to the right of the hole from which the yarn last emerged. Pull the yarn through.

9. Continue to make alternating long and short straight Gobelin stitches across the row; then repeat Step 6 to start a new row. Continue the pattern as shown for as many rows as your design requires.

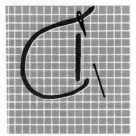

IF YOU ARE LEFT-HANDED...

1. Start at the top left-hand corner, slanting the needle downward and to the right as shown.

2. On the second row, insert the needle from right to left, keeping the yarn to the right of the stitches.

The infinite intrigue of monograms

There is almost no end to the variety of designs and impressions you can create from monograms. You may choose any style you want for the letters, and make them in embroidery, needlepoint or a combination of both. The "M" shown below, taken from the alphabet on the opposite page, was worked in the most basic monogram technique: simple embroidery on a fabric background.

To make your own monogram in this style, first enlarge and trace the letter on the fabric—in this case a swatch of satin. Directions for doing this appear in the Appendix. Next, using six-strand embroidery floss and a Size 5 to 10 crewel needle, fill in the letter with padded satin stitchery, worked over a filler of running stitches, as described on page 135. Finally, go around the edge in the outline stitch *(page 136)*, using six-strand floss in a contrasting color.

The result is a simple but elegant monogram suitable for handkerchiefs, towels or napkins. For a more startling monogram, turn the page.

ABCDE
FGHIJK
LMNOP
QRSTUV
WXYZ

Ingenious mixing of techniques

The bright, contemporary look of the monogrammed "H" shown below comes partly from its design and partly from the needlework techniques used to make it. The design, taken from the alphabet at right, has been worked in embroidery stitches with wool yarn and set off against a needlepoint background.

To reproduce a letter from this alphabet, use two-strand Persian wool yarn in any two contrasting colors you wish, and a Size 20 blunt tapestry needle. Begin by enlarging and tracing the letter on 14-mesh penelope canvas, as shown in the Appendix. (The stitches you will need are demonstrated on pages 134, 135, 145 and 192.) Then, using the darker-colored yarn, embroider the two heaviest lines in preliminary padded satin stitch, working the layer of padding with three rows of running stitch. Complete all the rest of the lines, both dark and light colors, in straight unpadded satin stitch. Finally, fill in the needlepoint background with old Florentine stitch.

ABCDE
FGHIJK
LMNOP
QRSTU
VWXYZ

A bit of personal bravura

The monogram on the tote bag at right owes its flamboyance to a combination of needlepoint and embroidery. To make a monogram from this alphabet, first enlarge and trace the letters on a 14-mesh penelope canvas, using the methods described in the Appendix. Next, with six-strand embroidery floss and a Size 5 to 10 crewel needle, make the white contour lines and the black shadows in padded satin stitch, using plain satin stitch for filler. Then fill in the colored areas, working from the largest to the smallest and adding the black edging last. Follow the stitch guide for each letter *(overleaf),* and the instructions on pages 134-145 or in the Appendix. Finally, complete the needlepoint background in a straight Gobelin stitch with a Size 20 blunt tapestry needle and three-strand Persian yarn.

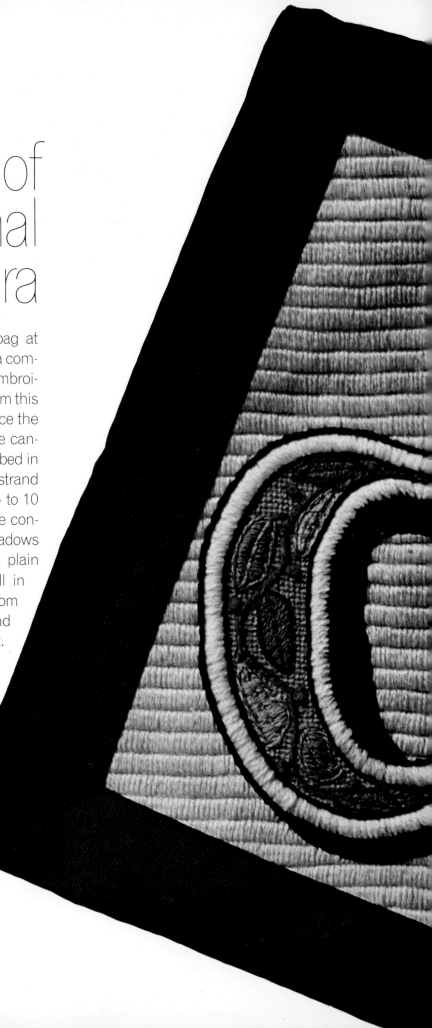

White contour lines of letter, and black shadows: padded satin stitch edged with split stitch. Solid white area: tent stitch. Black design motif: satin stitch. Black interior contour lines: chain stitch.

Outermost white contour line of letter and black shadows: padded satin stitch edged with split stitch. Black and white interior contour lines: outline stitch.

White contour line and black shadows: padded satin stitch edged with split stitch. Solid white area: tent stitch. Leaves: satin stitch. Black vines and swirl shapes: outline stitch. Black dots: French knots.

White kidney shapes, pointed ovals and black shadows: padded satin stitch edged with split stitch. Black dots: French knots. Black shade lines: outline stitch. Black and white stripes: anchored couching.

White contour line of letter, white oval shapes and black shadows: padded satin stitch edged with split stitch. Solid white areas: tent stitch. Black interior contour and shade lines: split stitch.

White contour line and center ring and black shadows: padded satin stitch edged with split stitch. Black band and circles: tent stitch. Leaves: satin stitch edged with chain stitch. Flowers: French knots.

White contour line and black shadows: padded satin stitch edged with split stitch. Solid black area: flame stitch. White triangles: satin stitch. Circles: padded satin stitch edged with anchored couching.

White and black swirls and black shadows and diamonds: padded satin stitch edged with split stitch. Black interior contour lines: outline stitch. White dots: French knots.

White contour lines and black shadows and circles: padded satin stitch edged with split stitch. Interior stripes: straight Gobelin stitch. White rings: chain stitch. White flowers and dots: French knots.

White contour line and ovals, black shadows and circles: padded satin stitch edged with split stitch. Black and white stripes: outline stitch. Black shade lines: stem stitch. White dots: French knots.

White contour line and flowers, black shadows and circles: padded satin stitch edged with split stitch. White motif: tent stitch. Stripes: straight Gobelin stitch. Black interior lines: outline stitch.

White contour line of letter, black shadows, bricks, diamonds and star: padded satin stitch edged with split stitch. White bands: tent stitch. Black shade lines: split stitch. Black and white dots: French knots.

White contour line of letter, white ovals, white and black clover leaves, black shadows and crescents: padded satin stitch edged with split stitch. Stripes: outline stitch. Shade lines: anchored couching.

White contour line of letter, white leaf designs and black shadows: padded satin stitch edged with split stitch. Solid white areas: tent stitch. Black dots: French knots. Black shade lines: split stitch.

Outermost white line, white band and egg shapes, and black shadows and crescents: padded satin stitch edged with split stitch. Black shade lines and black and white interior contour lines: outline stitch.

White contour line, black shadows and black design motifs: padded satin stitch edged with split stitch. Solid white area: tent stitch. Black interior contour lines: outline stitch. Black dots: French knots.

White contour line and black shadows: padded satin stitch edged with split stitch. Solid black areas: padded satin stitch. White dashes: French knots. Black and white interior contour lines: split stitch.

White contour line of letter, black shadows and black half moons and circles: padded satin stitch edged with split stitch. Black and white interior lines and stripes: split stitch. White band and rings: tent stitch.

White swirls and ovals: tent stitch. Black shadows, crescents and stars: padded satin stitch. Shadow edges and black interior lines: split stitch. Black shade lines: stem stitch. Dots: French knots.

White contour line of letter and black shadows: padded satin stitch edged with split stitch. Interior area: brick stitch.

White contour line of letter and black shadows: padded satin stitch edged with split stitch. Solid black area: tent stitch. White pointed oval shapes: padded satin stitch. White dots: French knots.

White contour lines and black shadows, black and white crescents and ovals: padded satin stitch edged with split stitch. Interior lines: outline stitch. Black and white dots and broken white lines: French knots.

White contour line of letter and black shadows and circles: padded satin stitch edged with split stitch. White band: tent stitch edged with outline stitch. Black and white interior contour lines: chain stitch.

White swirl shapes, circles and ring and black shadows: padded satin stitch edged with split stitch. Solid black interior areas: tent stitch. White flower: French knots. Black interior lines: split stitch.

White contour lines of letter, white ovals and black shadows: padded satin stitch edged with split stitch. Stripes: straight Gobelin stitch. Black swirls, contour and shade lines: split stitch.

White contour line, leaves and ring, and black shadows: padded satin stitch edged with split stitch. Black oval: tent stitch. White flower and black dots: French knots. Stripes: outline stitch.

Needlepoint take-offs

The art of needlepoint can bring strong personal accents to the decoration of a home. A design borrowed from the window curtains, for example, might be reproduced on pillow covers or table mats. Here, a pattern of chevrons taken from wall paper has inspired a set of needlepoint seat covers, thus transforming an ordinary director's chair into a bold individual statement.

The needlepoint artist worked the covers in a straight Gobelin stitch (page 142), relying on the Gobelin's ribbed effect to emphasize the geometric design of the chevrons. The finished covers were sewn by machine onto the canvas seat and back.

Using the repertory of basic needlepoint stitches described in this book, almost any decorative motif can be repeated. Backgrounds can be worked effectively in such stitches as brick, old Florentine or flame (pages 143-145). The tent stitch (Appendix) adapts beautifully to freeform, naturalistic subjects—say a leaf design from a drapery fabric or a rose from an Aubusson rug.

Instructions for copying, transferring any design to needlepoint canvas and for blocking the finished work appear in the Appendix.

A brilliant flight in embroidery

Free-form embroidery can enhance a commercial fabric design with unique decorative touches. Consider, for example, the segment of polished cotton print illustrated below. The embroiderer has zeroed in on a single butterfly from the print, and embellished it with yarn stitchery in subtly contrasting shades of lavender and blue green.

Five different stitches *(pages 135-141)* were used. Padded satin, chosen for its cushiony bulk, defines the major design areas. Two versions of the couching stitch, together with touches of squiggly bullion, lend contrast. Fuzzy-piled turkey stitching gives a strong design focus to the insect's body; and for a final fillip the embroiderer added antennae of split stitch. The end product *(right):* a novel personal emblem that can be used on such things as slipcovers, cushions or a lampshade.

Knit woolen streamers twine through honey - colored hair to produce a unique and extravagant coiffure.

6

FANCIFUL
WAYS WITH
WOOL

Envision a crocheted jacket that doubles as a perambulatory landscape painting. Up the body of the jacket, front and back, grows the craggy, brown-black bark of a stately tree. Around the tree's roots, along the jacket's hem, bloom red, pink and green forms suggesting flowers. Cool green leaf shapes swirl around the garment's neck and collar. To top off the landscape, puffy white clouds float in a glowing blue sky along the shoul-

WALKABOUT LANDSCAPES IN YARN

ders and sleeves. "When you wear the jacket," enthuses the owner of a New York City gallery that displays such fantasies in yarn, "you *become* the landscape and your head sticks out in the clouds above the trees."

The jacket's creator, a soft-spoken, sable-haired artist named Dina Schwartz, is one of a group of talented painters and draftsmen who have discovered the startling new art form of pictorial clothing. They have traded their painter's tools for colored yarn, knitting needles and crochet hooks. Instead of canvases they now turn out scarves, jackets, vests and skirts of vivid and unique design.

These artists in yarn stumbled upon their new medium almost by accident. One of the pioneers was a former abstract painter, Arlene Stimmel, whose first creative outlet was to fill canvases with color from automobile spray cans. While waiting for the paint to dry between coats, she taught herself to crochet. "Soon I was crocheting more and painting less," Arlene recalls. "At first I made only simple things; before I knew it, yarn had replaced paint, and I wanted to make paintings people could wear."

As Arlene and her fellow artists took hold of their new-found medium, they became fascinated with the mystique of woolcraft itself. Some bought spinning wheels and learned to make their own yarn. Then they explored the secrets of imparting color with natural dyes. These handmade wools became as precious, said one, "as fine oil paints you mix yourself."

While turning these special ingredients into garments, the artists developed an intriguing arsenal of individual techniques. Some, like Dina and Arlene, start with preliminary sketches, which they then execute with the crochet hook. Another method is to simply start crocheting and let the design take shape as the work progresses. Or the artist may begin by crocheting small, individual swatches—squares, circles, triangles—which he then pieces together.

Materials other than wool yarn may find their way into the work: swatches of alpaca or tweed, metallic threads, leather patches, beads, shells and feathers. Finally, to give shape to a complicated garment such as a vest or jacket, some artists pin the work to a seamstress' dummy (Dina has named hers Alice), which thus becomes a kind of easel for an opus in wool.

Some of these techniques are demonstrated in the section that follows: for example, the method for sewing together crochet swatches shown on page 185. (They will be helpful even if your urge to personalize does not extend to the creation of a knitted cape with jungle animals running through crocheted foliage.) You might do well to begin with a simple project such as the crocheting of trims and borders to decorate garments you are sewing *(pages 166-167)*. Then take off and let the trims grow wider or longer until they turn into belts, men's neckties, sleeve cuffs or collars. You may, as you gain courage and experience, copy a sewing pattern section by section, applying the principles described for transferring the pattern into knitting terms on pages 174-179, or you may, like some of the creators of pictorial vestments, even improvise as you go.

The instructions that follow will ease the way to finding your own form of personal expression in woolen stitches. Several sample knit and crochet pattern stitches are offered on pages 164-165 and 172-173, and the instructions on pages 174-179 will guide you in designing your own garments. The more fundamental techniques of knitting and crocheting are described in the Appendix.

So plunge in—and remember that you can always rip out.

vertical flame stitch

horizontal
flame stitch

162

vertical
banded
stripe

horizontal
banded stripe

multicolor shell

irregular tiered stripe

Colorful crochet trimmings

Unlike ribbons and ruchings that are ready-made, the trimmings you crochet for yourself will be one-of-a-kind creations. You can personalize them with your favorite colors. You can fashion them to the scale you fancy —enlarging or reducing the dimensions of the design by varying the weight of the yarn and the size of the hook. And you can produce them to the exact length and width you require in any one of the patterns shown on these pages.

For feminine clothes you might choose the multicolor shell pattern *(above)* or perhaps the flame stitch pattern *(left)*, worked either horizontally or vertically. For tailored clothes you might prefer the irregular tiered stripe pattern *(right)* or one of the straightforward banded stripes *(top right)*. These patterns can be made with standard crochet stitches, for which instructions appear in the Appendix. Detailed directions for the patterns start on the following page.

Instructions for the crochet patterns

The following instructions are for crocheting the patterns pictured on the preceding pages and used on the garments shown overleaf. The swatches were all made with basic crochet stitches and techniques (*Appendix*), using a Size G aluminum crochet hook and knitting worsted yarn.

THE HORIZONTAL FLAME STITCH PATTERN

Make a foundation chain of any multiple of 28, plus seven, depending on the length desired. *Row 1:* With color A, make 1 single crochet stitch in each of the next 3 chain stitches, 3 single crochet stitches in the next chain, 1 single crochet stitch in each of the next 3 chain stitches, skip 2 chain stitches, make 1 single crochet stitch in each of the next 8 chain stitches, 3 single crochet stitches in the next chain, 1 single crochet stitch in each of the next 8 chain stitches, skip 2 chain stitches. Repeat this sequence across the row, ending with 1 single crochet stitch in each of the next 3 chain stitches, 3 single crochet in the next chain, 1 single crochet stitch in each of the last 3 chain stitches. Chain 1 and turn. *Row 2:* Skip 1 single crochet stitch. Working through the back loops only of the stitches, make the pattern to be followed across the row in this sequence: 1 single crochet stitch in each of the next 3 stitches, 3 single crochet stitches in the next stitch, 1 single crochet in each of the next 3 stitches, skip 2 stitches, make 1 single crochet in each of the next 8 stitches, 3 single crochet in the next stitch, 1 single crochet in each of the next 8 stitches, skip 2 stitches. Repeat this sequence across the row, ending with 1 single crochet in each of the next 2 stitches, skip 1 stitch and make 1 single crochet in the last stitch. Chain 1 and turn. Repeat row 2 for the desired width, following this color sequence: 2 rows color A, 6 rows color B, 2 rows color C, 4 rows color D and 2 rows color A.

THE VERTICAL FLAME STITCH PATTERN

Make a foundation chain of any multiple of 28, plus seven, depending on the width desired. *Row 1:* With color A, make 1 single crochet stitch in each of the next 3 chain stitches, 3 single crochet stitches in the next chain, 1 single crochet stitch in each of the next 3 chain stitches, skip 2 chain stitches, make 1 single crochet stitch in each of the next 8 chain stitches, 3 single crochet stitches in the next chain, 1 single crochet stitch in each of the next 8 chain stitches, skip 2 chain stitches. Repeat this sequence across the row, ending with 1 single crochet stitch in each of the last 3 chain stitches; chain 1 and turn. *Row 2:* Skip 1 single crochet stitch. Working through the back loops only of the stitches, make the pattern to be followed across the row in this sequence: 1 single crochet stitch in each of the next 3 stitches, 3 single crochet stitches in the next stitch, 1 single crochet stitch in each of the next 3 stitches, skip 2 stitches, 1 single crochet stitch in each of the next 8 stitches, 3 single crochet stitches in the next stitch, 1 single crochet stitch in each of the next 8 stitches, skip 2 stitches. Repeat this sequence across the row, ending with 1 single crochet stitch in each of the next 3 stitches, 3 single crochet stitches in the next stitch, 1 single crochet stitch in each of the next 2 single crochet stitches, skip 1 stitch, 1 single crochet stitch in the last stitch. Chain 1 and turn. Repeat row 2 for the desired length, following this color sequence: 2 rows color A, 2 rows color B, 2 rows color C, 4 rows color D, 8 rows color A, 4 rows color B, 2 rows color C and 2 rows color D.

THE VERTICAL BANDED STRIPE PATTERN

Make a foundation chain of any number of stitches, depending on the length desired. *Row 1:* With color A, make a row of single crochet stitches. Chain 1 and turn. *Rows 2 and 3:* With color B, make a row of single crochet stitches through the back loops only of the stitches; chain 1 and turn. *Row 4:* With color A, make a row of single crochet stitches through the back loop only of the stitches; chain 1 and turn. *Row 5:* With color A, slip stitch across the row. Repeat rows 1-4 for the width desired. Finish the piece with row 5; fasten off.

THE HORIZONTAL BANDED STRIPE PATTERN

Make a foundation chain of any number of stitches, depending on the width desired. *Rows 1 and 2:* With color A, make a row of single crochet stitches; chain 1; turn. *Row 3:* With color B, make a row of single crochet stitches through the back loops only of the stitches; chain 1; turn. *Row 4:* With color B, make a row of single crochet stitches; chain 1; turn. *Row 5:* With color C, make a row of single crochet stitches through the back loops only of the stitches; chain 1; turn. *Row 6:* With color C, make a row of single crochet stitches; chain 1; turn. *Row 7:* With color A, make a row of single crochet stitches through the back loops only of the stitches; chain 1; turn. *Row 8:* With color A, make a row of single crochet stitches; chain 1; turn. Repeat rows 3-8 for the length desired; fasten off.

THE IRREGULAR TIERED STRIPE PATTERN

Make a foundation chain of any uneven number of stitches, depending on the length that you desire. *Row 1:* With color A, make 1 single crochet stitch in the first chain, then 1 double crochet stitch in the next chain. Repeat this sequence across the row, ending with 1 single crochet stitch in the last chain. Chain 2 and turn. *Row 2:* With color B, make 1 double crochet stitch in the first stitch and 1 single crochet stitch in the next stitch. Repeat this sequence across the row, ending with 1 double crochet stitch in the last stitch. Chain 1 and turn. *Row 3:* With color C, make 1 single crochet stitch in the first stitch and 1 double crochet stitch in the next stitch. Repeat this sequence across the row, ending with 1 single crochet stitch in the last stitch. Chain 2 and turn. Repeat rows 2 and 3, alternating colors A, B and C until you have achieved the width that you desire; then fasten off.

THE MULTICOLOR SHELL PATTERN

Make a foundation chain having any multiple of six, plus one, depending on the length desired. *Row 1:* With color A, make a shell in the third chain from the hook by making 3 double crochet stitches, chaining 1, and making 3 more double crochet stitches. Make the pattern to be followed across this row in this sequence: skip 2 chain stitches, make 1 single crochet stitch in the next chain, skip 2 chain stitches and make a shell in the next chain. Repeat this sequence across the row, ending with 1 single crochet stitch in the last chain; turn. *Row 2:* With color B, chain 3 and make 2 double crochet stitches in the first single crochet stitch. Make the pattern to be followed across the row in this sequence: skip 3 double crochet stitches, make 1 single crochet stitch in the next space that resulted from the chain 1 on the previous row, skip 3 double crochet stitches and make 1 shell in the next single crochet stitch. Repeat this sequence across the row, ending with 3 double crochet stitches in the top of the turning chain of the previous row; turn. *Row 3:* With color C, chain 2. Make the pattern to be followed across the row in this sequence: skip 3 double crochet stitches, make 1 shell in the next single crochet stitch, skip 3 double crochet stitches, make 1 single crochet stitch in the next chain-1 space. Repeat this sequence across the row, skipping the 2 double crochet stitches at the end; make 1 single crochet stitch in the turning chain of the previous row; turn. Repeat rows 2 and 3, alternating colors A, B and C until you have achieved the width desired; fasten off.

Novel touches in crochet

Crochet trimmings, inserted into seams and overlaid on hems and edges, bring bright individuality to the most straightforward fashion designs. A classic princess dress *(far left),* for example, takes on new chic when its seams flaunt crocheted bands. A casual wraparound skirt *(left)* becomes far more sophisticated with crocheted borders. And the quiet glamour of a pastel dress *(right)* is accentuated when its waistband is fashioned from vigorous flame stitch crochet. Instructions for the crochet patterns start on page 164. Directions for applying them to dressmaking projects like the ones shown here begin overleaf.

Instructions for crocheting and attaching trims

The crocheting instructions that follow are for the insets and borders shown on the preceding pages. Any of these trims can be applied to garments of different styles. The instructions for the pattern stitches used in making the trims are on pages 164-165; the basic crochet stitches are in the Appendix.

THE STRIPED INSET

You will need four ounces of knitting worsted in color A (black, in the dress on page 166) and two ounces of color B (white). Use an aluminum crochet hook Size C, and a tapestry needle to sew the seams. Crochet a sample swatch to check the gauge—which is 4 stitches to the inch.

The dress: Assemble the dress in the usual way, but leave the seams open where you plan to add the crocheted inset. Turn under the raw edges along the unstitched seam lines 1 1/4 inches and hem them, using a hemming stitch *(Appendix)*.

Using color A yarn, finish each hemmed seam edge with a row of blanket stitches as shown at right.

The trims: Measure the length of each of the open seams. Using the vertical band pattern, crochet a strip equal in length to each of the seams; if the seams connect, treat them as one long seam.

Attaching the trims: Using color A, join the crocheted strips to the open seams with a row of crocheted slip stitches as shown at right, inserting your hook through the crochet stitches of the strips and the blanket stitches along the edges of the seams.

THE MULTICOLOR SHELL BORDER

You will need four ounces of knitting worsted in color A (orange in the picture on page 166), two ounces of color B (beige) and two ounces of color C (purple); an aluminum crochet hook Size G; a hole puncher; a tapestry needle; two snap fasteners and a strip of narrow rolled elastic the length of your waistline measurement. Crochet a sample swatch to check the gauge—which is 4 stitches to the inch.

The skirt: If you are working with a firm fabric such as felt or leather, punch a series of holes along all edges to be trimmed. The holes should be about 1/2 inch in from the edge and 1/2 inch apart. If you are working on a fabric that ravels or is limp, make a 1/2-inch hem along the outer edge of the skirt and then punch the holes through both layers of fabric. Using color A, make a row of single crochet stitches through all of the punched holes except those around the waistband edge. Fasten off the yarn as shown at right.

The skirt trim: Starting at a top corner of the skirt, work 3 rows of the multicolor shell pattern around the outer edge of the skirt. Fasten off.

The waistband and tie: Using color A, chain 43 for one end of the tie. Then work single crochet stitches through the punched holes around the entire waistband. Chain 1 and turn. Work across these single crochet and chain stitches in the multicolor shell pattern for 6 rows. Fasten off. To make the other end of the tie, again chain 43 and work 6 rows of the multicolor shell pattern. Fasten off and tie to the waistband border at a point where it will lie comfortably with the other end of the tie.

The finishing touches: Sew two snap fasteners onto the waistband to hold the skirt closed at the waist. Draw the narrow elastic through the crochet stitches at the top of the waistband as inconspicuously as possible; then tack the elastic in place. If desired, use color A to embroider 2 rows of running chain stitches *(Appendix)* along the punched-hole edges.

THE WAISTBAND INSET AND CUFF

You will need two ounces each of knitting worsted in color A (deep pink, in the dress on page 167), color B (light pink), color C (orange) and color D (melon). Use an aluminum crochet hook Size G, and crochet a sample swatch to check the gauge—which is 4 stitches to the inch.

The dress: Assemble the dress until you reach the stage when you would attach the waistband. Fold under the raw edges of the skirt and bodice along the waistline seam markings; then press. Shorten the sleeves by 1 1/2 inches.

The inset: Measure the width of the waistband and allow for an extra 1 1/4 inches at the top and bottom for the openings between the pointed portions of the design. Make the horizontal flame stitch pattern in the desired width and length. To attach the waistband as inconspicuously as possible, hand sew the band to the skirt and the bodice, using color A and a conventional slip stitch *(Appendix)*.

The cuffs: Measure the width of the sleeve and make a trim in the horizontal flame stitch pattern of the desired width and length. Using color A, sew the cuffs in place with a slip stitch.

JOINING YARN

Join a new ball of yarn at the beginning of a row by drawing it through the first loop; leave a 1-inch-long end. Join a new color at the end of a row, working the last 2 loops on the hook with the new yarn *(drawing 1)*. After crocheting 2 or 3 rows, weave the loose ends of yarn through nearby stitches with the crochet hook *(drawing 2)*.

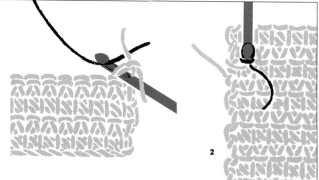

FASTENING OFF

Cut the yarn from the ball, leaving a 2-inch-long end. Pull this end through the loop on the hook to secure it as shown below. Then weave the loose end through one or two nearby stitches.

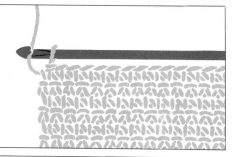

JOINING THE TRIM TO THE FABRIC

First create loops along the edges of the fabric by making a row of blanket stitches as follows: Draw a guide line with chalk 1/4 inch in from the edge to be joined. Using a knotted thread, insert the needle from the bottom piece of fabric to the top, at the far left edge of the line *(drawing 1)*. Holding the thread with your left thumb, insert the needle 1/4 inch to the right of the stitch made in Step 1 *(drawing 2)*. Keep the thread behind the needle, and pull the needle through the loop. Continue as shown *(drawing 3)*, ending with a fastening stitch *(Appendix)*.

Join the trim and the crochet strips with a crocheted slip stitch as follows: Insert the crochet hook from front to back through a loop at the edge of the trim and through one of the blanket stitches at the edge of the fabric. Draw the yarn through, leaving a loop on the hook *(drawing 4)*. Insert the hook through the next loop at the edge of the trim and the next blanket stitch. Bring the yarn over the hook and draw it, in one motion, through these stitches—as well as through the loop on the hook *(drawing 5)*. Continue in this manner until the pieces are joined.

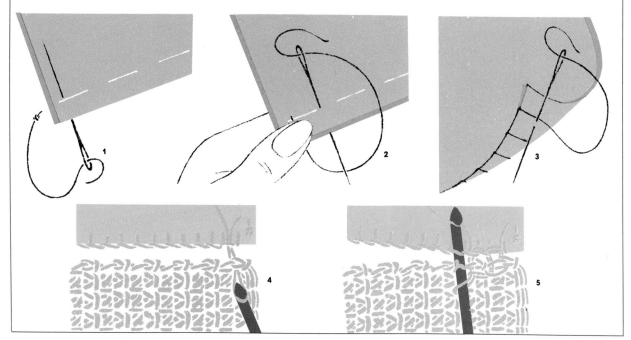

diagonal twist

diamond

banded reverse stockinette

High-style knits in a low key

Thanks to their small scale and subtle design, the knitting patterns used for the swatches illustrated at left and below can be repeated yard after yard without losing their elegance. For that reason, they are ideal patterns from which to create a stylishly understated fabric for a dress like the one shown on pages 180-181. Yet the designs themselves are simple enough so that the patterns could also serve for any other kind of garment where fine knits are in order: a man's or woman's pullover sweater, for example, a formal scarf, or even a baby's jacket or cape.

Both the diagonal twist pattern *(top left)* and the double seed *(below)* form soft three-dimensional textures, and the diamond pattern *(bottom left)* creates an overall design with no discernible direction. Any of these three can be used interchangeably in whatever garment you decide to make. However, the banded reverse stockinette pattern *(top center)* produces a horizontal striped effect. The garment in which it is used should be planned so that the stripes run in the most flattering direction—to broaden the shoulders, say, or accentuate the bust.

All four patterns can be knitted with lightweight sport yarn on small needles; complete directions for the patterns follow overleaf.

double seed

Instructions for knitting the patterns

The following instructions are for knitting the patterns pictured on pages 170-171. These swatches have a relatively fine gauge —6 stitches per inch—and were made with Size 6 needles and lightweight sport yarn. Directions for the basic knitting stitches can be found in the Appendix.

THE BANDED REVERSE STOCKINETTE PATTERN

Cast on the desired number of stitches, making sure that the total is a multiple of three, plus one. *Row 1:* Purl 1 stitch and slip 2 stitches with the needle in the purl position *(drawing, right)*. Repeat this sequence across the row, ending with purl 1. *Rows 2,4,6,8,10 and 12:* Make a row of knit stitches. *Rows 3 and 5:* Make a row of purl stitches. *Row 7:* Purl 2. Slip 2 with the needle in the purl position, then purl 1; repeat this sequence of slip 2, purl 1 across the row, ending with purl 2. *Rows 9 and 11:* Make a row of purl stitches. Repeat rows 1-12 to complete the pattern.

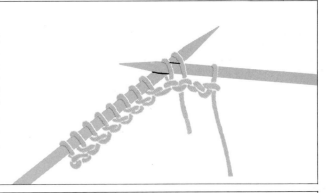

THE DIAGONAL TWIST PATTERN

Cast on the desired number of stitches, making sure that the total is a multiple of four. *Row 1:* Knit 2 stitches, then knit the second stitch that is on the left-hand needle *(drawing 1)* without dropping it from the needle. Now knit the first stitch that is on the left-hand needle *(drawing 2)* and drop both stitches from the needle. Repeat this sequence across the row. *Rows 2 and 4:* Make a row of purl stitches. *Row 3:* Knit the second stitch on the left-hand needle but do not drop it from the needle. Now knit the first stitch and drop both stitches from the left-hand needle. Knit 2 stitches. Repeat this sequence across the row. Repeat rows 1-4 to complete the pattern.

1

2

THE DOUBLE SEED PATTERN

Cast on the desired number of stitches, making sure that the total is a multiple of four. *Rows 1 and 2:* Knit 2 stitches, then purl 2 stitches. Repeat this sequence across the row.

Rows 3 and 4: Purl 2 stitches, then knit 2 stitches. Repeat this sequence across the row. Repeat rows 1-4 to complete the pattern.

THE DIAMOND PATTERN

Cast on the desired number of stitches, making sure that the total is a multiple of four, plus one. *Rows 1,3,5 and 7:* Make a row of purl stitches. *Row 2:* Knit 1 stitch. Bring the yarn in front of your work *(drawing 1)* as if to purl and, keeping it in front, slip 3 stitches from the left-hand needle to the right-hand needle *(drawing 2)*. Now move the yarn back to its normal knit position *(drawing 3)* and knit 1 stitch. Repeat this sequence across the row. *Row 4:* Knit 2 stitches. Slide the right-hand needle under the horizontal strand that was formed in row 2 *(drawing 4)*; then insert the needle into the next stitch on the left-hand needle *(arrow)*. Knit both loops as if they were one loop *(drawing 5)*. Knit 3 stitches. Repeat this sequence across the row—sliding the needle under the strand, knitting it together with the loop

on the left-hand needle, and knitting 3 stitches. End with knit 2. *Row 6:* Knit 3 stitches. Bring the yarn in front of your work as if to purl and, keeping it in front, slip 3 stitches from the left-hand needle onto the right-hand needle. Place the yarn back in the normal knit position and knit 1. Repeat this sequence across the row—slipping the 3 stitches and knitting 1. End the row with knit 3. *Row 8:* Knit 4. Slide the right-hand needle under the horizontal strand formed in row 6, then insert the needle into the next stitch on the left-hand needle and knit both loops as if they were one loop. Knit 3. Repeat this sequence across the row —sliding the needle under the strand, knitting it together with the loop on the needle, and knitting 3 stitches. End with knit 4. Repeat rows 1-8 to complete the pattern.

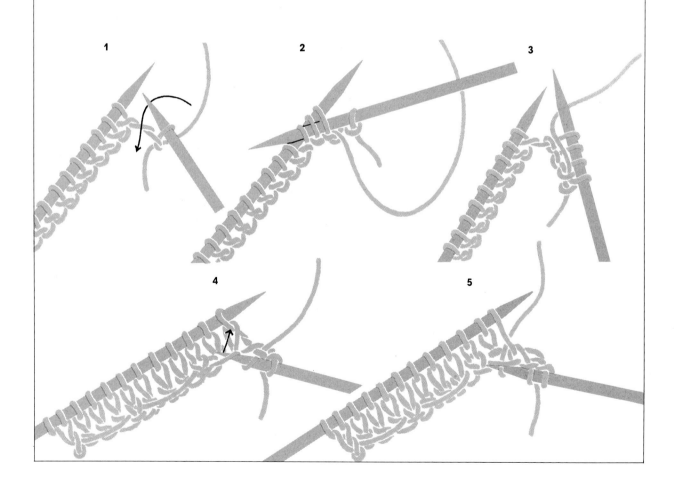

Adapting a sewing pattern for knitting

Almost any commercial sewing pattern can be converted into a guide for knitting—as demonstrated by the sprightly Geoffrey Beene design that is interpreted in knit stitches on pages 180-181.

First, choose the pattern you wish to adapt for knitting. Then select the yarn—your yarn shop can help estimate how much you will need. Choose the needle size recommended on the yarn label, if there is one, or follow these rules: use Size 1 to 3 for 2-ply lightweight yarn, Sizes 3 to 5 for 3-ply mediumweight yarn or Sizes 5 to 14 for 4-ply yarn of a heavier weight. Select a pattern stitch from among those shown on pages 170-171, or use a simple stockinette pattern—knit one row; purl one row.

Then to translate the pattern pieces into knitting instructions, all you need to do is measure each of the pattern pieces and multiply the measurements by your knitting gauge, which can be determined by the method explained below.

General principles for measuring typical pattern pieces are given here and on the following pages. Each principle is then illustrated by a specific example, using a knitting pattern that would be appropriate for the Beene dress—diagonal twist pattern—and a hypothetical gauge of six stitches and eight rows to the inch.

DETERMINING THE GAUGE

Knit a sample swatch that measures at least 4 by 4 inches. Remove the swatch from the needles without binding off and lay it on a flat surface. Count the number of stitches to the inch across the swatch; this figure is your stitch gauge when using the yarn, needles and pattern stitch you have selected to make your garment. Then count the number of vertical rows to the inch; this figure is your row gauge.

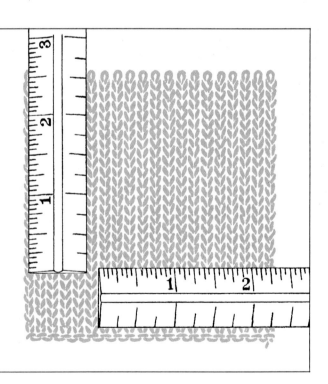

174

ADJUSTING THE PATTERN PIECES TO FIT YOUR FIGURE

Lay out all the pieces of the pattern you have chosen, discarding those for facings or interfacings. Fold under any darts on the pattern pieces and tape them down. Measure the pattern's total circumference at the bust, waist and hips; then measure the total length of the garment and sleeves, excluding seam and hem allowances. Compare these measurements to your own and adjust each pattern piece, following the instructions on pages 42-43. Keep in mind, however, that knitted garments have considerable give and the additional inches included in commercial sewing patterns to provide wearing ease are therefore not needed. Compare your measurements to the actual pattern pieces rather than to the standardized measurements that appear on the pattern envelope (as you would if you were adjusting a pattern for sewing).

If you plan to weave the seams of the finished garment together to achieve an almost invisible seam (page 185), cut off the seam allowances of the pattern; if you plan to use the easier method of sewing the seams together (page 185), cut off all but 1/4 inch of the seam allowances. Cut off the hem allowances.

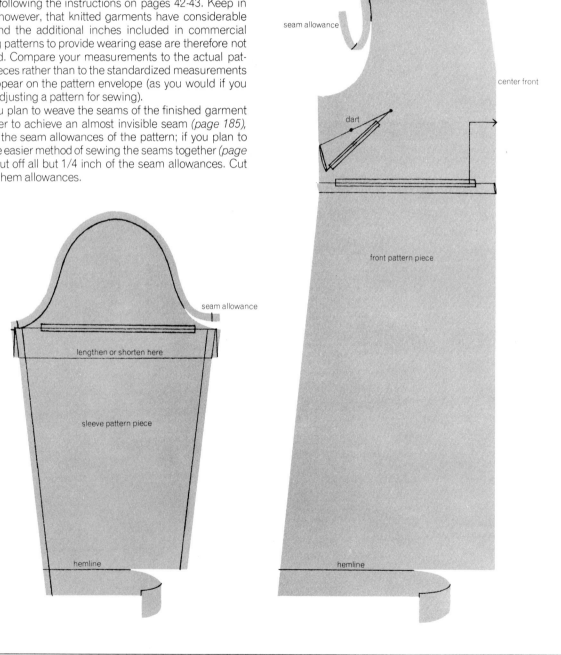

seam allowance

center front

dart

front pattern piece

seam allowance

lengthen or shorten here

sleeve pattern piece

hemline

hemline

KNITTING THE GARMENT BACK

To determine how many stitches to cast onto your needles, measure the width of the pattern at the hem edge, doubling the measurement if the piece is for half the back only. To get the total number of stitches required, multiply this measurement by your stitch gauge. Then check to see if the stitch multiple called for in your pattern stitch divides evenly into the total number of stitches. If it does not, increase the number you are casting on to accommodate the stitch multiple.

As you increase or decrease the number of stitches on your needle to shape the garment, the stitch multiple may not divide evenly into the number of stitches on your needle. If this happens, complete your pattern stitch as far as you can, then begin at that same point on the return row.

Example: If the hem illustrated here measures 13 inches, double it and multiply 26 by 6; cast on 156 stitches. Since the stitch multiple in this example is 4, the figures work out evenly. If the stitch multiple were 5, you would have to add 4 stitches to the number cast on.

In determining how to shape the back between the hem and the underarm, first measure the width of the back at the underarm, doubling the measurement if the pattern piece is for half of the back only. To determine the number of stitches you should have when you reach the underarm, multiply this measurement by your stitch gauge.

Example: If the underarm measures 9, multiply 18 inches by 6 to find you have 108 stitches at the underarm.

To find out how many stitches you will have to decrease as you knit the back, subtract the number of stitches at the underarm from the number cast on. Since you will be decreasing evenly on both sides of the garment, divide this figure in half. Then measure the length of the back from the hem edge to the underarm and select an appropriate interval between the rows where you will be decreasing —1/2 inch or more depending on the length of the piece.

Example: There is a difference of 48 stitches between the hem (156) and underarm (108), and the length to the underarm is 27 inches. You will have to decrease by 48 stitches—or 24 times in 27 inches. The most gradual way to do so is to decrease 1 stitch on each side every inch, then work on 108 stitches until the garment back measures 27 inches to the underarm.

To determine how many stitches you will need at the shoulders, first measure across the shoulders on the pattern, doubling this measurement if the pattern piece is for half the back only. Then measure across the back of the neck on the pattern—again doubling this measurement if the pattern piece is for half of the back only. Add the measurements together. Multiply the total by your stitch gauge to determine the number of stitches you should have at the top of the back.

Example: If each shoulder is 4 inches, and the total back of the neck is 4 1/2 inches, the number of stitches that should be at the top of the back is 75. That means you will have to decrease from the 108 stitches you had at the underarm to the 75 stitches required at the shoulders; but—since it is easier to decrease an even number of stitches—to end up with 76 stitches simply add 1 stitch to your estimate for the measurement of the top of the back.

To determine how to shape the back between the underarm and the shoulder at the sleeve edge, first measure the distance from the underarm to the shoulder. Then bind off a number of stitches equal to 1 1/2 inches at the beginning of each of the next two rows, starting on the outside —the side that will show in the finished garment. Decrease

at appropriate intervals—usually every other row—to reach the proper number of stitches for the top of the back.

Example: If the underarm-to-shoulder measurement is 7 1/2 inches, bind off 10 stitches at the beginning of each of the next two rows. This will leave 12 stitches to be decreased to reach 76 stitches. Decrease 1 stitch at the beginning and end of every other row 6 times. Work on 76 stitches until the armhole measures 7 1/2 inches.

In order to shape the shoulders and neckline, first subtract the number of stitches that will be needed for the back of the neck from the total number of stitches now on your needles. To determine the number of stitches you will be working with on each shoulder, divide the number remaining in half. To shape the shoulders, bind off stitches equal to 1 inch at the beginning of every row, again starting on the outside of the work. To shape the back of the neck, bind off the remaining stitches all at once, straight across the row.

Example: Subtract the number of stitches needed for the back of the neck (since the total in this example is 27— 4 1/2 inches multiplied by the gauge of 6—add on 1 stitch so that the number is even) from the 76 stitches at the top of the back. Divide this figure of 48 in half; you have 24 stitches per shoulder to bind off. Since this involves 4 inches (24 stitches divided by the gauge of 6) for each shoulder, bind off 12 stitches at the beginning of each of the next 4 rows, then bind off the remaining 28 stitches for the back of the neck.

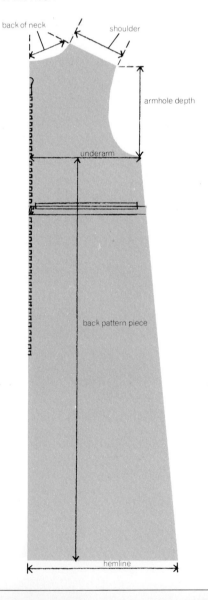

back of neck · shoulder · armhole depth · underarm · back pattern piece · hemline

KNITTING THE GARMENT FRONT

Knit the front, following the basic instructions for knitting the back, until you reach the point between the underarm and the shoulder where the shaping for the front neckline must begin. Determine that point by measuring up from the bottom edge of your pattern to the lowest point of the neckline. Then make the neckline as follows, allotting to it the same number of stitches as you bound off for the back neckline.

To shape a round neck, plan to decrease 1 stitch at both sides of the neck opening three to five times at appropriate intervals. To this number add the number of stitches that will be required to make the two shoulder measurements. Subtract this total from the number of stitches on your needle to find the number of stitches to be bound off for the base of the neckline.

Example: Add 5 stitches to the number of stitches for each shoulder (24), then double the 29 stitches for a total of 58 stitches for both shoulders. If there are 76 stitches on your needles at the point where you must begin shaping the neckline, subtract 58 for a figure of 18 to be bound off for the base of the neckline. Work across 29 stitches. Join another ball of yarn (Appendix) to work both sides of the neck at once, and bind off the center 18 stitches. Work across the remaining 29 stitches. Now decrease 1 stitch at each side of the neck edge every other row five times.

To shape a V neck, bind off 1 stitch at the point of the V if you are working with an odd number of stitches. If you are working with an even number of stitches, do not bind off any stitches. Then use your row gauge to calculate the number of rows you will be working until you reach the shoulders, and decrease 1 stitch at each side of the neckline every few rows until you have the required number of stitches for each shoulder.

Example: If the V neck shaping begins at the top of the armhole, you will have 76 stitches on your needle. Subtract the number needed for the shoulders (48); this means you will have to lose 28 stitches, or 14 on each side of the neckline. If there are approximately 6 inches (or 48 rows) to work with, proceed as follows: knit across 38 stitches, join another ball of yarn, and knit across the remaining 38 stitches. Working on both sides of the neckline at once, at each neck edge decrease 1 stitch every fourth row 10 times, and then every other row 4 times.

To complete the front, continue knitting until the front measures the same as the back. Then shape the shoulders as you did on the back.

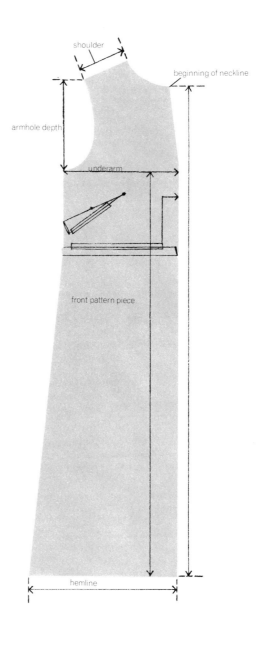

KNITTING A SET-IN SLEEVE

To determine how many stitches to cast onto your needles, measure the width of the sleeve at the hem edge. Multiply this measurement by your stitch gauge to determine the number of stitches to be cast on. Then check to see if the stitch multiple called for in your pattern stitch divides evenly into the total number of stitches. If it does not, increase the number of stitches you are casting on to accommodate the stitch multiple.

Example: If the sleeve is 9 inches wide at the hem edge and your stitch gauge is 6 to the inch, cast on 54 stitches. Since the stitch multiple in this example is 4, cast on 2 more stitches to make a total of 56.

To determine how to shape the sleeve between the hem and the widest part, measure the width of the sleeve at its widest point and multiply this measurement by your stitch gauge.

Example: If the widest part of the sleeve is 14 inches, you will need 84 stitches.

In order to know how many stitches you will have to increase as you knit the sleeve, subtract the number of stitches cast on from the number at the widest part of the sleeve. Since you will be increasing evenly on both sides of the sleeve, divide this figure in half. Then measure the length of the sleeve from the hem edge to the widest part, and decide on an appropriate interval between the rows on which you will be decreasing—usually 1 to 2 inches for a sleeve.

Example: There is a difference of 30 stitches between the hem (54) and the widest part of the sleeve (84)—and the length between them is 15 inches. You will have to increase 30 stitches, that is, 15 times in 15 inches. Increase 1 stitch on each side every inch 15 times. Then work on 84 stitches until the sleeve measures 17 inches, the length to the underarm.

To start shaping the sleeve cap, first measure from the dot indicating the center top of the sleeve to the point where you will begin to shape the cap. Then bind off the same number of stitches as you did when beginning to shape the armhole on the back and front pieces. Continue to shape the cap by decreasing 1 stitch at the beginning and end of every other row until you are 1 to 1 1/2 inches short of the cap length.

Since a number of stitches equivalent to 1 or 2 inches should be left at the very top of the cap to keep it rounded, count the number of stitches remaining on your needle. Subtract the number that must remain and dispose of the difference by binding off a few stitches at the beginning of each of the next 4 to 6 rows.

Example: Bind off 10 stitches at the beginning of each of the next 2 rows, leaving 64 stitches on your needle. If the cap is 6 inches long, and you wish to knit to within 1 inch of the top, you will be decreasing over the next 40 rows (5 inches multiplied by the row gauge of 8). At that point you will have 24 stitches left on your needle. Since you should have about 12 stitches (2 inches) at the very top of the cap, bind off 2 stitches at the beginning of each of the next 6 rows, then loosely bind off the remaining 12 stitches.

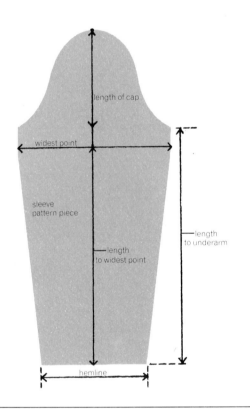

Figure labels: length of cap, widest point, sleeve pattern piece, length to widest point, length to underarm, hemline

KNITTING A GARMENT WITH A RAGLAN SLEEVE

KNITTING THE GARMENT BACK

Knit the back up to the underarm, following the instructions for a garment with a set-in sleeve. Compare the number of stitches on your needles to the number of stitches you will need for the back on the neck. The difference constitutes the number of stitches you must plan to decrease at regular intervals on both sides of the armhole.

Example: If there are 108 stitches on your needle at the underarm, and the back of the neck calls for 28 stitches, this leaves 80 stitches—or 40 for each side—to be decreased. If the armhole measures 8 inches, and the row gauge is 8 rows per inch, you will have 64 rows in which to decrease the 80 stitches. Bind off 4 stitches at the beginning of each of the next 4 rows, leaving 64 stitches on your needle. You will have to lose 32 stitches on each side in the remaining 60 rows. Do this by decreasing 1 stitch on each side of every other row 28 times, then every row 4 more times.

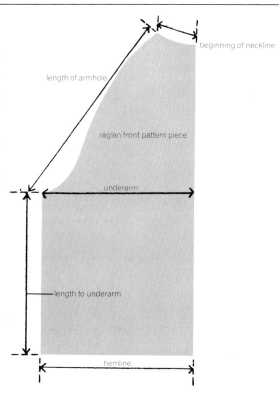

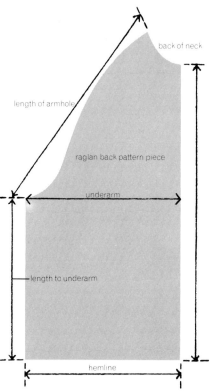

KNITTING THE GARMENT FRONT

Knit the front of the garment, following the instructions for knitting the garment with a set-in sleeve.

KNITTING THE SLEEVES

Knit the sleeve, following the instructions for the set-in sleeve but stopping where the shaping of the cap begins. Then bind off the same number of stitches as you did when beginning to shape the armhole on the back and front pieces. Now decrease 1 stitch at the beginning and end of every other row, conforming as closely as possible to the raglan shaping on the armholes. When the sleeve measures about 2 inches less than the full length of the armhole, count the number of stitches on your needle. Now decrease as frequently as necessary until the finished cap measures the same as the armhole.

Example: If the number of stitches at the beginning of the sleeve cap is 90, bind off 4 stitches at the beginning of each of the next 2 rows. If the sleeve cap is 6 inches long, knit 4 inches (32 rows with a gauge of 8). Of these 32 rows you now have 30 remaining on your needle, 2 rows having been bound off at the beginning of the cap. Decrease 1 stitch at the beginning and end of every other row 15 times. Now 52 stitches are on your needle; you must decrease all of these in the next 2 inches (16 rows) as you shape the top of the cap. Bind off 3 stitches at the beginning of the next 16 rows. Then bind off the remaining 6 stitches.

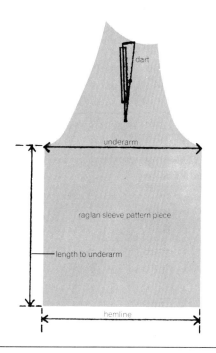

Colorful twist on a sewing design

The free-swinging, candy-colored dress at right, an interpretation of a Geoffrey Beene original, is a delightful example of the look you can achieve by knitting a garment that was originally designed to be sewed together in cloth.

In making the knit dress, the diagonal twist pattern shown here provides an intriguing texture that does not detract from the basic simplicity of the dress. A line of trimming that duplicates the swooping curve of a seam in the cloth dress produces a yoke effect around the top and accentuates the dolman sleeve. Finally, the dress is topped off with a hat and scarf of the same texture and color.

Charts indicating the measurements needed to convert the pattern for knitting are shown overleaf. With them are standard knitting instructions for the dress, hat and scarf.

Instructions for knitting the dress ensemble

The pattern pieces shown here are the basic pieces needed for the dress pictured on the preceding pages. The accompanying dimensions are for sizes 8 to 16. Using these figures—and the principles on pages 174-179—you can compute your own knitting instructions. As a double-check compare them to the directions that follow.

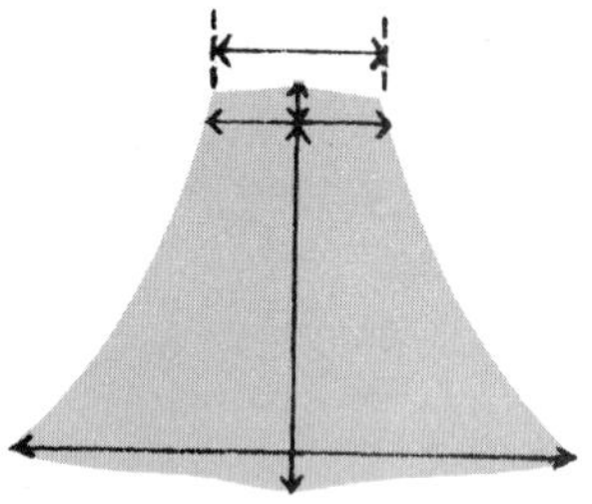

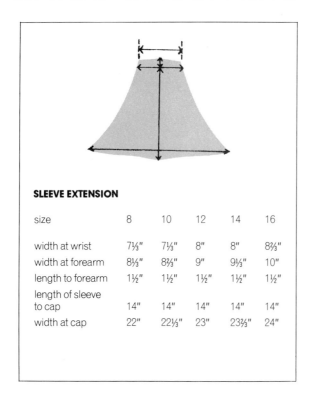

SLEEVE EXTENSION

size	8	10	12	14	16
width at wrist	7⅓"	7⅓"	8"	8"	8⅔"
width at forearm	8⅓"	8⅔"	9"	9⅓"	10"
length to forearm	1½"	1½"	1½"	1½"	1½"
length of sleeve to cap	14"	14"	14"	14"	14"
width at cap	22"	22⅓"	23"	23⅔"	24"

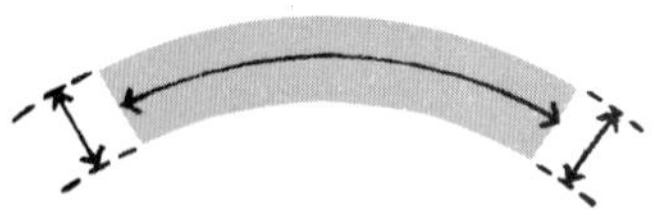

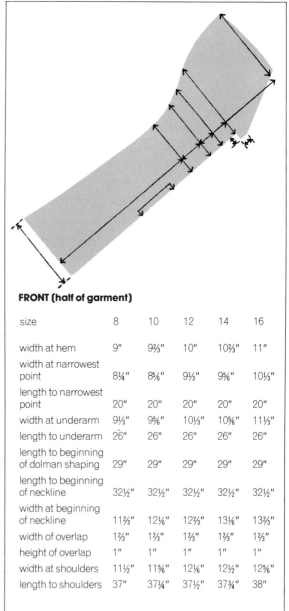

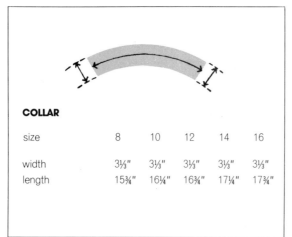

COLLAR

size	8	10	12	14	16
width	3⅓"	3⅓"	3⅓"	3⅓"	3⅓"
length	15¾"	16¼"	16¾"	17¼"	17¾"

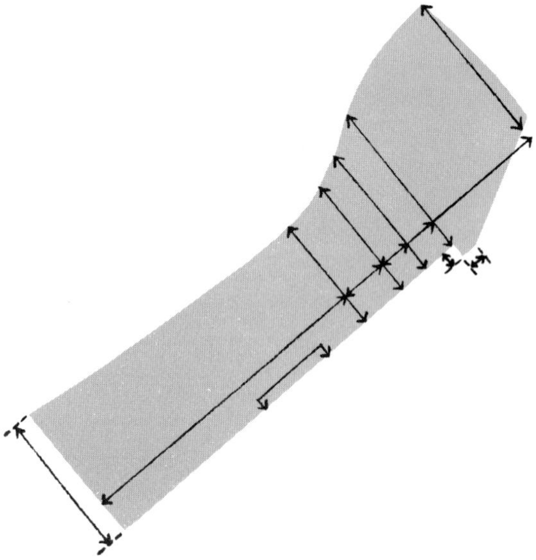

FRONT (half of garment)

size	8	10	12	14	16
width at hem	9"	9⅔"	10"	10⅔"	11"
width at narrowest point	8¼"	8⅚"	9⅓"	9⅚"	10⅓"
length to narrowest point	20"	20"	20"	20"	20"
width at underarm	9⅓"	9⅚"	10⅓"	10⅚"	11⅓"
length to underarm	26"	26"	26"	26"	26"
length to beginning of dolman shaping	29"	29"	29"	29"	29"
length to beginning of neckline	32½"	32½"	32½"	32½"	32½"
width at beginning of neckline	11⅔"	12⅙"	12⅔"	13⅙"	13⅔"
width of overlap	1⅔"	1⅔"	1⅔"	1⅔"	1⅔"
height of overlap	1"	1"	1"	1"	1"
width at shoulders	11½"	11⅚"	12⅙"	12½"	12⅚"
length to shoulders	37"	37¼"	37½"	37¾"	38"

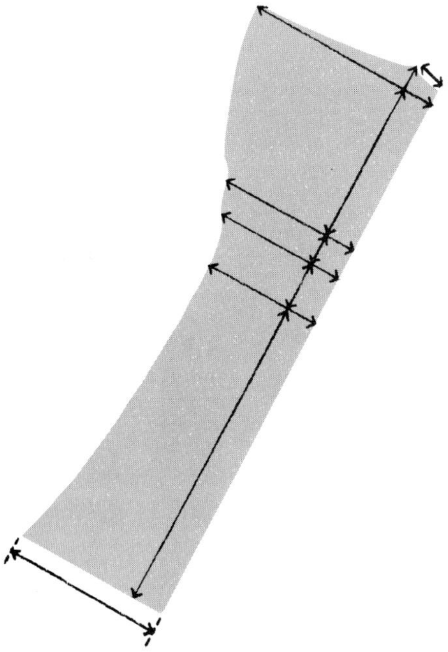

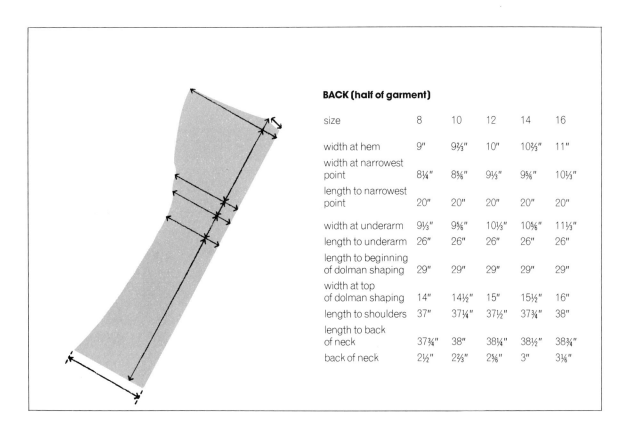

BACK (half of garment)

size	8	10	12	14	16
width at hem	9"	9⅔"	10"	10⅔"	11"
width at narrowest point	8¼"	8⅚"	9⅓"	9⅚"	10⅓"
length to narrowest point	20"	20"	20"	20"	20"
width at underarm	9⅓"	9⅚"	10⅓"	10⅚"	11⅓"
length to underarm	26"	26"	26"	26"	26"
length to beginning of dolman shaping	29"	29"	29"	29"	29"
width at top of dolman shaping	14"	14½"	15"	15½"	16"
length to shoulders	37"	37¼"	37½"	37¾"	38"
length to back of neck	37¾"	38"	38¼"	38½"	38¾"
back of neck	2½"	2⅔"	2⅚"	3"	3⅙"

THE DRESS

Directions given here are for size 8; changes for sizes 10, 12, 14 and 16 appear in parentheses, in that order. To make the dress, you will need 13 (or 14,16,17,19, according to size) two-ounce skeins of fingering yarn. You will need straight knitting needles in Size 6, an aluminum crochet hook in Size F and a tapestry needle. Before you start, knit a sample swatch in the diagonal twist pattern *(page 172)* to check the gauge—which is 6 stitches and 8 rows to the inch. Note: The seams in this dress have been woven; consequently no additional stitches have been added for seam allowances.

The back: With the Size 6 knitting needles, cast on 108 (116, 120,128,132) stitches. Work in the diagonal twist pattern *(page 172)* for 5 (4,5,4,5) inches. (The number of inches required at certain points in the shaping does not necessarily increase as the size grows larger.) Decrease 1 stitch at the beginning and end of the next row. Repeat this decrease every 5 (4,5,4,5) inches, 3 (4,3,4,3) times more.

There are now 100 (106,112,118,124) stitches on the needle, and the piece measures 20 inches. Work for 1 inch, then increase 1 stitch at the beginning and end of the next row. Repeat this increase every 1 inch, 5 times more. There are now 112 (118,124,130,136) stitches on the needle, and the piece measures 26 inches. Work on these stitches for 3 inches more, then increase for the dolman shaping in the following manner: Increase 1 stitch at the beginning and end of the next row and repeat this increase every other row until there are 168 (174,180,186,192) stitches in all. Work on these stitches until the piece measures 8 (8 1/4, 8 1/2, 8 3/4, 9) inches above the point where the dolman shaping began.

The shoulders: Bind off 23 (23,25,25,26) stitches at the beginning of each of the next 2 rows; 23 (24,24,25,26) stitches at the beginning of each of the next 2 rows; and 23 (23,24, 24,25) stitches at the beginning of each of the next 2 rows. Bind off loosely the remaining 30 (32,34,36,38) stitches for the back of the neck.

The front: Work exactly as you did for the back, until you have started the dolman shaping—at which point there are 140 (146,152,158,164) stitches on the needle. To shape the neckline, work across 70 (73,76,79,82) stitches; cast on 10 stitches for the underlap part of the neckline and slip the remaining 70 (73,76,79,82) stitches onto a holder, making 80 (83,86,89,92) to be worked later.

Continue to increase at the side edge as on the back. At the same time, work at the neck edge for 1 inch, then decrease 1 stitch at that edge every other row, 24 (26,27,28, 29) times. When there are 69 (71,73,75,77) remaining on the needle and the piece measures the same as the back—from the bottom edge to the beginning of the shoulders—shape the shoulder the same way you did the back. Then return to the stitches on the holder and, reversing all shaping, work the other side of the front to correspond to the side just completed.

The sleeves: Cast on 44 (44,48,48,52) stitches. Work in the pattern stitch for 3 rows. Increase 1 stitch at the beginning and at the end of the next row. Repeat this increase every fourth row until there are 50 (52,54,56,60) stitches. Then increase 1 stitch at the beginning and at the end of every other row until there are 132 (134,138,142,144) stitches. Work on these stitches until the piece measures 14 inches. Bind off loosely.

The collar: Cast on 20 stitches. Work in the pattern stitch for 2 rows, then decrease 1 stitch at the beginning and increase 1 stitch at the end of the next row. Repeat this sequence every other row until the piece measures 7 3/4 (8, 8 1/4, 8 1/2, 8 3/4) inches, ending at an increase. Work 2 rows, then decrease 1 stitch at the beginning and increase 1 stitch at the end of the next row. Repeat this sequence every other row for 7 1/2 (7 3/4, 8, 8 1/4, 8 1/2) inches more. Work 2 rows and bind off.

The finishing touches: Using the tapestry needle, weave the shoulder seams together and weave the side seams, leaving an opening of 11 (11 1/4, 11 1/2, 11 3/4, 12) inches on each side of the dress between the top of the side seam and the start of the shaping for the shoulder. Weave the top of the sleeve to the opening. Tack the neckline overlap in place, over the underlap, as shown in the photograph. Weave the collar in place. Work 2 rows of single crochet stitches (Appendix) around the bottom and sleeve edges of the dress.

The trim: For the sleeve joinings, cast on 132 (134, 138, 140, 144) stitches. Knit 1 row, purl 1 row, then bind off.
For the front of the dress, cast on 70 (72,74,76,78) stitches and knit 1 row, purl 1 row, then bind off.
For the neck opening and outer edges of the collar, cast on 216 stitches and knit 1 row, purl 1 row, then bind off.
Sew the trim in place along the sleeve joinings and the front of the dress, as shown in the photograph. Turn the neck opening approximately 1/2 inch to the outside of the dress and tack it into place; then sew the trim on top of the folded edge and around the outside edge of the collar. Weave the seams together as shown on the opposite page and block (Appendix).

THE SCARF
You will need 3 two-ounce skeins of fingering yarn. Use straight knitting needles in Size 6, and an aluminum crochet hook Size F. Knit a sample swatch in the diagonal twist pattern (page 172) to check the gauge, which is 6 stitches to the inch.

The scarf: Cast on 42 stitches. *Row 1:* Purl 1 stitch, knit 1 stitch, purl 1 stitch, then work 36 stitches in the diagonal twist pattern. End the row with purl 1, knit 1, purl 1. *Row 2:* Knit 1 stitch, purl 1, knit 1, then work 36 stitches in the diagonal twist pattern. End the row with knit 1, purl 1, knit 1. Repeat these 2 rows until the piece measures 66 inches; bind off loosely.

The finishing touches: Block the scarf (Appendix) and work 1 row of single crochet stitches (page 190) along one short end, then along the other.

The fringe: Cut several strands of yarn, each measuring 8 1/2 inches. Knot 6 of the strands in every other single crochet stitch along the two edges. Trim the ends of the strands evenly.

THE CAP
You will need 1 two-ounce skein of fingering yarn. Use knitting needles in Sizes 4 and 6, and a tapestry needle. First, knit a sample swatch in the diagonal twist pattern (page 172) to check the gauge, which is 6 stitches to the inch on the Size 6 needles. Using the Size 4 needles, cast on 102 stitches. Knit 1, purl 1 in ribbing for 1 inch, then change to Size 6 needles. Work in the diagonal twist pattern stitch for 4 1/2 inches, then work to completion the following sequences in a stockinette stitch (knit 1 row, purl 1 row).

Decrease 1 stitch at the beginning and end of the next row, work 1 row, then begin to decrease in the following sequence. *First decrease row:* Knit 8 stitches, knit 2 together. Repeat across the row, thus decreasing 10 times. Work 3 rows on 90 stitches. *Second decrease row:* Knit 7 stitches, knit 2 together Repeat across the row, thus decreasing 10 times. Work 3 rows on 80 stitches. *Third decrease row:* Knit 6 stitches, knit 2 together. Repeat across the row, thus decreasing 10 times. Work 3 rows on 70 stitches.

Continue in this manner, decreasing 10 stitches evenly spaced on every fourth row and leaving 1 stitch less between each decrease, until 60 stitches remain. Then decrease every other row until 10 stitches remain. Break off the yarn, leaving a long thread.

The finishing touches: Draw the loose thread through the remaining 10 stitches. Then weave the back seam and block (Appendix).

PICKING UP STITCHES AT AN EDGE

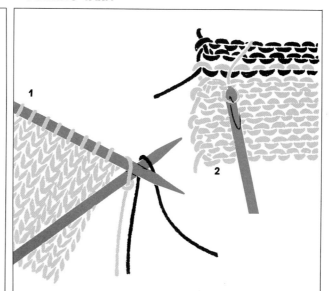

To add a sleeve, a collar or a ribbing to a knit piece, you will have to pick up stitches along the finished edge. To do so, insert the needle into the first stitch to be picked up. Then wrap a strand of yarn around the needle and draw the yarn through the stitch (drawing 1). Continue in this manner along the edge, drawing the yarn through each successive stitch to be picked up (drawing 2).

JOINING YARN

To introduce a new ball or color of yarn at any point along a row, wrap the yarn around the working needle, leaving 2- or 3-inch-long ends, and use the new yarn to knit the next stitch (drawing 1). When you have knitted 2 or 3 rows with the new yarn, weave the loose ends (drawing 2) through nearby stitches on the wrong side of the piece, using a crochet hook.

JOINING KNITTED PIECES

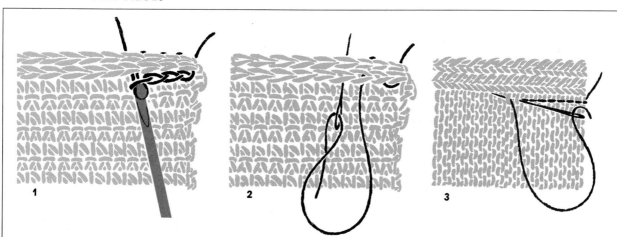

Knitted garments can be seamed in three ways: by crocheting, weaving or sewing. In each case, begin by placing the edges together, wrong sides out, and aligning the stitches and rows.

If you choose to use the crochet method (drawing 1), begin by inserting a crochet hook through the first stitch below each edge. Catch a fresh strand of yarn with the hook and draw it through both edges, thus forming a loop on the hook. Then insert the hook through the next pair of stitches, catch the yarn and draw it through these stitches as well as through the loop that was formed on the hook.

To weave two pieces together (drawing 2), insert a blunt-tipped tapestry needle through the outermost stitch of each edge, which is made up of four loops. Then turn the needle and repeat weaving back and forth until the pieces are joined.

To sew two pieces together (drawing 3), insert a blunt-tipped tapestry needle through both pieces 1/4 inch down and in from the edges to be joined. Leaving a 2-inch-long end of yarn, insert the needle 1/4 inch to the right of the first stitch and bring it out from back to front 1/4 inch to the left of the first stitch.

Whichever method you choose, make sure to weave any loose ends into nearby stitches.

GLOSSARY

ADJUSTMENT LINE: A double line printed on a pattern piece to indicate where the piece may be lengthened or shortened.

BACKSTITCH: To make several machine stitches in reverse at the beginning or end of a seam line for reinforcement.

BASTE: To stitch pieces together temporarily, or to indicate pattern markings on both sides of a piece of fabric. Basting stitches can be made by hand or by machine—generally at six stitches to the inch—and are removed when permanent stitching is completed.

BIAS: A direction diagonal to that of the threads forming woven fabric. If the bias is at a 45° angle it is called a true bias.

BIAS TAPE: A folded strip of nylon, rayon or cotton, cut diagonally to the fabric threads—on the bias—so that the strip will stretch smoothly to cover curved and straight edges of a garment piece. Double-folded bias tape is usually called bias binding; made only of cotton, it is used to bind raw edges.

BLOCK: To set the final shape of finished knitting, crocheting or needlepoint. For knitting or crocheting, the work is pressed with a warm iron through a damp cloth. For needlepoint, the finished work is tacked on a board, dampened, rubbed and then allowed to dry.

CLIP: A small straight cut made into the seam allowance, often up to the line of stitching, to help the seam lie flat around curves and at corners.

CLOSURE: The part of a garment on which fasteners—such as buttons or zippers—are placed; also, the fasteners themselves.

COUCHING: The embroidery technique of tying down long strands of thread by taking small stitches with another thread at evenly spaced intervals over the strands.

CROCHETING: The process of making fabric by using a hook to knot strands of yarn into a series of connected loops.

CROSSWISE GRAIN: See GRAIN.

DART: A stitched fabric fold, tapering to a point at one or both ends, that shapes fabric around curves.

DRESSMAKER'S CARBON: A marking paper, available in a range of colors, used to transfer pattern markings to fabric.

EASE: An even distribution of fullness in fabric, without perceptible gathers or tucks, that enables one section of a garment to be smoothly joined to another slightly smaller section—as in the seam joining a sleeve to its armhole or in the hem of a flared skirt.

EDGE STITCH: Machine stitching that is made on the visible side of the garment very close to the finished edge.

EMBROIDERY: The decoration of fabric or leather executed with a needle and thread, often in a combination of colors and a wide variety of stitches. When wool yarn is used the embroidery is called crewel.

FACING: A piece of fabric, frequently the same as that used in the garment, that is sewed to the raw edge of a garment at an opening such as the neckline and armhole.

FASTENER: Any device that opens and closes a garment—button, hook and eye, snap or zipper, See also CLOSURE.

FOOT: See PRESSER FOOT.

GAUGE: The number of stitches or rows per inch in a piece of knitted or crocheted material.

GODET: A triangular piece of fabric inserted into a seam or into a slash cut up from a hemline to change the style and add fullness to a garment.

GORES: Skirt panels, tapered from the hemline to the waist.

GRADING: Trimming each seam allowance within a multilayer seam—the fabric, facing, interfacing, etc.—to a different width so as to reduce bulk and make the finished seam lie flat.

GRAIN: The direction of threads in woven fabrics. The warp—threads running from one cut end of the material to the other—forms the lengthwise grain. The woof, or weft—the threads running across the lengthwise grain from one finished edge of the fabric to the other—forms the crosswise grain.

HOOP: A circular, two-piece wood, metal or plastic frame for embroidery, one adjustable ring fitting snugly around the other to hold a section of the embroidery fabric taut.

INTERFACING: A fabric sewed between two layers of garment fabric to stiffen, strengthen and support parts of the garment. Interfacing is typically used around necklines, in collars, cuffs, pockets and waistbands.

KNITTING: The process of making fabric by using two or more pointed needles to knot strands of yarn into a series of connected loops.

LAP: To extend one piece of fabric over another, as at the connection of the ends of a belt.

LENGTHWISE GRAIN: See GRAIN.

LINING: A fabric, usually lightweight, covering the inside of part or all of a garment.

MACHINE BASTE: To insert temporary stitching for marking or preliminary seaming, by machine rather than by hand.

MACHINE STITCH: To stitch permanent seams or finish edges by machine.

MONOGRAM: A decorative initial or group of initials, commonly executed in embroidery or needlepoint stitches.

MUSLIN: An inexpensive, plain-woven cotton fabric used for making prototypes of garments (called muslins) as an aid to styling and fitting.

NAP: The short surface fibers on a fabric that have been drawn out and brushed in one direction —such as on velvet or corduroy.

NATURAL FIBERS: The fibers of animal and vegetable substances; most commonly cotton, silk, linen (from flax) and wool.

NEEDLE BOARD: A board embedded with short, blunt needles that is used while pressing pile fabrics. When the fabric is placed wrong side up over the board, the needles prevent the pile from being flattened or marred by the pressing.

NEEDLEPOINT: Designs created by working yarn through the meshes of stiff canvas, covering the canvas completely.

NEEDLEWORK: A comprehensive term including all work done with a needle and thread, including embroidery, knitting, crocheting and sewing.

NOTCH: A V or diamond-shaped marking made on the edge of a garment piece as an alignment guide, intended to be matched with a similar notch or group of notches on another piece. Also a triangular cut into the seam allowance of a curved seam to help it lie flat.

OVERLAP: The part of the garment that extends over another part, as at the opening of a blouse, jacket or waistband.

PADDING: An embroidery technique for giving finished work a three-dimensional effect by working a layer of foundation stitching, or filler, under and at right angles to the final covering stitches.

PILE: A surface of upright yarns that usually lie in a particular direction, found on fabrics such as corduroy, velvet and terry cloth.

PIVOT: A technique of machine sewing for making angular corners by stopping the machine, with the needle down, where the direction of a seam line changes, raising the presser foot, pivoting the fabric and lowering the presser foot before continuing to stitch again.

PLACEMENT LINE: A line printed on a pattern to indicate where buttonholes, pockets, trimming and pleats are to be placed.

PLACKET: A garment opening with an overlapping edge covered by a visible strip of fabric running the length of the opening. Used with openings that are equipped with fasteners.

PLEATS: Folds of fabric used to control fullness.

PRESHRINK: The process of treating fabric to shrink it to an irreducible size before cutting. Washable fabric is immersed in water and pressed when almost dry. Nonwashable fabric should be preshrunk by a dry cleaner.

PRESSER FOOT: The part of a sewing machine that holds down fabric at the sewing point while the fabric is being advanced under the needle. An all-purpose, or general-purpose, foot has two prongs of equal length and is used for most stitching. A straight-stitch foot has one long and one short prong and can be used for straight stitching and stitching over fabrics of varying thicknesses. A zipper foot has only one prong and is used to stitch zippers and cording.

REINFORCE: To strengthen an area that will be subjected to strain, such as a waistline with seam ribbon, a seam with extra stitches, or a corner seam or a pocket with a small patch of fabric.

RIBBING: In knitting, an alternately raised-and-

lowered effect created by a combination of knit and purl stitches across each row.

ROLL: To manipulate fabric between the fingers, usually along a seam line, in order to bring the line of seam stitching out to the edge, or beyond the edge to the wrong side of the garment.

SEAM: The joint between two or more pieces of fabric, or the line of stitching that makes a fold in a single fabric piece, e.g., a dart.

SEAM ALLOWANCE: The extra fabric—usually 5/8 inch—that extends outside a seam line.

SEAM TAPE: A flat tape of finishing fabric—typically rayon or nylon with a woven edge, or nylon or polyester stretch lace—usually 1/2 to 5/8 inch wide. The tape is used to attach hems or is sewed over a seam to reinforce it. Lace seam tape may also be used for ornamentation.

SELVAGE: The lengthwise finished edges on woven fabric.

SKEIN: A length of yarn or thread packaged for knitting or crocheting.

SLIDE FASTENER: See ZIPPER.

STAY STITCH: A line of machine stitches sewed at 12 stitches to the inch along the seam line of a garment piece before the seam is stitched. Stay stitching is used as a reinforcement to prevent curved edges from stretching and as a guide for folding an edge accurately.

SYNTHETIC FIBERS: Man-made fibers produced by forming filaments from chemical solutions; among the familiar synthetic fibers are rayon, nylon and Dacron.

TACK: Several stitches made in the same place, usually on the wrong side of the garment, used to hold garment pieces such as cuffs permanently in the correct position. See also TAILOR TACKS.

TAILOR TACKS: Hand stitches used for marking pattern seam lines and symbols on delicate fabrics such as silks, which might be damaged by other marking methods.

THROAT PLATE: A flat metal piece with a hole through which a sewing-machine needle passes as it stitches. A general-purpose throat plate has a wide hole that will accommodate any sideways motion of the needle; many machines also have a

second throat plate with a smaller hole, which prevents soft fabrics and knits from being pulled down into the machine and puckering during stitching.

TOPSTITCHING: A line of machine stitching made on the visible side of the garment and parallel to a seam for ornamentation.

TRACING WHEEL: A small wheel attached to a handle, used in conjunction with dressmaker's carbon paper, to transfer markings from pattern pieces to fabric. Tracing wheels with serrated edges can be used for most fabrics; plain edges are used for knit fabrics to prevent snagging.

TRIM: To cut away excess fabric in a seam allowance after a seam has been stitched. Also, a strip of fabric—such as braid or a knitted or crocheted strip—that is sewed on the surface or into the seams of a garment for decorative purposes.

TRUE GRAIN: Fabric is said to be aligned on the true grain when the warp and woof threads are at right angles to each other. See also GRAIN.

UNDERSTITCHING: A line of machine stitches sewed alongside a seam, attaching the seam allowance to the facing and preventing the facing from rolling out.

WARP: See GRAIN.

WEFT: See GRAIN.

WITH NAP: A cutting direction on patterns indicating how the pattern is to be aligned. Used with fabrics that, because of their surface, napped weave or printed design, change in appearance with the direction in which they are set.

WOOF: See GRAIN.

YARN: A continuous strand of textile fibers, spun from short fibers or long filaments, and used in needlework, in woven fabric and in the manufacture of thread.

ZIGZAG STITCH: A serrated line of machine stitching used as decoration or to prevent raveling of raw edges, particularly on knits.

ZIPPER: A mechanical fastener consisting of two tapes holding parallel lines of teeth or coils that can be interlocked by a sliding bracket, or slider. See also CLOSURE.

ZIPPER FOOT: See PRESSER FOOT.

BASIC STITCHES

The diagrams below and on the following pages show how to make the elementary hand stitches, knitting, crocheting, embroidery and needlepoint stitches referred to in this volume.

THE FASTENING STITCH

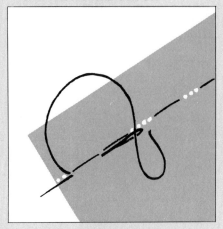

To end a row with a fastening stitch, insert the needle back 1/4 inch and bring it out at the point at which the thread last emerged. Make another stitch through these same points for extra firmness. To begin a row with a fastening stitch, leave a 4 inch loose end and make the initial stitch the same way as an ending stitch.

THE RUNNING STITCH

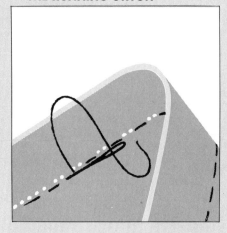

Insert the needle, with knotted thread, from the wrong side of the fabric and weave the needle in and out of the fabric several times in 1/8-inch, evenly spaced stitches. Pull the thread through. Continue across, making several stitches at a time, and end with a fastening stitch. When basting, make longer stitches, evenly spaced.

THE CATCH STITCH

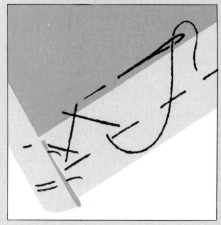

Working from left to right, anchor the first stitch with a knot inside the hem 1/4 inch down from the edge. Point the needle to the left and pick up one or two threads on the garment directly above the hem, then pull the thread through. Take a small stitch in the hem only (not in the garment), 1/4 inch down from the edge and 1/4 inch to the right of the previous stitch. End with a fastening stitch.

THE SLIP STITCH

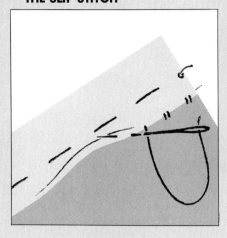

Fold under the hem edge and anchor the first stitch with a knot inside the fold. Point the needle to the left. Pick up one or two threads of the garment fabric close to the hem edge, directly below the first stitch, and slide the needle horizontally through the folded edge of the hem 1/8 inch to the left of the previous stitch. End with a fastening stitch.

THE HEMMING STITCH

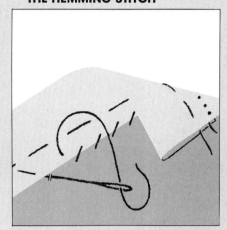

Anchor the first stitch with a knot inside the hem; then pointing the needle up and to the left, pick up one or two threads of the garment fabric close to the hem. Push the needle up through the hem 1/8 inch above the edge; pull the thread through. Continue picking up one or two threads and making 1/8-inch stitches in the hem at intervals of 1/4 inch. End with a fastening stitch.

THE OVERCAST STITCH

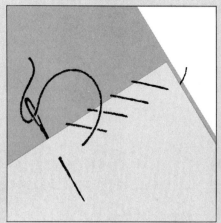

Draw the needle, with knotted thread, through from the wrong side of the fabric 1/8 to 1/4 inch down from the top edge. With the thread to the right, insert the needle under the fabric from the wrong side 1/8 to 1/4 inch to the left of the first stitch. Continue to make evenly spaced stitches over the fabric edge and end with a fastening stitch.

1. Form a slipknot in the yarn, leaving a free end long enough for the number of stitches to be cast on (allow about 1 inch per stitch).

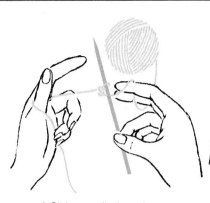

2. Slide a needle through the slipknot and hold the needle in your right hand. Loop the yarn attached to the ball over your right index finger and loop the free end of the yarn around your left thumb.

3. Insert the tip of the needle through the loop on your left thumb and bring the yarn attached to the ball under and over the needle from left to right.

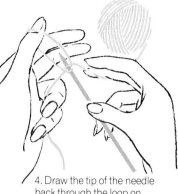

4. Draw the tip of the needle back through the loop on your thumb, then slip the loop off your thumb. Pull the short end of the yarn down to tighten the loop, which is now a stitch. Repeat Steps 2-4 for the required number of stitches.

THE KNIT STITCH

1. Insert the right needle in the front of the stitch closest to the tip of the left needle, as shown. Bring the yarn under and over the right needle.

2. Pull the right needle back through the stitch, bringing with it the loop of yarn. Slide this loop—which is now a stitch—off the left needle and onto the right. Repeat Steps 1 and 2 for each knit stitch.

THE PURL STITCH

1. Insert the right needle into the stitch closest to the tip of the left needle, as shown. Bring the yarn around and under the right needle.

2. Push the needle back through the stitch, bringing with it the loop of yarn —which is now a stitch. Transfer this new stitch to the right needle, letting it slip off the left needle as you do so. Repeat Steps 1 and 2 for each purl stitch.

INCREASING STITCHES

1. On a knit row, insert the right needle through the back of a stitch. Knit the stitch, but do not drop it off the left needle.

2. Knit the same stitch in the ordinary way, and transfer the two stitches to the right needle.

1. On a purl row, insert the right needle from right to left through the horizontal loop at the bottom of a stitch. Make a purl stitch but do not let it slide off the left needle.

2. Now insert the right needle into the vertical loop above the horizontal one. Purl the stitch in the ordinary way, and slide both loops onto the right needle.

DECREASING STITCHES

1. Insert the right needle into two stitches instead of one, either from front to back as shown, for a knit stitch, or from back to front as for a purl stitch. Proceed as though you were knitting or purling one stitch at a time.

BINDING OFF STITCHES

1. Knit (or purl) two stitches. Then insert the left needle through the front of the second stitch from the tip of the right needle.

2. With the left needle, lift the second stitch on the right needle over the first stitch and let it drop.

1. Form a loose slipknot around the crochet hook, about 1 inch from the end of the yarn. Grasp the yarn attached to the ball with the tip of the hook and pull the yarn through the slipknot with the tip of the hook, as shown.

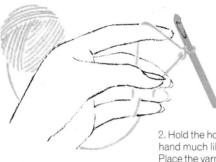

2. Hold the hook in your right hand much like a pencil. Place the yarn from the ball around the left little finger, then up and over the left index finger. Grasp the free end of the yarn between the thumb and middle finger of the left hand.

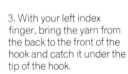

3. With your left index finger, bring the yarn from the back to the front of the hook and catch it under the tip of the hook.

4. Pull the tip of the hook through the loop on the hook, bringing the yarn with it to create the first chain stitch in the foundation chain. Repeat Steps 1-4 to form a chain of the desired length.

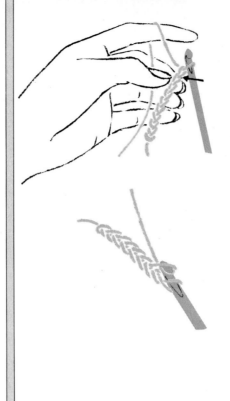

1. To single crochet the first row after a foundation chain, insert the hook through the second chain stitch from the hook (arrow)—do not count the loop on the hook.

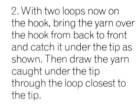

2. With two loops now on the hook, bring the yarn over the hook from back to front and catch it under the tip as shown. Then draw the yarn caught under the tip through the loop closest to the tip.

3. Bring the yarn over the hook again and draw it through both of the loops that were on the hook; there is now only a single loop on the hook. Insert the crochet hook into the next chain stitch and repeat Steps 1 and 2. At the end of each row, chain one stitch if the next row is to be worked in single crochet, two stitches for a double crochet pattern, and three stitches for a triple crochet pattern.

4. Turn the work to crochet back across the previous row. Insert the hook through both loops of the second stitch from the edge, as shown, and all subsequent stitches on this and all rows after the foundation chain.

THE DOUBLE CROCHET STITCH

1. To double crochet the first row of stitches after a foundation chain, count back to the third chain stitch from the hook (arrow)—do not count the loop on the hook. Swing the yarn over the hook from back to front, then insert the hook through this third chain stitch.

2. Bring the yarn over the hook again and draw it through the loop closest to the tip. Bring the yarn over the hook again and draw it through the two loops closest to the tip.

3. Bring the yarn over the tip again and draw it through the remaining two loops on the hook. At the end of each row, chain one stitch if the next row is to be worked in single crochet, two stitches for double crochet and three stitches for triple crochet.

4. Turn the work to crochet back across the previous row. Bring the yarn over the hook and insert the hook through both loops of the second stitch from the edge (arrow) on this and all rows after the first.

INCREASING STITCHES

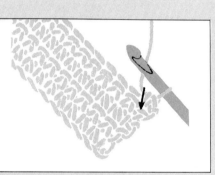

To increase stitches, work one stitch—either a single, double or triple crochet, as called for in the instructions—then insert the crochet hook back into the same loop or loops (arrow) and repeat the stitch.

DECREASING STITCHES, SINGLE CROCHET

1. To decrease in a row of single crochet stitches, insert the hook into both loops of a stitch. Bring the yarn over the hook and draw it through the two loops closest to the tip; this leaves two loops on the hook.

2. Insert the hook through both loops of the next stitch. Bring the yarn over the hook and draw it through the two loops closest to the tip. Bring the yarn over the hook again and draw it through the three remaining loops on the hook.

DECREASING STITCHES, DOUBLE CROCHET

1. To decrease in a row of double crochet stitches, bring the yarn over the hook and insert it through both loops of a stitch. Bring the yarn over the hook again, as shown, and draw it through the two loops closest to the tip. Then bring the yarn over the hook again and insert it through both loops of the next stitch.

2. Again bring the yarn over the hook and draw it through the two loops closest to the tip, as shown; there are now five loops on the hook. Bring the yarn over the hook again and draw it through the two loops now closest to the tip. Repeat the process until there are three loops remaining on the hook. Then pull the yarn through the three remaining loops.

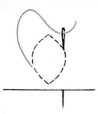

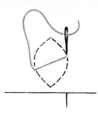

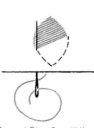

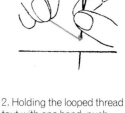

THE SATIN STITCH

1. Using a knotted thread, bring the needle up from the wrong side of the material held in the hoop; then, at the angle desired, insert it down to the wrong side at a point diagonally across the design.

2. Bring the needle straight up from the wrong side just above the first hole and insert it above the hole made in Step 1.

3. Repeat Step 2 until the top is filled. Then bring the needle from the wrong side just below the filled part and make diagonal stitches until the bottom is filled. Secure the last stitch on the wrong side (Ending Off, *below*).

THE FRENCH KNOT

1. Using a knotted thread, bring the needle up from the wrong side of the material held in the hoop. Put down the hoop and loop the thread once around the needle.

2. Holding the looped thread taut with one hand, push the needle tip into—or just next to—the hole made in Step 1. Slide the loop down to the fabric. Then push the needle through to the wrong side of the fabric.

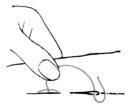

3. Bring the needle up from the wrong side at a point that suits your design, and repeat Steps 1 and 2. Secure the last stitch on the wrong side (Ending Off, *below*).

THE STEM STITCH

1. Using a knotted thread, bring the needle up from the wrong side of the material held in the hoop.

2. With your left thumb, hold the thread away from the needle. Point the needle to the left, but take a stitch to the right of the hole made in Step 1. The needle should emerge midway between the beginning of this stitch and the hole made in Step 1.

3. Pull the thread through taut and take another stitch to the right the same size as the one made in Step 2. Continue making similar stitches along the design and secure the last stitch on the wrong side (Ending Off, *below*).

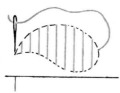

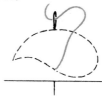

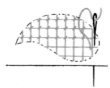

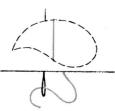

THE CHAIN STITCH

1. Using a knotted thread, bring the needle up from the wrong side of the material held in the hoop. Pull it through and loop the thread from left to right.

2. With your left thumb, hold the thread in a loop of the desired size and insert the needle in the hole from which it emerged in Step 1. Keeping the loop under the needle point, bring the needle out directly below. Pull the needle through.

3. Again loop the thread and hold it. Insert the needle in the hole from which it last emerged and bring it out through the loop. Complete the design and anchor the last stitch by inserting the needle below its loop. Secure on the wrong side (Ending Off, *below*).

THE SQUARED FILLING STITCH

1. Using a knotted thread and with the material held in a hoop, bring the needle up from the wrong side of the material in the middle of one edge of the design. Insert the needle down to the wrong side at a point directly across the design.

2. Bring the needle up from the wrong side just to the left of the previous hole on the same side of the design. The distance between stitches should be consistent.

3. Continue making parallel stitches, starting each on the side of the design where the previous stitch ended. Complete the left-hand area, then bring the needle up to the right of the center stitch made in Step 1, and fill the right-hand area.

4. Bring the needle up from the wrong side of the fabric at the center of the far right end of the design, and insert the needle at a right angle across the design to the far left end. Complete the right-left stitches as in Steps 1-3.

5. To lock, bring the needle up in the upper right corner where the 2 stitches cross. Insert the needle diagonally over the intersection. Work 1 right-left stitch at a time. Secure on the wrong side (Ending Off, right).

ENDING OFF

On the wrong side of the material, slide the needle underneath the nearest 3 or 4 consecutive stitches and pull it through. Snip off the excess thread.

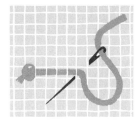
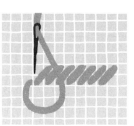
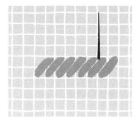
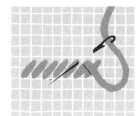
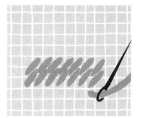

THE HORIZONTAL TENT STITCH
1. Using knotted yarn, insert the needle from the front of the canvas, 5 holes from the hole where the pattern will begin. Bring the needle out through the beginning hole; insert it into the canvas 1 hole above and 1 hole to the right. Slant the needle downward and bring it out 1 hole to the left of the beginning hole.

2. Continue, working from right to left, to the end of the row; when you reach the knot, cut it off. Then insert the needle diagonally 1 hole above—and 1 hole to the right of—the one from which the yarn last emerged. Pull the needle through to the back of the canvas.

3. Rotate the canvas 180° so the last stitch made is on the right; bring up the needle from the back, 1 hole above the hole through which the yarn entered the canvas in Step 2.

4. Insert the needle 1 hole above and 1 hole to the right of the hole through which the yarn last emerged, continuing as before across the row.

5. At the end of the row, rotate the canvas 180° so the last stitch made is on the right. Bring up the needle from the back, 1 hole below the hole through which the yarn last entered the canvas. Continue the pattern. At the end of each piece of yarn, run the last 1 1/2 inches through the stitches on the back of the canvas.

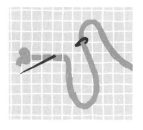
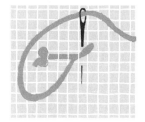
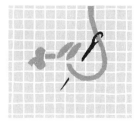
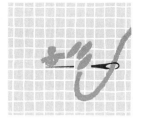
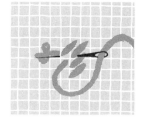

THE DIAGONAL TENT STITCH
1. Insert the needle into the canvas 1 hole above and 1 hole to the right of the beginning hole. Slant the needle downward diagonally and bring it out 1 hole to the left of the beginning hole.

2. Insert the needle into the canvas diagonally, and bring it out vertically 2 holes below.

3. Insert the needle diagonally, this time bringing it out 2 holes down and 1 to the left, in the hole below the one from which the yarn emerged in Step 2.

4. Insert the needle diagonally and bring it out horizontally 2 holes to the left.

5. Insert the needle diagonally and bring it out horizontally 2 holes to the left.

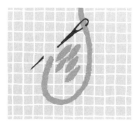
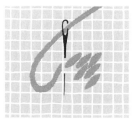
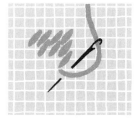

6. Insert the needle diagonally and bring it out diagonally 1 hole to the left of the hole from which the yarn last emerged.

7. Repeat Step 2 three times, inserting the needle diagonally each time, and bringing it out vertically.

8. At the bottom of the diagonal, repeat Step 3 —i.e., insert the needle diagonally and bring it out at a slant 2 holes down and 1 to the left. Then repeat Step 4 four times, inserting the needle diagonally and bringing it out horizontally 2 holes to the left. Then repeat Step 6.

9. Continue to follow the pattern. Repeat Step 2, working vertically as many times as necessary to get to the bottom of the diagonal. Repeat Step 3 at the bottom. Repeat Step 4, working horizontally back up the diagonal, and then repeat Step 6 once at the top to complete the pattern.

1. Tape the drawing, print or photograph to be traced to a table top or board. Center a sheet of tracing paper over the design and tape it at the top.

2. Trace the design with a fine-tipped black pen. If you are making a tracing for needlepoint be sure the line is strong enough to be seen through the canvas.

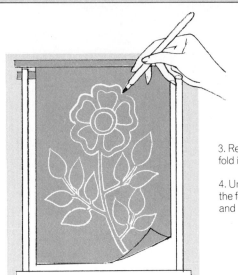

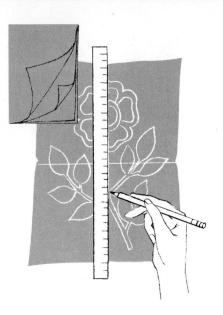

3. Remove the tracing and fold it into quarters.

4. Unfold it and lightly mark the fold lines with a ruler and pencil.

ENLARGING OR REDUCING A DESIGN

1. Trace the design onto a square piece of paper—it must be square to preserve proportions in rectangular designs—and fold the tracing in half across its width, then across its length. Unfold and fold it in quarters and eighths across its width and length to make a grid with eight squares on each side. (For an elaborate design, the paper may be folded into a 16-square grid.) With a ruler and pencil draw lines along the fold marks.

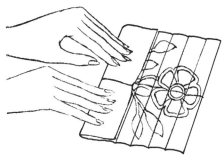

2. Identify horizontal and vertical coordinates as on a map, by penciling letters (A to H) along the top and numbers (1 to 8) down the side.

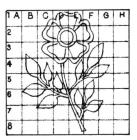

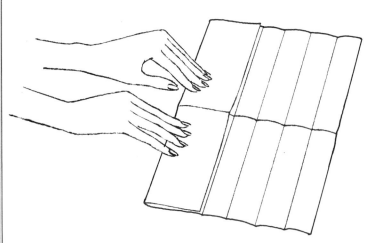

3. Cut a sheet of drawing paper into a square approximately the size you want the embroidery or needlepoint to be.

4. Fold it just as you folded the original and pencil in the same lines and coordinates.

5. Using the coordinates to locate matching squares, copy the design freehand, square by square.

6. Transfer the enlarged or reduced design to the fabric as shown on page 196.

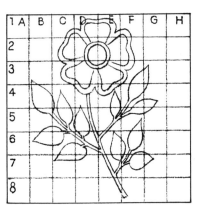

TRANSFERRING A DESIGN TO EMBROIDERY FABRIC

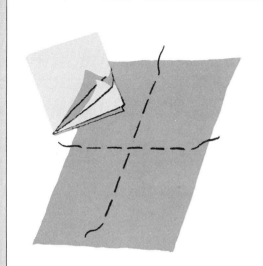

1. Fold the embroidery fabric into quarters and crease the fold lines with your fingers or an iron.

2. Unfold the fabric and baste along the creases, taking long stitches on the visible side for easily followed guide lines.

3. Tape the fabric, wrong side down, to the work surface.

4. Lay the paper tracing over the fabric, aligning its center fold lines with the basting on the fabric, and tape the tracing down along the top. At the bottom corners, put tabs of tape that can easily be lifted as you work.

5. Insert dressmaker's carbon paper, carbon side down, between the tracing or enlarged or reduced drawing and the fabric. (If the carbon paper is smaller than the design, move it as you work.)

6. Trace the design with a dull pencil, pressing hard. From time to time lift the paper and check that the design is coming through distinctly on the fabric. Avoid smudging by working from top to bottom. Remove the fabric and baste around the edges to prevent fraying.

TRACING A DESIGN ONTO NEEDLEPOINT CANVAS

1. Cut a piece of needlepoint canvas at least 2 or 3 inches larger than your design on each side. Fold it in quarters; then unfold it and mark the fold lines with a pencil.

2. Place the tracing under the canvas and align the marked center fold lines on the design with the fold lines made on the canvas in Step 1. Tape the tracing and the canvas in place with masking tape.

3. Trace the design directly onto the canvas with a fine-tipped pen and indelible ink, which will not rub off or stain the finished needlepoint. (You may want to use several colors of indelible ink as a helpful stitching guide.) Minor details may be drawn on the canvas freehand or be stitched in at will. Draw a border limiting the area of the design.

4. Remove the canvas from the design and attach masking tape to the edges to prevent the canvas from unraveling as you work.

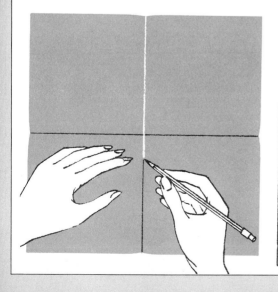

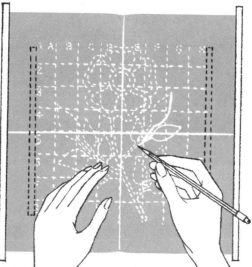

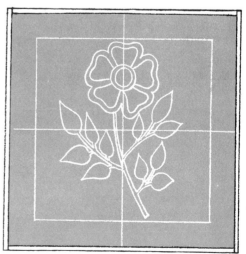

CREDITS

Sources for the illustrations in this book are shown below. Credits from left to right are separated by semicolons, from top to bottom by dashes.

6,7—Dan Budnik. 10—Mary Evans Picture Library. 11—Copyright © by Philippe Halsman; Pictorial Parade; United Press International. 12,13—Bettmann Archive; Press Association; Pictorial Parade; Paul Schutzer, Time-Life Picture Agency, © 1972 Time Incorporated; Wide World Photos; Pictorial Parade. 14 through 19—Dan Budnik. 20,21—Tasso Vendikos. 25—The Bettmann Archive. 26 through 31—Richard Noble. 34,35—Drawings by Raymond Skibinski. 36,37—Ken Kay. 40,41—Drawings by May Routh. 42,43—Drawings by John Sagan. 44 through 51—Drawings by Raymond Skibinski. 52,53—Tasso Vendikos. 57—Sharland from Black Star, Time-Life Picture Agency, © 1972 Time Incorporated. 58,59—Drawings by Antonio, dress designs by Carol Horn. 60 through 65—Drawings by Raymond Skibinski. 66 through 73—Drawings by John Sagan. 74,75—Drawings by Antonio, top designs by Carol Horn. 76 through 85—Drawings by Ted Kliros. 86,87—Drawings by Antonio, pants designs by Carol Horn. 88 through 97—Drawings by John Sagan. 98,99—Drawings by Antonio, skirt designs by Carol Horn. 100 through 109—Drawings by John Sagan. 110,111—Drawings by Antonio, skirt designs by Carol Horn. 112 through 123—Drawings by Raymond Skibinski. 124,125—Needlework by Meredith Gladstone. 129—Courtesy Editions Verve, Paris. 130—R. Guillemot from Top—Victoria and Albert Museum, London. 131—Victoria and Albert Museum, London—M. Desjardins from Top; Bulloz. 132—Al Freni courtesy Mrs. Stevens Baird. 133—Robert Colton courtesy Mrs. Theodore Roosevelt III. 134 through 141—Drawings by John Sagan. 142 through 145—Drawings by Raymond Skibinski. 146,147—Ken Kay, embroidery by Meredith Gladstone; Letters by Photo Lettering Inc. 148—Herbert Orth, embroidery by Lucy Ciancia, needlepoint by Meredith Glad-stone. 149—Letters by Photo Lettering Inc. 150,151—Ken Kay, needlepoint and embroidery by Meredith Gladstone. 152,153—Letters by Photo Lettering Inc. 154,155—Tasso Vendikos, needlepoint by Erica Wilson. 156,157—Herbert Orth, embroidery by Lucy Ciancia. 158,159—Tasso Vendikos. 162,163—Ken Kay, crochet by Annette Feldman. 166,167—Tasso Vendikos, crochet by Annette Feldman. 169—Drawings by John Sagan. 170,171—Ken Kay, knitting by Annette Feldman. 172 through 179—Drawings by John Sagan. 180,181—Richard Noble, knitting by Annette Feldman. 182 through 192—Drawings by John Sagan. 193—Drawings by Mulvey/Crump Associates, Inc. 194—Drawings by Raymond Skibinski—drawings by John Sagan. 195—Drawings by Raymond Skibinski—drawings by John Sagan.

ACKNOWLEDGMENTS

For their help in the preparation of this book the editors would like to thank the following individuals: Angela Alleyne; Mrs. Stevens Baird; Jane Beatty; Karen B. Booth; Penny Burnham; Lucy Ciancia; Janet Dubane; Anne Fogarty; Audrey C. Foote; Cynthia Gold; Carol Horn; Carolyn Mazzello; Carmen Mercadal; Issey Miyake; Marjorie Miller; Belle Conway Rivers; Mrs. Theodore Roosevelt III; Mrs. Janet Tiso.

The editors would also like to thank: Geoffrey Beene, Inc.; Bloomingdale's; Butterick Fashion Marketing Company; Consolidated Canvas; Cherie Dervin; Duplex International Ltd.; Echo Scarfs Co.; David E. Evins; Fe-Ro Fabrics, Inc.; Galanos; The Grand Hotel; Greeff Fabrics, Inc.; Held Fabrics; Henri Bendel, Inc.; Julie: Artisan's Gallery; The McCall Pattern Company; Marimekko Fabrics courtesy of Design Research; Sally Gee, Inc.; F. Schumacher & Co.; So-Good, Inc.; Staron-Lafitte; Scarves by Vera, Inc.; Weller Fabrics.

INDEX

Numerals in italics indicate an illustration of the subject mentioned.

198

✗ Printed in U.S.A.